Rhythmicity and Deleuze

Rhythmicity and Deleuze

Practice as Research in the Musical-Philosophical

Steve Tromans

LEXINGTON BOOKS
Lanham • Boulder • New York • London

Published by Lexington Books
An imprint of The Rowman & Littlefield Publishing Group, Inc.
4501 Forbes Boulevard, Suite 200, Lanham, Maryland 20706
www.rowman.com

86-90 Paul Street, London EC2A 4NE

British Library Cataloguing in Publication Information Available

Library of Congress Cataloging-in-Publication Data

Names: Tromans, Steve, author.
Title: Rhythmicity and Deleuze: practice as research in the
musical-philosophical / Steve Tromans.
Description: Lanham: Lexington Books, 2023. | Includes bibliographical
references and index.
Identifiers: LCCN 2023009423 (print) | LCCN 2023009424 (ebook) | ISBN
9781666926064 (cloth) | ISBN 9781666926071 (ebook)
Subjects: LCSH: Music—Philosophy and aesthetics. | Improvisation
(Music)—Philosophy. | Music—Performance—Philosophy and aesthetics. |
Time in music. | Deleuze, Gilles, 1925–1995—Influence.
Classification: LCC ML3800 .T77 2023 (print) | LCC ML3800 (ebook) | DDC
781.1/7—dc23/eng/20230306
LC record available at https://lccn.loc.gov/2023009423
LC ebook record available at https://lccn.loc.gov/2023009424

To the Gods of Future Possible: a concept

Contents

Introduction

This book brings together my music improvisation and composition and Gilles Deleuze's philosophy of time, for the purpose of creating a musical-philosophical concept I am calling *Rhythmicity*. In three practice-as-research projects, I set out to investigate how music and philosophy can work together to make a fresh contribution to both fields, as well being of relevance to scholarship in practice as research in music, Deleuze studies, experimental music, and Performance Philosophy.

I argue that the relationship between music and philosophy can be understood in rhythmic terms, as a complex interdisciplinary movement operating in multiple dimensions. Rhythmicity is evolved by incorporating the insights of each project and accompanying chapters into the apparatus of its successor(s). In this way, the temporal dimensions of Rhythmicity are plotted in a series of interlinked movements: in the first practice-as-research project (chapters 3–5), as a simultaneous "cyclical" and "hyperbolic" movement of the musical-philosophical as experienced by the reader-listener; in the second project (chapters 6–8), as a complex folding of multiple possible movements and harmonic combinations in what I call a "tonality of time"; and, in the final project (chapters 9–11), as a temporal line-cycle intertwining the musical and the philosophical expressed in the triple perspective of composer, performer, listener, and what I call the "Rhythmicity of silences."

Alongside offering a concept of the ways in which music and philosophy interact, I conclude that Rhythmicity provides a way to rethink the temporal in respect to how we model its movements and relationships. Through the models of temporal interaction devised in each project, Deleuze's concepts are transformed via their incorporation into the musical-philosophical mix. In addition, music improvisation and composition are shown to be utilisable for more than the making of music alone, with the book providing fresh insight for the fields of music practice as research and Performance Philosophy in respect of its uniqueness of process and output.

My enquiry is predicated on the notion that creative processes of music-making can provide insights into philosophical questions otherwise unavailable through more traditional research practices. I utilise my own practice in solo piano improvisation and composition, in conjunction with audio documentation, music transcription, and writing in a range of registers, to investigate selected concepts from Deleuze's philosophical oeuvre across the three practice-as-research projects.[1] Specifically, I undertake these projects to explore and transform our understandings of Deleuze's philosophy of time as it is expressed through his concepts of difference and repetition, the fold and the incompossible, and Chronos and Aion. In the course of the investigation, I perform a series of solo piano improvisations (for the first project) and compose two new works, *In the Garden of the Incompossible* and *The Time Is out of Joint*, as well as giving improvised performances of these (for the second and third projects, respectively). Through experimenting with ways of bringing different modes of investigation and presentation together, I undertake the creation of the concept of Rhythmicity, which is developed as a multimodal means of expressing a musical-philosophical movement between the practices of music-making (my own) and Deleuze's philosophy of time (via the concepts listed above).

I capitalise Rhythmicity throughout the book in order to make instances of its use (and concept) noticeably distinct from the more commonplace "rhythm," "rhythmic," and so on. In its basic definition (via the online dictionary, Lexico), "rhythmicity" describes a "rhythmical quality or character," and my decision to coopt the term comes from this suitability in conveying a sense of rhythmic movement beyond narrow definitions of rhythm as something belonging specifically to (for instance) music.[2] In this book, Rhythmicity's interrelation of music practices and Deleuze's philosophy of time takes influence from a methodological suggestion in Brian Massumi's (2002) *Parables for the Virtual*. In the introduction to this hugely influential treatise on movement, affect, and sensation in philosophy and cultural/critical studies, Massumi advocates a strategy of conceptual "poaching": "When you uproot a concept from its network of systemic connections," he stresses, "you still have its *connectibility*" (20). Massumi describes this connectibility as "the rhythm without the regularity, or a readiness to arrive and relay in certain ways"; an experimental state of affairs leading to a "creative tension that may play itself out in any number of ways" (20). In the three practice-as -research projects presented and analysed in chapters 4–5, 7–8, and 10–11, such creative conceptual tension is most definitely encouraged—and is enabled via each project's construction in the multiple modes of Rhythmicity.

On account of its multimodal expression, Rhythmicity can be conceived of as a conceptual *practice* in addition to its function as a concept per se (i.e., as an abstract means of understanding). It is well known that Deleuze (in his individually authored work as well as in his collaborations with Félix Guattari) developed a radical notion of what constitutes a concept, and to what uses concepts could and should be put. In their final publication,

What Is Philosophy?, Deleuze and Guattari (1994) define the concept as a multiplicity, always consisting of more than a single component (15) and having "a *becoming* that involves its relationship with concepts situated on the same plane" (18). For the authors, concepts are incorporeal (thus abstract in the more traditional sense of the term: concept) at the same time as being intermixed with the specific state of affairs in which they are "effectuated" (21). In this manner, all concepts are connected both to one another, in terms of the history of concepts and their usage, and to the conditions of their creation. Deleuze and Guattari denied the possibility of concept creation in any disciplinary field other than philosophy, stating that concepts "belong to philosophy by right, because it is philosophy that creates them and never stops creating them" (33). However, in this book, I am arguing (and demonstrating) that Rhythmicity can be experienced as expressing a movement between musical and philosophical practices, making its concept interdisciplinary and most certainly not confined to the field of philosophy alone.

Throughout this book, the concept of Rhythmicity is practised, and investigated, in the modes of what I am calling the "musical-philosophical." I use this hyphenisation in order to convey the dynamic nature of the relationship between music and philosophy engendered in what follows. On occasion, I use the terms "the musical" and "the philosophical" as nominalised adjectives, as a means of indicating my musical-philosophical appropriations of certain of the practices of music (improvisation, composition, analysis) and philosophy (conceptual creation, argument, analysis) from their respective disciplinary fields. In other words, I am arguing for (and practising) an interdisciplinary approach to the ways in which research in music and philosophy is undertaken.

In respect to these particular uses of the terms "the musical" and "the philosophical," the notion of the metaphorical, and its problematisation, is instructive. As McGrath (2018) makes clear, ontologies of music are ever resistant to being pinned down to any kind of "definite set of identity conditions" or solely as an "analytical object" (2). For an enquiry such as mine—where I am interested in employing "the musical" outside its strict disciplinary connotations and experimenting with what it can *do* (rather than what it *is*)—such ontological "pinning down" is both futile and unnecessary. Via its metaphoric qualities, "musicality" (or the musical, as I am calling it in this book) signifies something that, as McGrath puts it, is "inexpressible in words alone" (2). Rather than being a hindrance to understanding, that very inexpressibility is key to "the idea of music," in its centuries-old elucidation from the age of Enlightenment to twentieth-century modernism and beyond: an epistemological trajectory of music's ideation "from sound to metaphor" (6).

Similar to, though not identical with, this perspective on the interdisciplinary, intermedial usefulness of thinking in terms of the metaphoric and (not exclusively) the ontologic, the practice of philosophy can also be considered "musical" in the sense that it can function dynamically, affectively, rhythmically. Likewise, the practice of music can be "philosophical" in a similar way—although differently articulated. Where one discipline has historically used words as its primary epistemological vehicle, the other uses sounds—and silences, as I address in the third project (chapters 10–11). As Cull Ó Maoilearca (2019) understands it, the relationship between music and philosophy (in terms of the epistemological power dynamic between the two) is not about music living up to the ideal of philosophy, but how music can change our understanding of what philosophy is, and does.[3] My concept/conceptual practice of Rhythmicity draws together and utilises the dynamic, affective, and rhythmic aspects of the musical and the philosophical, and thus becomes key to how the book's chapters are articulated, as well as being the ongoing focus of its development.

Since my undertaking explicitly sets out to practise musical-philosophical expression, there are certain instances where the reader is required to listen to audio recordings at the same time as reading the text. This is an important means of experiencing the musical-philosophical Rhythmicity I am investigating, and conceptualising—and, in the case of the first and second projects (chapters 4–5 and 7–8), this process of reading-listening is crucial to the analyses undertaken. The practice of reading at the same time as listening is not a simple task at first, but I have found that it becomes more comfortable with repeated engagement—and, I should also add, this was the way in which I myself wrote and read the words that make up the analyses of each project: listening while writing, writing while listening. As McGrath (2018) acknowledges, new ways of being able to listen (via new technology or new modes of artistic presentation) have enabled listeners to pursue "new modes of listening" (50). McGrath makes plain that the act of listening is itself not without philosophical interest. In his own definition, listening pertains to the act of "concentrated musical attention" (13). Hearing, on the other hand—or at least what we understand by its term—is a different (though not unrelated) issue. In this regard, the work of Jonathan Sterne stands as exemplar of the issues surrounding the distinction between listening and hearing, in respect of a focus on problematising the relationship between audience and artist (or artwork). For Sterne (2012), his "audiovisual litany" of Sound Studies points out the fact that "hearing places you inside an event" (9)—the implicit suggestion being that listening is less of an all-consuming act in its affective status. And my own blend of listening-reading/reading-listening, here in this book, is most certainly intended to pursue—and encourage—a programme of novel ways to approach the musical-philosophical questions raised, investigated, and presented (in multimodal fashion).

From my own experiences, I would argue that any remaining difficulty experienced in listening to the musical-philosophical, at the same time as reading about it, is a positive reflection on the originality of such expression. In other words, the differences between the modes of engagement utilised help to maintain the creative tension, and the Rhythmicity, that bringing together my music and Deleuze's philosophy as musical-philosophical expression occasions.

The reader-listener is not required to be fully conversant with Deleuze's philosophy in order to understand, and experience, my concept of Rhythmicity. Neither are they expected to be expert in the music practices employed (such as improvisation, for example). In both these cases, there is ample provision for explanation of the concepts and practices involved. As noted later, each project begins with an overview of the Deleuzian concepts interrogated (in chapters 3, 6, and 9). These overviews are given for the purpose of providing context for the musical-philosophical enquiries that follow. Similarly, the analyses made of each practice as research project draw repeatedly on self-reflection on the music-making undertaken, in order to offer an "insider" perspective for the reader-listener. Rhythmicity is a multimodal concept/conceptual practice, and should be approached as such—where the musical and the philosophical are equal partners in its expression. In addition, it should be remembered that, as indicated earlier (and demonstrated in this book), "the musical" is not necessarily the sole province of music practices, and, likewise, that "the philosophical" can also be practised in music.

CONTRIBUTIONS

As noted by a range of writers including Parr (2010a), the field of Deleuze studies has, in recent years, experienced "a tremendous proliferation of scholarship" (vii). Across a wide array of disciplines (including, but not limited to, theatre, dance, film, architecture, politics, and cultural studies), theorists have drawn on various aspects of Deleuze's oeuvre in order to provide fresh insights in their chosen field/s of study. However, as Hulse and Nesbitt (2010a) point out, "very little response" by way of Deleuzian output has emerged from the field of music research (xv)—beyond a few key exceptions such as Campbell (2013), Criton and Chouvel (2015), and Assis and Giudici (2017, 2019). In similar fashion, the (also relatively nascent) field of practice as research in music has been slow to embrace the potential of Deleuze's work as a focus for its various projects. Notable exceptions include: Paulo de Assis' *Deleuzabelli Variations* that form part of the *Music Experiment*

21 project (2013–2018) at the Orpheus Research Centre in Music, Ghent, Belgium; the *Deleuzian Music Research* project (2012–2016) headed by Pirkko Moisala at the University of Helsinki, Finland; and the diverse group of Deleuze-inspired practitioner-researchers gathered together in the biannual *Deleuze and Artistic Research* conferences (inaugurated in 2015 and hosted by the Orpheus Research Centre in Music), and the related collections of papers and presentations of participants of these conferences edited by Assis and Giudici (2017, 2019).

Although a large proportion of my work in music has tended to be cat-egorised in terms of jazz and improvised music, in more recent years I have increasingly explored parallels in my practice with certain of the concerns of experimental music. In the 1950s, John Cage, as one of the first to talk about a music that could be considered experimental (as opposed to "modern" or "avant-garde," for instance), the experimental (in the making of experimental music or any other experimental act) is "simply an action the outcome of which is not foreseen" (Cage 1978, 69). Echoing Cage's words more than a half-century later, Gottschalk (2016) has argued that experimental music is best understood as operating from a position of "openness": of musical enquiry oriented towards discovery, towards the unknown (1). At the time of writing, I identify much of my recent output in these terms (while still utilis-ing processes of improvisation as part of my creative apparatus, as demon-strated in this book and its practice as research projects). My music-making undertaken for this enquiry most definitely aligns with an experimental atti-tude to the potential function, and use, of music.

In studies of experimental music, the dominant approaches in the fields to date have tended to revolve around historical and ontological issues—that is, who practices/has practised it, and how it can be defined. Nyman (1974), for instance, is well known as being the first attempt at a comprehensive definition of what experimental music is and does, as well as providing an overview of its practitioners and their work at the time of its original pub-lication.[4] More recently, Saunders (2017), Nicholls (1990), and Gottschalk (2016) have followed Nyman's lead, with Saunders providing a contempo-rary account of experimental music practitioners and their practice (includ-ing such notables as long-time Cage associate Christian Wolff, the British free-improvising saxophonist Evan Parker, and Manfred Werder from the Wandelweiser Collective), and Nicholls taking a retrospective, and specifi-cally North American, look at the work of Charles Ives, Charles and Ruth Seeger, and Henry Cowell. The example of Gottschalk (2016) is of particular interest to a project such as mine, since, alongside continuing the historiog-raphy of experimental music from the 1970s into the twenty-first century, she expands the purview of experimental music research to include issues of a phenomenological nature. For example, she writes of the experience of experimental music—including in relation to the perception of time—and of the research undertaken by practitioners themselves, rather than research into their work by others. Of this latter issue—experimental music considered *as* research—the collections edited by Crispin and Gilmore (2014) and Coessens (2017), where each chapter is written by practitioner-researchers, are important examples of the overlap between the fields of practice as research/artistic research and experimental music studies. And it is in this overlap that one often finds experimental musicians/researchers who have a keen interest in utilising aspects of the philosophy of Deleuze (see chapter 1 of this book for more in respect of such exponents).

In existing studies focused on improvisation, pedagogical, phenomenological, and ontological concerns predominate much of the literature. For instance, in pedagogical terms, there are the various study guides and "how to" books one finds in any music library which are, for the most part, focused on issues of jazz practice. Popular examples of these guides include Levine (1995) and Rawlins and Bahha (2005), alongside exemplary publications by Nachmanovitch (1990) and Stevens (2007). With regards to the phenomenology of improvisation, key publications in the field are those of Sudnow (1993), and Benson (2003). And in respect of studies concerned with the ontology of improvisation, Davies (2011), Borgo (2007), and Bailey (1992) are exemplary.[5] In addition to these concerns, researchers in and into music improvisation have recently begun to explore the potential of Deleuze's work to provide new perspectives on how we understand the practice and its creative process (with implications for the ontological, phenomenological, and pedagogical issues investigated by the researchers indicated above, and others). This more recent interest is exemplified by Peters (2009, 2017), Costa (2011), and certain of the contributors to Buchanan and Swiboda (2004), Hulse and Nesbitt (2010), and Assis and Giudici (2017, 2019).

My own enquiry contributes to the above fields in respect of continuing this widespread interest in engaging with the philosophy of Deleuze, as well as in more general philosophical terms. As I detail in the conclusion, my concept of Rhythmicity, in its musical-philosophical movements (via the three practice-as-research projects), provides fresh insight into how we conceive the way time operates other than in its conception in terms of Deleuze's three syntheses (chapters 3–6) and the Chronos-Aion system (chapters 9–11), McTaggart's A-theory or B-theory, or Henri Bergson's durational multiplicity (see chapter 1 for discussion of both McTaggart's and Bergson's theories in this respect). As noted earlier, the uniqueness of Rhythmicity in each of the three projects presents a way of conceptualising the temporal in respect of a cyclical and hyperbolic movement (in the first project), a multifurcating tonality of time (in the second project), and a line-cycle movement via three interlinked subjectivities (in the third project). All three of these complex, interdisciplinary, musical-philosophical movements theorise time in, and through, practice (as research). As a result, Rhythmicity provides the opportunity to experience facets of the temporal that may previously have been hidden or less well known. This is an assertion to which I return in the conclusion.

A further contribution this book provides, to our understandings of how different practices can interact with philosophy, concerns its exploration of what has been termed the "problem of application": where the epistemological apparatus of one field is used to understand/explain the practice or ontology of another. This is an area of ongoing debate in Performance Philosophy: see, for instance, my discussions in chapters 1 and 2 around the question of applying philosophical notions/concepts to the practices of art/music raised by Cull Ó Maoilearca (2014) and Bowie (2007). It is also a major point of concern in practice as research with regard to the balance of practically oriented and theoretically oriented research methods (as well as in the terminology of both practice and research, themselves—see later). By mixing the modes of research process and presentation in my enquiry (music improvisation and composition; literature and practice review; audio recordings and transcriptions of performances given; written reflections, analyses), the core trajectory of my enquiry is (purposefully) articulated *between* the investigative practices of music and philosophy. This is the constantly-in-flux, interdisciplinary zone of the musical-philosophical, in which my concept of Rhythmicity is expressed. This concept is developed throughout the course of the three projects of my enquiry, with a view to exploring the ways in which music and philosophy can resonate together to produce a novel contribution to our understandings of both fields—and where neither assumes hierarchical importance over the other. Therefore, my experiment and its concept have implications for how we approach and utilise the practices of diverse fields in conjunction with one another, in addition to the novel perspectives on the nature of time and temporal relation that this book offers.

PRACTICE AS RESEARCH: A BRIEF OVERVIEW

As is well documented in the growing body of literature focused on this nascent field of academic enquiry (see, for instance, Barrett and Bolt [2010], Biggs and Karlsson [2011], Borgdorff [2012], Coessens et al. [2009], Doğantan-Dack [2015a], Frayling [1997], Freeman [2010], Hannula et al. [2005], Nelson [2013], Smith and Dean [2009b]), practice as research (or whichever of its alternative terms the various authors promote/prefer to use—see later) began to emerge in the 1990s. As indicated by Doğantan-Dack

(2015b), the fields of design and the visual arts in the UK were the first to embrace the notion that creative practice in the arts could offer a viable method of undertaking research, leading to similar instances of academic investigation in/through the arts in Europe, and eventually to interest among scholars and practitioners in other art forms—including music (1). This interest has spread rapidly. As Kershaw (2009) notes, by the end of the first decade of the 2000s, research specifically utilising "creative performance as a method of enquiry" was being practised "in the UK, Australia, Canada, Scandinavia, South Africa and elsewhere" (105).

From the outset of this new approach to arts research, there has been debate surrounding how best to qualify its process(es) of enquiry. In his terminological overview of the field, Jullander (2013) provides a useful list of some of the more common ways of describing the new paradigm, including "practice-led" and "practice-based" research, "practice as research" (popular in the UK since the 1990s, and my preferred term for describing my own project—as I will discuss), "research in the arts," "artistic research" (a term much favoured on the continent), and "research through" and "research by" practice (13).[6] Jullander points out the fact that, despite some geographical preferences, none of these terms (or any others) have been universally embraced in academic parlance (13).

For the researcher(s) concerned, then, the choice of terms utilised tends to be reflective of how the relationship between "practice" and "research" is conceived in their own particular enquiries. In the polarised terms proffered by Smith and Dean (2009a), for instance, the degree to which what they call "scholarly research" forms the *modus operandi* of the investigation points towards its qualifying as either "practice-led research" or "research-led practice"—where the latter involves methods and outcomes of a more traditional, "scholarly" nature (7). A criticism of Smith and Dean's polarising of practice and research in this manner is that, despite their assertions otherwise, the knowledge component of the enquiry tends to be implied as being located towards the *research* end of the spectrum—with practice providing, for the most part, a means by which research insights can potentially be created, before being "documented, theorised and generalised" in order to fulfil "all the function of research" (7). From the perspective provided by Smith and Dean, the problem of practice being seen (inadvertently or otherwise) as the lesser of the two terms, with respect to providing original contributions to knowledge, remains relatively unaddressed and certainly not helped by the terminology that their book promotes.

In contrast, of the alternative ways of defining this new research paradigm, the terms "research in the arts," "practice research," and "artistic research" offer what seem to be useful general qualifiers under which to gather a rapidly diversifying array of research practices in various art-making fields.

Borgdorff (2011), for example, draws attention to the usefulness of the term "artistic research" in that it "unites the artistic and the academic in an enterprise that impacts on both domains" (44). For their part, Coessens et al. (2009) describe artistic research as oscillating between two modes of exploration: embracing, on the one hand, the "structure, rigour and even constraints" of what they call "formal research" and, on the other, being true to the "wide-eyed, experiential way of being in the world" that is the practice of "artistic creativity" (56–57).

What unites Coessens et al. (2009), Borgdorff (2011), Smith and Dean (2009a), and other commentators, then, is a desire to express a sense of the fluidity, rather than the exclusivity, of the relationship between artistic and academic endeavour. The appeal of methods of research that explicitly utilise dynamic relations between seemingly disparate practices resonates with my own concerns regarding the musical-philosophical and Rhythmicity. However, in spite of the usefulness of many avenues of thought in the extant body of research in this nascent field, I would argue that the older term "practice as research" remains the most representative of my project's concerns. Since I am investigating the notions that (1) music-making can be used as both method and mode of presentation of research, (2) that there can be such a thing as the musical-philosophical, and (3) that the dynamic between music and philosophy can be conceptualised as a rhythmic quality (Rhythmicity), it is the *practical* aspects of the enquiry that underlie the investigation at all stages of the research process. As Nelson (2013) defines it, practice as research is "a key method of enquiry where, in respect of the arts, a practice (creative writing, dance, musical score/performance, theatre/performance, visual exhibition, film or other cultural practice) is submitted as substantial evidence of a research enquiry" (8–9). In the next section, I turn to address these practical methodological aspects of my own project.

MY PRACTICE AS RESEARCH

According to standard methodological approaches, a research project might be premised on the question: What can Deleuze's philosophy of time contribute to our understanding of music practice? However, as indicated earlier, my project seeks to reverse or invert this methodological tendency in order to ask, in addition: What can practice as research in music composition and improvised performance contribute to our understandings of Deleuze's philosophy of time (as expressed via the three pairs of Deleuzian concepts interrogated in this book—difference and repetition, the fold and the incompossible, and Chronos and Aion)? In order to explore these questions, the principle methods of research utilised in this enquiry are as follows: (1) first-person reflections on/analyses of my practices of improvisation and composition; (2) the interrelation of these reflections/analyses with aspects of Deleuze's conceptual apparatus (i.e., the three pairs of concepts indicated earlier); and (3) the musical-philosophical as a means of bringing all these together in a multimodal expression (Rhythmicity).

In all three projects, I chose to restrict my music performance to the solo piano. This restriction was deliberate and is a methodological (and creative) decision according to the manner in which I decided to investigate the concepts pertinent to each project. For instance, in the first project, exploring Deleuze's concepts of difference and repetition, I wanted to begin from first basics, first principles, in order that my investigation could be grounded in the musical-philosophical in a similar (though different) way to how Deleuze grounded each of his three syntheses of time in the basic terms of time: present, past, future (see chapters 3–5). For this reason, I deliberately chose a limited set of notes and intervals with which to investigate difference and repetition from the piano. The solo nature of that musical-philosophical investigation fed directly into the pared-down minimalism of (on the surface, simple, but at depth, endlessly complex and convoluted) differences and repetitions in and for themselves and suited my enquiry's first steps toward constructing the Rhythmicity of this initial Deleuzian conceptual pairing.

In the second project, which involves Deleuze's concepts of the fold and the incompossible, I considered the fact that, as a pianist with two hands, I am able to utilise that fact in the exploration of folding the various combinations of chords in various possible ways (grounded in a notion of incompossibility—see chapters 6–8). If I had engaged with other musicians in the performance of the composition written for this particular project (*In the Garden of the Incompossible*), the elegant simplicity of that two-handedness would have been lost. This is not to say that I would not be delighted to explore how two or more musicians would navigate their ways through "the garden" of the piece's score—but, for the requirements of this enquiry, the solo-pianist, two-handed approach worked best.

Similarly, in the third project, which draws Deleuze's concepts of Chronos and Aion into the musical-philosophical mix, the nature of my composition, *The Time Is out of Joint*, with its alternating sections of silence and sound (see chapter 10), meant that a solo-piano (or solo in general) approach was best. As with *In the Garden*, I would certainly be interested, in future, to discover how multiple musicians might express the alternating silences and sounds of *The Time Is out of Joint* both individually and collectively, but—again, for the express requirements of this enquiry—found that solo performance aided my specific needs.

Improvisation and composition are interlinked in the second and third of the three projects. In the first of the three projects, it is improvisation, alone, that is used. In the second and third projects, improvisation is used to articulate certain notes or chords: in the first instance, groups of three or four notes exploring a range of intervals, differently and repeatedly; in the second, various ways of articulating compound chords composed of major and minor triads that each share at least one common note (which comprise the labyrinth-like grid score of my composition, *In the Garden of the Incompossible*). In the third project, I use improvisation as a way of populating the second of each of the two, alternating sections (of silence and sound) that make up the form of my composition, *The Time Is out of Joint*. Unlike the improvisational practice adopted for the first and second projects (which are improvisations *on*, or *with*, something—some basic materials that pre-exist the improvisations), the way I utilise improvisation in the final, third project, is in terms of what tends to be known as "free" improvisation—that is, I play without reference to any pre-existing notes or chords or directions from the score (other than to silently count to ten while playing—see chapter 10).

As Bailey (1992) notes, free improvisation is, inevitably, a broad church in terms of its definition as music practice: "freely improvised music is an activity which encompasses too many different kinds of players, too many different attitudes to music, too many different concepts of what improvisation is, even, for it all to be subsumed under one name" (83). This situation leads Bailey to coin his famous neologism, "non-idiomatic music," in order to describe these fundamentally diverse approaches to the act of improvisation that can, yet, somehow be unified under one umbrella notion: that such activity tends not to be "tied to representing an idiomatic identity" (xii). Objections have, inevitably, been raised as to the validity of Bailey's new term. For instance, Hamilton (2000) argues, convincingly, that Bailey's own creative practices as "a highly idiomatic and individual improviser" has meant that he has built up a set of "favourite stylistic or structural devices," the existence of which would seem, thus, to preclude the possibility of his actually being able to practice non-idiomatic improvisation, in spite of it being his declared ideal as a free-improvising musician (182). Peters (2017), for his part, expands Bailey's original binarism of idiomatic and nonidiomatic improvisation into six new categories of classification: fixed idiomatic, semi-fixed idiomatic, unfixed idiomatic, unfixed cross-idiomatic, fixed nonidiomatic, and unfixed nonidiomatic (76). For Peters, these variants are applied to the act of music made in performance with regard to how closely (fixed) or not (unfixed) the improvisation relates to the norms of the idiom or idioms in question and, in respect of the fixed or unfixed nonidiomatic labels, whether or not the improviser improvises with a sense of commitment (a fixed nonidiomatic approach) or a sense of irony (an unfixed approach) in respect of their attitude to the music as made and its potential resonances with past musics made (2017, 87). Davies (2011) is also instructive in respect of how free improvisers are free to draw on "various musical traditions as ingredients in their improvisation" while remaining untied to notions of their actually performing a pre-existing work or operating exclusively within a specific musical tradition (160).

Arguments over precise definition aside, the general idea that free improvisers are relatively unrestricted with regard to what they actually play when they perform—and that such freedom is more in abundance in the act of freely improvising than it is in improvisations undertaken in the practice of bebop in jazz, or in Baroque-era figured bass, or in the North Indian raga system—stands as a useful working definition of the music-making process known as free improvisation.

In each of the three practice research projects of this enquiry, I employ first-person reflection in order to elucidate aspects of the music practices utilised. As Jullander (2013) points out, despite the relative nascence of practice as research and the inevitable lack of a widely accepted, stable methodology for practitioner-researchers to draw, reflection on one's own artistic work is one of the most consistently utilised methods across the field of practice as research/artistic research (15). While examples of a bias in more traditional research against the use of self-reflection and the subjective are plentiful in the literature, Haseman and Mafe (2009) articulate the issue particularly succinctly when they summarise the more standardised position thus: "most established research strategies are carefully structured to exclude the researcher, based on the belief that researcher subjectivity stands to infect the objective 'truth' and universal applicability of research findings" (212). In answer to criticism that reflection on one's own practice effectively nullifies the (supposedly essential) objective distance between researcher and researched adopted in older/more established research practices, practitioner-researchers argue that such "personal interest and experience" presents, instead, "an advantage to be exploited," as opposed to a hindrance to the enquiry in hand (Barrett 2010, 5). This unique situatedness of the practitioner-researcher thus provides an opportunity for the inherently ongoing, emergent quality of one's understanding of one's practice to bring fresh insight to that which is being explored (for example, the Deleuzian concepts I am investigating and transforming).

Regardless of whether one is concerned with music practice considered as practice alone, or music practice *as* research, understanding one's own ways of practising (in the case of this book, my processes of improvisation and composition) is a continual process for a musician, in much the same way that mastering an instrument is an open-ended undertaking. In fact, as the improvising drummer and educator John Stevens has pointed out, the two are not mutually exclusive activities: "Improvisation is the basis of learning to play a musical instrument. . . . It has to be realised that a person's own investigation of an instrument—his [or her] exploration of it—is totally valid" (Bailey

1992, 98). And when the practices of improvisation (and composition) are utilised in making an argument for the validity of the musical-philosophical via Rhythmicity (as in this book), the experience of exploring how to turn one's musical practices and techniques to the research in hand becomes a part of the enquiry—one that is just as valid as the more traditional methods utilised (literature review, music analysis, transcription).

The next major component of my multifaceted enquiry involves the utilisation of aspects of Deleuze's conceptual apparatus. I use Deleuze "as" method not so much as "influence" or "inspiration," but in order to bring the concepts selected into direct relation with my music-making on the level of a two-way process of transformation: the musical-philosophical expression I am investigating and enacting in this book and its practice as research projects. As I discuss in chapters 1 and 2, I am critical of certain other music projects involving Deleuze as offering little beyond an application of his philosophy, or as name-checking his concepts while not necessarily engaging with them on a more meaningful level. Accordingly, in the projects undertaken in this enquiry, Deleuze's concepts are drawn into the musical-philosophical mix, functioning as elements in that mix rather than as ways of understanding imposed from without.

Deleuze created an array of concepts during his lifetime—some of which were repeated (though differently) in more than one publication. The concepts of his that I have chosen to investigate in my enquiry are each selected on the basis of their potential contribution to the development of Rhythmicity. In addition, they are chosen based on their resonance with the music practices and practitioners that have influenced my own music-making (both historically and in the projects undertaken for this book). For instance, in chapters 3–5, I investigate difference and repetition, beginning with these concepts since they form the foundation of Deleuze's philosophical system.[7] A second reason for choosing difference and repetition is that they resonate strongly with my long-standing interest in using music-making techniques from American Minimalism (as I discuss in chapters 3–5). In chapters 6–8, I draw on Deleuze's concepts of the fold and the incompossible.[8] These are selected on account of their relevance to, firstly, the process of mixing together the diverse practices of philosophical conceptualisation and music-making; and, secondly, their pertinence to the radical activities of a set of music collectives and musicians that have been influential to my practice (again, both historically and in relation to the second project of this enquiry).[9] Finally, in chapters 9–11, I target Deleuze's philosophy of time via his concepts of Chronos and Aion. These are chosen in order to consolidate certain of the insights of the previous two projects and their chapters: namely, the usefulness of multiple analytical perspectives and multimodal enquiry in transforming Deleuze's conceptual apparatus, as well as our understandings of the music practices utilised (not to mention the continued evolution of Rhythmicity as concept/ conceptual practice). Generally speaking, Chronos and Aion relate to conceptions of measured and unmeasured time, respectively—and, in Chronos-Aion, the interrelation of both (as I explore in the chapters themselves). Through providing multiple perspectives on the third project in practice as research (via the composer-me, the performer-me, the listener-me), I find, in Deleuze's Chronos-Aion, a resonance with the temporal experience of composing, performing, and listening to, the music for that project. In so doing (as with each of the three projects), I also find a way of transforming our understandings of Deleuze's concepts as much as also to highlight the unique perspective they offer our understandings of the music practices employed. This pursuit of an equality of voice (musical, philosophical) is at the heart of Rhythmicity.

My enquiry is Deleuzian in the sense that I have found, in Deleuze's work, a useful set of concepts to approach in a musical-philosophical manner, drawing aspects of his philosophy into my music-making—for the purpose of transforming both in the process. As Flaxman (2017) highlights, for many artists involved in academic research, "One does not set out to be a Deleuzian"; it is, rather, that one finds one's art-making process and Deleuze's conceptual apparatus becoming the site of what Flaxman (paraphrasing Deleuze on his attraction to the philosophy of Spinoza) calls "an 'unprepared encounter' that grips the artist, and then 'it is as if one discovers that one is' a Deleuzian" (14). As Colebrook (2002) notes, one of the prime difficulties in understanding Deleuze's philosophy in terms of method lies in the fact that he tended to reinvent his "style and vocabulary with each new project" (4). However, by adopting this approach in his research, Deleuze was able to tackle again and anew the problem of thinking difference and "the dynamism and instability of thought" (Colebrook 2002, 4). For Deleuze, the concepts he created evolved as a result of the encounters between diverse fields of practice, and he is in/famous for drawing on a wide range of disciplines alongside philosophy in pursuit of the themes of his research. It is this focus on the emergent and the repeatedly different in Deleuze's creative process, then, that makes the multifarious process of his conceptual creation so appealing to an enquiry like my own, investigating the musical-philosophical as a rhythmic quality of interdisciplinary research (Rhythmicity).

While the Deleuzian notions of difference and repetition, the fold and the incompossible, and Chronos and Aion, are not necessarily familiar to musicians (at least in terms of how they verbally articulate—if at all—their own practice), this process of taking a philosophical theme and exploring how it might receive fresh insight via the modes of the musical opens the practices of both fields to novelty. This is, of course, one of the aims of my book: to investigate a notion of the musical-philosophical, and to express its perpetual disciplinary "in-between-ness" in terms of my developing concept of Rhythmicity.

Artistic reflection in practice as research, in its capacity for learning/reflection as part of its *modus operandi*, offers a useful epistemological ground for this enquiry—one through which the danger of merely applying the concepts of Deleuze's philosophy to the practices of my music-making is lessened (or theorised otherwise) on account of the two-way process engendered.

The final aspect of practice as research that I utilise in the three projects and their resulting chapters is focused on the emergent, ongoing nature of the musical-philosophical undertaking itself. It is, of course, not uncommon for research undertakings to evolve/diverge in various ways from their original posited methods of enquiry through the experiences garnered in the course of an investigation. Indeed, as Gritten (2015) suggests, it may indeed be more enticing for practitioners involved in research to "simply get on with it" and "spend less time on determining the nature" of artistic practice as research (80). However, in the case of my own enquiry, the very act of engaging in musical-philosophical practice as research necessitates a repeated return to methodological issues as a core aspect of the investigative process, since the focus of my attention is, in its interdisciplinary constitution, in an ever-emergent, unstable state of becoming; a nascent (or newly recognised) mode of research practice.

That practice as research, more generally, should explicitly embrace the emergent nature of its methods is argued by Barrett (2010) to be a major imperative of its enquiry. Barrett explicitly encourages the ever-evolving, creatively unstable nature of its investigative process as part-and-parcel of the wider methodological issues themselves—since these "are *necessarily* emergent and subject to repeated adjustment, rather than remaining fixed throughout the process of enquiry" (6). Accordingly, a feature of my three projects as a whole is the ongoing exploration of practice as research methodology. In this manner, my enquiry benefits from the actual experience of undertaking practice as research, rather than (simply or otherwise) writing about it from a theoretical position outside the enquiry. This latter perspective tends to be the case in, for instance, the first part of Nelson (2013), who, despite (or indeed, because of) aiming to provide a wide-ranging "how-to" guide to practice as research (or "research in the arts" in his terminology), spreads the generality a little too thinly, resulting (to my eye) in an unnecessary move away from stressing the importance of the actualities of practitioner-researchers' singular experiences of their own projects.

Note: In order to facilitate the analyses that make up chapters 4, 7, and 10, the reader is requested to download the audio tracks available at the link provided later. For the analyses in chapters 4 and 7, the relevant tracks should ideally be listened to in "shuffle mode" (and on repeat). The reasons for this are explained in the chapters themselves. The tracks are available to listen to/download via the following link: https://tinyurl.com/4v5k8wpj.

NOTES

1. As I discuss further, I am qualifying my undertaking as "practice as research," in distinction to several other terms in common usage (for example, artistic research, practice-led research, practice-based research) that describe an investigation such as mine—that is, one that mixes artistic practice with various other modes and methods of enquiry.

2. See the section, "Rhythm," in chapter 2 for an overview of the study of rhythm in various disciplines to date.

3. Unpublished correspondence with the author, 6 June 2019.

4. Alongside its comprehensive overview of the multifaceted work of John Cage (who is directly referenced in the book's subtitle), Nyman's book was among the first to introduce the pioneers of the North American minimalists (Terry Riley, La Monte Young, Steve Reich, and Philip Glass), and the British free improvisation and experimental music scenes centred around the composer Cornelius Cardew and the AMM music ensemble, to a wider audience/readership. Each of these artists have been hugely influential in respect of my own music practice (as I frequently reflect on in the chapters of this book).

5. Addressing issues across a number of these concerns is the collection edited by Lewis and Piekut (2016) and, for example, the journals *Critical Studies in Improvisation*, *Creativity Research Journal*, and *Perspectives of New Music*.

6. A recent addition to this list is "practice research," a term utilised for a research event at Goldsmith's College, London, in 2015 (see http://www.gold.ac.uk/news/the-future-of-practice-research/). I should also include the aforementioned field of Performance Philosophy, since one aspect of the work undertaken in PP is to consider artistic performance (in a range of disciplines) to be able to engage in higher-level research of the kind practised in philosophical enquiry.

7. As I note in chapter 3, *Difference and Repetition* was the book in which Deleuze began to build his conceptual apparatus—to "do philosophy" of his own design (Deleuze 2004a, xiii).

8. As discussed in chapters 6–8, the incompossible is a concept rooted in divergence—a multiplicity of possible worlds coexisting as the "play in the creation of the world" (Deleuze 2004a: 62).

9. I am referring to the likes of Cornelius Cardew and the Scratch Orchestra, AMM Music, Derek Bailey and Company, Ornette Coleman's Prime Time, and Anthony Braxton—as I discuss in chapter 6.

Chapter 1

Why Deleuze?

Why is Gilles Deleuze such an important philosophical figure, and why is his work so relevant to music research (and artistic research more generally)? For my own part, Deleuze's philosophy of time has proven to be a fertile breeding ground for my various musical-philosophical projects of the last decade or so. But I am not alone in my appreciation of the extraordinary potential of his ideas to aid our understandings of many things in and of the world. In the early 1970s, Michel Foucault famously (and provocatively) declared that, in the future, twentieth-century philosophy would eventually come to be regarded as "Deleuzian" (Foucault 1970). In support of this prophecy, while at the same time extending the scope to include early-twenty-first-century thought, Moisala et al. (2017) call Deleuze "one of the most influential philosophers of our time" (1). It is certainly widely recognised that Deleuze has come to be a major philosophical figure for many researchers across an impressive range of disciplines. As Smith (2008) notes, in his entry under "Gilles Deleuze" for the *Stanford Encyclopedia of Philosophy*: "along with a growing influence in philosophy, Deleuze's work is approvingly cited by, and his concepts put to use by, researchers in architecture, urban studies, geography, film studies, musicology, anthropology, gender studies, literary studies and other fields."

By any account, over the last few decades, Deleuze's philosophy has become of increasing importance to researchers across a number of fields, including a growing interest among scholars in the field of research in the arts. In support of this assertion, the pianist and artistic researcher Paulo de Assis (2017b) points to how Deleuze's work (either alone, or in his collaborations with the radical psychoanalyst and political activist, Félix Guattari), "acts as a key reference for many artist-researchers, who engage in knowledge production both in academic and non-academic fields of practice" (9). I discuss the relevance of Deleuze to music research and music researchers later in this chapter, but first I provide an overview of Deleuze's work and influences, with special focus on his contribution to the philosophy of time, which is of direct importance to my concerns in this book and its projects in practice as research.

GILLES DELEUZE AND THE PHILOSOPHY OF TIME

Gilles Deleuze (1925–1995) was a French philosopher, active in the second half of the twentieth century, who became most widely known for his philosophy of difference. In his early magnum opus, *Difference and Repetition* (first published in 1968), Deleuze elevated difference from its more typical supporting role as an indicator of the difference between two or more things. In place of this notion, he created a concept wherein difference is considered as ungrounded in anything else; a difference that is released from its subservience to notions of identity and sameness: a *difference-in-itself* (Stagoll 2010a: 75).[1] The radicality of this conception cannot be overstated. As Colebrook (2002) highlights, until Deleuze introduced his concept of difference-in-itself, "the history of Western thought had been based on being and identity"—that is, the idea that "there is some *being* that then goes through becoming or is then differentiated" (2). Through Deleuze, difference becomes a creative force for change, or change itself. In constructing his philosophy of difference, Deleuze created a series of further concepts (alone, and together with Guattari), some of which appear multiple times in his oeuvre, some of which feature only sparingly. These concepts include (in alphabetical order, not order of hierarchical importance, and certainly not an exhaustive list): actuality, affect, assemblage, becoming, body without organs, deterritorialisation, event, fold, haecceity, immanence, movement-image, multiplicity, nomadism, repetition, rhizome, simulacrum, time-image, univocity, and virtuality.

The thing that links all these concepts, no matter the diverse uses Deleuze puts them to in his various publications, is that they are each a means of expressing Deleuze's philosophy of *process*: his keen interest, throughout his career, in a philosophy that is grounded in change; not how things change, but conceptualising change itself, as process, in and of time. His philosophy of time is thus processual—and at odds with much of the mainstream ideas in the wider philosophy of time as championed for the last one hundred years and more (while taking influence from the work of Henri Bergson notion of duration [*la durée*] and Nietzsche's concept of the eternal return, as I will discuss).

In the well-known and widely referenced McTaggart model of time as either "A-theory" or "B-theory" (coined by the philosopher J. M. E. McTaggart in the early twentieth century), there are two distinct ways of conceptualising time. In the A-theory model, the future is anticipated and the past is remembered; all events begin first in the future, become part of the present, and ultimately make their way into the past. In the B-theory model, all times are equally real, there being no major distinction between past, present, and future—the differences we experience between them merely highlighting our lack of knowledge of the future compared to the past. A-theorists understand time as a process of ongoing transformation; B-theorists consider time akin to the Einsteinian space-time, wherein time is a fourth dimension that can be plotted in much the same way as its three-dimensional spatial cousins. The first theory is dynamic, the second static (mirroring the polarised positions taken by the Ancient Greeks in respect of Heraclitus and his ephemeral never-the-same-river-twice, and Parmenides and his timeless, unchanging reality).[2]

In contrast, Deleuze's own philosophy of time is conceptualised via his three syntheses (in *Difference and Repetition*) and the Chronos-Aion relation (in *The Logic of Sense*). Where the three syntheses construct a model of time that is passive in terms of a subject's inability to act, think, or intend, due to the fracturing of conceptions of "free will" into a manifold of temporal processes opening the future and transforming the past (Williams 2011, 16–17), the Chronos-Aion relation theorises any given activity as an interrelation of the bodily conditions of the present and the incorporeality of the past and the future (18; 150).[3] Deleuze therefore models time as neither subjective nor objective, but in terms of process.

True to his interest in understanding and expressing a philosophy that takes account of process and change over time, Deleuze often used his concepts in different ways in different publications. In this way, throughout his philosophical investigations, Deleuze explored the major notion that a philosophy of change must *itself change*. As Smith (2008) notes, as much as Deleuze can be labelled a philosopher of difference, he is also a philosopher of *process* (as a key aspect of difference and its mechanisms of change). This interest in process is an important reason why Deleuze's philosophy appeals so strongly to artistic researchers in music, since any conceptualisation of process introduces the question of temporality into the heart of the enquiry at hand. This is not to suggest, of course, that musicians are the only artists who practice their art in time, or that musician-researchers are somehow uniquely placed to investigate the philosophy of time where their fellow performing artists (for instance) are not. I am merely talking in terms of musicians and music-making, here, on account of the primary concerns of my enquiry and the fact that I am a musician. Musicians, like other artists, are keenly aware of the importance of time in the making of their work. This is especially true for performers especially so, given their intimate relation to the timeframes of a given performance; but it is also the case for composers, who work with time at a certain remove from the time of concert performance, yet are still connected to it by virtue of the work of composition and its relation to its event-to-come. Deleuze's philosophy of time, in particular, then, holds a definite attraction to artist-researchers investigating the various processes inherent in music-making.

For Deleuze, process, and the concepts he develops as a result of investigating its philosophy alongside that of difference, offered him a way to counter the dominant *structuralist* perspectives that had held sway in philosophy (and in other fields of research) for a number of years prior to his first major publications in the late-1960s and beyond. At the time of Deleuze's earliest writings, the major movement in (so-called continental, typically French) philosophy was that of structuralism. Via the structuralist perspective, leading thinkers of the mid-twentieth century, such as Jacques Lacan, Claude Lévi-Strauss, Roland Barthes, and Louis Althusser, sought to map the underlying structures of things and practices as diverse as the self and society, human behaviours in different cultures, writing, and Marxism. Taking inspiration from the semiology of Ferdinand de Saussure, structuralists sought to identify the underlying "sign-systems" by means of which, as Sarap (1993) attests, "the general structures of human activity" could be isolated and, as a result, understood (39).

Key post-structuralist thinkers like Deleuze, alongside Michel Foucault, Jacques Derrida, Jean-François Lyotard, and Pierre Bourdieu, criticised the structuralist worldview in respect of its tendency, intentional or not, to omit or suppress that which did not easily fit within its epistemological structures (Sim and Van Loon 2009, 87).[4] One such rogue element, elusive to the sign-system models of the structuralists (who, essentially, chose to therefore ignore it in their analyses), was that ultimate agent of change itself: *time*. "For the analyst, time no longer counts," argues Bourdieu (1977); "To restore to practice its practical truth, we must therefore reintroduce time into the theoretical representation of a practice which, being temporally structured, is intrinsically defined by its *tempo*" (8).

Taking up the baton in favour of such a necessary reintroduction of time into our understandings of practices, the formative Deleuze (re)turned to the (at that time long-dismissed) work of Bergson—in particular, to aspects of his philosophy of time.[5] In early publications such as the essay on Hume (Deleuze 1991), "La conception de la difference chez Bergson" (Deleuze 1956), and *Bergsonism* (Deleuze 1988a), Bergson's philosophy became a vital touchstone in the development of Deleuze's original thought. In his afterword to the book on Bergson, Deleuze (1988a) calls this "return to Bergson" not only an indication of "renewed admiration" for Bergson's philosophy, but also "a renewal or extension of his project today" (115). In later publications, Deleuze retained his Bergsonian tendency, drawing on his predecessor's work on perception and memory in both of the *Cinema* books written in the last full decade of his life (Deleuze 1986; 1989). The main conceptual influence Deleuze took from Bergson's philosophy relates to their shared interest in conceptualising time and change in terms of heterogeneity, radical difference, and becoming—most notably, the latter's (interlinked) concepts of duration and multiplicity. With duration, Bergson theorised a concept of lived time in opposition to the quantified time of the clock, for instance. Clock time, for Bergson, spatialises time, distorting it from its continuity (Stagoll 2010b, 82). Such time is merely a fourth dimension of space—a "homogenous time" through which one counts simultaneities (such as the movements of the hands of a clock) rather than measuring duration itself (Bergson 2001, 107–109). Bergson's concept of duration, on the other hand, theorises a heterogeneous time: an internal experience of time "without moments external to one another, without relation to number"; "a process of organisation or interpenetration of conscious states . . . which constitutes true duration" (108). As Deleuze (1988a) states, the conception of time in terms of a Bergsonian duration is that of a particular kind of multiplicity: "an internal multiplicity of succession, of fusion, of organisation, of heterogeneity, of qualitative discrimination, or of *difference in kind*" (38).[6]

This conception of multiplicity and its multifarious, temporally grounded, and intensive nature, could equally well describe Deleuze's own conceptual apparatus and its use, as formulated and reformulated across his oeuvre.[7] In other words: as noted earlier, Deleuze's concepts are not fixed in their usage, and he is inclined to adopt and adapt his own prior work as much as that of others.' For example, Deleuze is well-known for his practice, throughout his career, of taking other philosophers' concepts and recasting them for his own purposes—such as the aforementioned Bergson and Hume, along with the likes of Nietzsche, Spinoza, Kant, Foucault, and Leibniz (the last two of whom receive more detailed attention in chapters 6–8 of this book).[8] Added to this creative practice of adopting/adapting others' concepts, he is equally well-known for generating concepts through philosophical "encounters" with the work of practitioners in fields other than that of philosophy—for instance, in the books on the paintings of Francis Bacon (Deleuze 2005) and the writings of Franz Kafka (Deleuze and Guattari 1986), and, of course, the various directors referenced in the two *Cinema* books (Deleuze 1986; 1989). As I discuss in more detail in the next section, musical encounters were also a key source of conceptual creation for Deleuze. For example, Deleuze took particular influence from the composers Pierre Boulez and Olivier Messiaen—both of whom feature in, among other publications, Deleuze (2005) and Deleuze and Guattari (2004, 1994).

As Deleuze and Guattari (1994) argue, the practice of philosophy is characterised by creation, not discovery: "The object of philosophy is to create concepts that are always new"; "Concepts are not waiting for us ready-made" (5). In a project such as my own, this definition of philosophical practice is instructive—in particular with respect to the importance of the *novelty* of conceptual creation. In order for my concept of Rhythmicity to develop the flexibility to provide insights across a number of Deleuzian concepts and musical and artistic-research practices (my own and those related to the fields most closely related to my enquiry), its definition and the way in which it is practised necessarily changes and develops/evolves over the course of the book. "The concept speaks the event, not the essence or the thing" (Deleuze and Guattari 1994, 21)—and it is the event of the musical-philosophical in the practice as research projects in this book that provides, in different ways, the opportunity for Rhythmicity not so much to *speak* (given that the modes of expression of the musical-philosophical are not confined to words alone), but to *perform* its concept.

If Deleuze's philosophy is characterised by a series of interrelated and ever-changing enquiries into, for instance, process, difference, becoming, event, and time, then I would argue that my own musical-philosophical enquiry, via the development and expression of the original concept of Rhythmicity, can be considered Deleuzian—at least in the sense that the definition and use of my central concept is interrelated and ever-changing across the three projects of this book. It is also Deleuzian in the sense that I am concerned with processes of time—through my investigations into the series of Deleuze's concepts selected in each project, and also given the temporal nature of my new concept of Rhythmicity (being a rhythmic quality expressed in multimodal and musical-philosophical fashion in various ways across the book). My enquiry is *not*, however, Deleuzian in the limited sense of (simply or otherwise) applying Deleuze's philosophy and concepts to "explain away" the processes and practices of the music-making undertaken. Instead, I utilise Deleuze's concepts in the process of developing Rhythmicity, as elements alongside other elements (such as music-making, the writings of others, analysis, and transcription) in the musical-philosophical makeup of my original concept and its expression in this book.

This issue of application and utilisation is one that I return to at key moments throughout the course of what follows. But, at this point, I want to turn to address the use of Deleuze's work in the music research (and certain instances of music practice) of others to date, in order to further contextualise my own enquiry.

DELEUZE AND MUSIC PRACTICE AND/AS RESEARCH

Since the early 2000s, a number of theorists have investigated music from the perspective of the philosophy of Deleuze. Of these, publications by Bogue (2003) and Campbell (2013), alongside collections edited by Buchanan and

Swiboda (2004), Hulse and Nesbitt (2010), MacArthur et al. (2016), Moisala et al. (2017), and Assis and Giudici (2017, 2019), provide key insights concerning how our understandings of a wide variety of styles, concepts, practices, and practitioners can be expanded and enriched via Deleuze's conceptual apparatus. In respect of improvisation (alongside composition, one of the predominant music-making practices in the three projects of this book), authors in these publications tend to focus their engagements with Deleuze around a set of concepts emphasising process over product, dynamism over stasis. Given improvisation's openness to the conditions and contingencies of its acts of performance, this is hardly surprising, of course, and Deleuze's concepts of assemblage, becoming, de/re/territorialisation, difference/repetition, event, nomadism, and rhizome are among those regularly drawn on by music theorists to express a sense of the process/dynamism of improvised music-making.

However, my own undertaking both links up with, and contributes something fresh to, extant Deleuzian research in respect of the particular use I make of Deleuze's conceptual apparatus—and in respect of the concepts selected. My strategy of treating these concepts as elements in the musical-philosophical mix means that they take their place alongside the music practices involved, rather than standing as epistemological apparatus for restricting the music to mere illustration of the philosophical ideas concerned. Of the concepts themselves, while difference and repetition (which I utilise in chapters 3–5) receive widespread attention in Deleuzian music scholarship, the fold and the incompossible (see chapters 6–8), and Chronos and Aion (see chapters 9–11), are less frequently referenced. Hence, my project provides an opportunity in Deleuze studies, and in music research that utilises Deleuze, to explore what these lesser-known Deleuzian concepts can add to an enquiry such as mine, investigating a musical-philosophical expression in which neither music nor philosophy (considered in purely disciplinary terms) take privilege over one another, but are equal partners in the interdisciplinary interrelation.

In terms of the relationship between philosophy and music in Deleuze's own work, Deleuze's writings on music draw on a relatively small set of composers from the Western canon: a majority of whom operated within the modernist paradigm (Campbell 2013, 2; Moisala et al. 2017, 4). Of these, the most commonly cited are Boulez (see Deleuze 1995; 2006a; 2006b; and Deleuze and Guattari 1994, 2004) and Messiaen (Deleuze 2005; and Deleuze and Guattari 1994; 2004). However, alongside these two, one also finds references to Cage, Debussy, and Stravinsky (Deleuze 2006a; and Deleuze and Guattari 1994, 2004), Berio, Stockhausen, and Wagner (Deleuze 2006a; and Deleuze and Guattari 2004), Varese (Deleuze and Guattari 2004), Webern (Deleuze 2006b; and Deleuze and Guattari 2004), and the American

Minimalist La Monte Young (Deleuze and Guattari 2004). The use Deleuze makes of the music/music-theory of these composers relates, in the most part, to his notions of music as a "cosmic" force/assemblage of different forces: "the essential thing is no longer forms and matters, or themes, but forces, densities, intensities" (Deleuze and Guattari 2004, 378). Deleuze focuses on modernist music in particular, given its propensity for bringing together disparate elements in its multi-layered compositions—practising a "heterophony" of difference via folding (cf. Deleuze 2006a).[9] One only has to consider works such as Boulez's *Pli selon pli* (1957–1989), Cage's *Concert for Piano and Orchestra* (1958) or *4'33"* (1952), and Messiaen's *Chronochromie* (1960), to get a sense of the appeal of these ("cosmic") compositional approaches to Deleuze in constructing his conceptual apparatus in respect of, for example: (1) heterophony (as in the Boulez); (2) relating music to other sounds/acts in the concert hall (à la Cage); or (3) opening the concept of music to include sounds from the wider world/nature (thinking of Cage, again, and Messiaen's use of birdsong).

As with his references to novelists, painters, and film directors, Deleuze takes what he requires by way of conceptual inspiration from the musicians he draws on. In contrast, a number of music-researchers utilising Deleuze often provide little more than a commentary on the work Deleuze has already carried out, before (simply or otherwise) applying his ideas to their chosen field/subject.[10] Consider, for instance, Swiboda (2004). Declaring the so-called electric period music-making techniques of the trumpeter Miles Davis in the 1970s to be resistant to conventional musicological analysis (201), Swiboda, instead, employs Davis as "a worthwhile 'mediator,' both for Deleuze and Guattari's own concepts, but also for their philosophical approach" (213). In providing this mediation, Davis's 1975 albums *Agharta* and *Pangaea* function as music examples for Deleuze and Guattari's (2004) concept of the "cosmic refrain" (and related concepts such as de/re/territorialisation and assemblage). This kind of approach certainly broadens the appeal and relevance of Deleuze to music research, with theorists expanding the styles of music considered to include, among others, jazz, improvised music, pop, metal, Indian classical, and—in the case of Campbell (2013)—Gaelic psalm singing. However, it succeeds less in making an original contribution in the musical-philosophical terms I am interested in exploring in my book. One major area where such approaches fail is in respect of the fact that they tend to consider Deleuze's (and Deleuze and Guattari's) conceptual apparatus as a means of understanding the music concerned differently, rather than exploring how the music itself may be able to offer something fresh to Deleuze studies. As with the problem of application discussed earlier (and elsewhere in this book), the direction of epistemological flow in such approaches is all too often one way (i.e., from philosophy to music and not, or rarely, vice versa).

In contrast to the growing body of theoretical writings on music (and other art forms) utilising Deleuze, instances of practitioner-researchers in music engaging with his philosophy is not only more recent but also more tentative.[11] An instructive example is provided by Crispin and Gilmore (2014). In this impressive anthology of artistic experimentation/research across the field of music practice (e.g., composition, electronic music, jazz, improvisation), the use of Deleuze is limited to only five of the thirty-five collected essays. Of those five, in not one is Deleuze approached as anything other than a means of *applying* an extant conceptual model to a particular music practice. In Schwab (2014), there is mere passing reference to "affect" and classical music performance (115); in Coessens et al. (2014), Deleuze is used to conceptualise rehearsal and performance, and the relationship between composer and performer, in terms of "repetition" and (a Bergson-influenced) "intuition" (349, 352); and, in Coessens and Östersjö (2014a), "difference" is applied to the ways of exploring the relations between the unknown and the known in artistic experimentation (365–366).

Of course, it can be argued that there is no particular reason for musician-researchers to draw on the philosophy of Deleuze (or any other philosopher, for that matter) in their experiments in practice as research—and there is certainly a logic to such an argument. However, given the shared interest in investigating processes of creation in practices that operate in and of time, the concerns of the artist-researcher and the concerns of Deleuze overlap to an extent that, in my estimation, makes an engagement with Deleuzian concepts almost inevitable. The important issue, then, given such an overlap, becomes *how* one balances the relationship between one's music-making and Deleuze's philosophical concepts without allowing either to dominate (i.e., being mindful of the problem of application).

Alongside the nascent body of artistic research exploring Deleuzian themes, it should also be noted that there are, to date, certain music practitioners who have engaged with, or more generally name-checked, aspects of Deleuze's work. As Campbell (2013) references, the composer Brian Ferneyhough has indicated influence from Deleuze's book on Bacon (Deleuze 2005) and Deleuze and Guattari (2004) on their concepts of the refrain and deterritorialisation (see Campbell 2013, 166). Drawing inspiration from Deleuze's concepts of difference and repetition, and also Deleuze's philosophical engagement with the "monadology" of Gottfried Leibniz, the composer and improviser Bernhard Lang has produced a series of works titled *Differenz/Wiederholung* (1998–, ongoing) and *Monadologies* (2007–, ongoing). These pieces explore processes of repetition of minute fragments of extant musical works (by Haydn, Puccini, Bob Dylan, and Miles Davis), using computer programs to generate extended iterations of aspects of these fragments which are then scored for performance by ensembles (see Rutherford-Johnson 2017, 258–259; Gottschalk 2016, 141).

In addition to the Deleuzian influence cited by Ferneyhough and Lang, the various artists whose work is gathered in tribute to Deleuze on the albums *Folds and Rhizomes for Gilles Deleuze* (released not long after Deleuze's death in 1995 by the label Sub Rosa) and *In Memoriam Gilles Deleuze* (released in 1996 on the Mille Plateaux label) provide further examples of how Deleuze's concepts have functioned as catalysts for music-making (though not specifically practice as research, as with my enquiry). (See Murphy [2004] for a comprehensive overview of the music on, and Deleuzian themes of, these two albums.) A more recent example is that of the 2019 duo-improvisation project *The Orchid and the Wasp* by the electric guitarist Chris Sharkey and the drummer/percussionist Mark Sanders. Again, though, as with Ferneyhough, Lang, and the artists on the aforementioned tribute albums, the relevance of Deleuze's work to the music-making of Sharkey and Sanders is more along the lines of inspiration and application than that of a two-way transformative process (as I undertake in the practice as research projects in this enquiry). By this I mean that, while Deleuze is directly referenced as having been an inspiration in the making of these various musics, there is no subsequent move (or desire) to use what is performed as a way of contributing to our knowledge of the concepts in question. Deleuze's work becomes, in these instances, a means of generating new music, but music is not considered as a means of generating new philosophy.

Despite the relative scarcity of artistic practice and artistic research in music involving Deleuze—and given, even in the little work that does exist, the tendency to apply (rather than transform) the concepts borrowed—the inauguration of the *International Conference on Deleuze and Artistic Research* in Ghent, Belgium, in 2015 (hosted by the Orpheus Research Centre in Music, with subsequent conferences in 2017 and 2019), bears testament to the recent, and increasing, relevance of Deleuze to musicians who conduct research in and through their own practice. An important example of music practitioner-researchers utilising the work of Deleuze in their own projects is that provided by certain instantiations of the pianist Paulo de Assis's *Diabelli Machines*[x].[12] Instantiations of *Diabelli Machines*[x] are typically multimodal in their manner of presentation, given that they encompass "a series of performances, lectures, articles, or installations" focused on exploring various artistic-research approaches to Beethoven's *Diabelli Variations*, op. 120.[13] Of these, the second, third, and fourth manifestations deal explicitly with concepts from Deleuze—and are, accordingly, subtitled *Deleuzabelli Variations I–III*. The abstract/programme note for the last of these three describes its creative process as utilising "diverse techniques of elimination, substitution, and replacement" in relation to Beethoven's original, with Deleuze's (linked) concepts of difference and repetition (from Deleuze 2004a) providing "a sort of method related to processes of continuous transformation and permanent becoming."[14]

A key way in which Assis's approach to making *Deleuzeabelli Variations* is pertinent to my own research lies in how he declares his use of Deleuze to be a *method* ("sort of" or otherwise) in the making of new music.[15] The "sort of" qualifier is important when considering Deleuze's own attitudes to method/ology as a way of creating insights in philosophy. Deleuze eschewed any notion of having or utilising a method or methodological set, preferring instead to consider each new project/book as a means of reinventing philosophy and its concepts. "If Deleuze has a method," cautions Colebrook (2002), "it is that we should never have *a* method, but should allow ourselves to *become* in relation to what we are seeking to understand" (46). His approach, therefore, is more along the lines of an *anti*-method. My own use of Deleuze is in these terms. Certain of his concepts form part of the methodological apparatus I am using in this book, but they do not provide its method of enquiry alone.

Deleuze "as" method ("sort of" or anti-) is also an approach flagged by Moisala et al. (2017) as an important avenue of thought for interrelating Deleuze and music. In the introduction to their edited collection, the authors indicate the importance of exploring the "methodological implications" of Deleuze's work for music researchers (2). As with the case of my enquiry, an approach that utilises Deleuze as part of a method/ology of music research, or music practice as research, differs from much of the theoretical work on Deleuze and music which (as I suggest, above) has a tendency to apply Deleuze's concepts to music practices/practitioners—often with little or no concern as to how these may also transform our understandings of the former.

This problem of application brings me, in the next chapter, to consideration of the relationship between music and philosophy in extant research, and how my enquiry addresses this pertinent matter in current research in music and the performing arts.

NOTES

1. See chapters 3–5 of this book for a more detailed overview of difference as a Deleuzian concept, given that it is one half of the conceptual pairing, difference and repetition, investigated in the first of my practice as research projects.

2. This overview of McTaggart's A- and B-theories of time draws from Mautner (2005) in respect of the entry under "A-theory and B-theory" and related entries (e.g., the entry under "Perdurantists" with regard to the timeless, spatialised model of time as part of a four-dimensional space-time).

3. See chapters 3–5 and 9–11 for a detailed study of, respectively, Deleuze's three syntheses of time and his concepts of Chronos and Aion and their relevance to my enquiry and my concept of Rhythmicity.

4. Depending on the source one consults, the list of philosophers belonging to the structuralist and post-structuralist movements is often cross-populated. Foucault, for instance, is sometimes included among the names of key structuralists, while Barthes sometimes gets a mention among the post-structuralists. Sarap (1993) is among those who notes the similarities, alongside the differences, of the two movements in mid- to late-twentieth-century thought (1–3). What is clear, across the distinctions, is that all these thinkers tend to have both structuralist and post-structuralist aspects to their thought, articulated at various points in their careers.

5. Of the contempt in which Bergson was held at the time of Deleuze's early writings on his work, the latter said, of certain of his contemporaries, that "there are people these days who laugh at me simply for having written about Bergson at all. It simply shows they don't know enough history" (Deleuze 1995, 6).

6. See my discussions in chapters 3 and 4, concerning Bergson's (2004) conception of present/actual perception and past/pure memory in terms of a difference in kind (rather than a difference in degree) for more on this important aspect of Bergson's thought.

7. See Deleuze and Guattari (1994), for instance, when they argue that every concept "is a multiplicity, although not every multiplicity is conceptual" (15); and "a concept also has a *becoming* that involves its relationship with concepts situated on the same plane" (18).

8. In an infamous passage from a letter reproduced in Deleuze (1995), he speaks of this practice in terms of a kind of "immaculate conception": "taking an author from behind and giving him a child that would be his own offspring, yet monstrous" (6).

9. See chapters 6–8 for my own full-length enquiry into Deleuze's concept of the fold and the use it can be put to in a musical-philosophical Rhythmicity interrelating music composition, performance, and writing.

10. Indicative of this tendency are the collected essays in Buchanan and Swiboda (2004), Hulse and Nesbitt (2010), and Moisala et al. (2017)—as even a glance at the title pages of each will elucidate.

11. As discussed earlier, and returned to later, the *Deleuze and Artistic Research* conferences and publications spearheaded by Assis and Giudici are welcome exceptions to this tentativeness on the part of the wider music practice as research community to give relevance to Deleuze's work and its usefulness to the field.

12. *Diabelli Machines*[x] forms part of the *Music Experiment 21* project initiated by Assis in 2013 (and which ran until 2018). See https://musicexperiment21.eu/projects/diabelli-machines.

13. See https://www.researchcatalogue.net/view/302790/302791.

14. See https://www.researchcatalogue.net/view/241121/241122.

15. As detailed in *Logic of Experimentation* (Assis 2018), the 2013–2018 *Music Experiment 21* project (of which *Deleuzabelli Variations* was a part) made use of a "three-step methodology" (110)—the final step of which was inspired by Deleuze and Guattari's (1980/2004) concept of the *assemblage*. Similarly, Assis's ongoing

RASCH project (which began in 2011 with *RASCH 0—Schumann's BWO*) employs a Deleuzian–Guattarian approach to the creation of concepts as primary philosophical task (cf. Deleuze and Guattari 1991/1994, and my discussion of this issue earlier in this chapter). In the case of the *RASCH* project, the conceptual creation is also influenced by the work of Roland Barthes (his writings on the music of Robert Schumann, specifically), and Barthes's concept of the *somatheme* (Assis 2017c, 16), alongside Deleuze and Guattari's (2004) concepts of *strata* and *assemblage* in the building of a new ontology of the musical "work" (*sic*) (Assis 2018, 67). At the time of writing, full details of the *RASCH* project (now in its twenty-seventh instantiation) can be found online at: https://www.researchcatalogue.net/view/64319/64320.

Chapter 2

Philosophy, Music, and Rhythm

Bringing together aspects of music and philosophy is not, in itself, a new project in academia. Music, as Gracyk and Kania (2014) point out, "has long been an object of philosophical enquiry since the beginning of philosophy" (xxii), while Scruton (1997) also points to the philosophy of music as being "the oldest branch of aesthetics" (vii). For these theorists, and many others (for example, Alperson 1986; D. Davies 2011; S. Davies 2002; Goehr 1992; Kivy 2002; Levinson 1990; Peters 2009; Ridley 2004), music provokes a series of philosophical questions worthy of detailed investigation—questions concerning, for instance: the ontology/ies of the musical work/music performance; music as *mimesis*/representation; the relationship between musical form/content/expression; and how music can have meaning and value and express/elicit emotions.

However, in terms of establishing productive relations between the research practices of *both* disciplines, it is only in more recent years that music has begun to be considered less as an *object* for philosophical study and more as a means of actually *doing* philosophy. For example, the aforementioned collection edited by Gracyk and Kania (2014) is noticeably silent on the question of what the making of music can contribute to our understandings of philosophy. Indeed, despite the breadth of its collected musical and philosophical knowledge on a range of matters—including musical aesthetics (for example, Scruton [2014] on the concept of rhythm), kinds of music (Brown [2014b] on the nature of jazz and its practice), and musical practices (Brown [2014a] on the ontology of improvisation and the notion of "spontaneous creation," and Benson [2014] on improvisation as a key to the relationship between the performer and the performed)—none of its fifty-six chapters consider the idea of music-making *as* a philosophical practice.

This issue of whether music/musicians can provide philosophical insights is developed at book-length by Bowie (2007), when he suggests that "using philosophy to look at music puts rather too much faith in philosophy, and too little in music itself" (2). In response to this critique, Bowie proposes an alternative conception of the relationship between music and philosophy, writing, instead, of "the philosophy which is conveyed by music itself" (xi), or (memorably) the philosophy of music "in the subjective genitive," where such philosophy emerges *from* music, rather than the latter being merely the former's object of interest (415). Bowie's arguments are frequently illuminating—especially in his discussions on the pertinence of rhythm as a concept connecting music and philosophy (which I draw on at greater length in the section on "Rhythm," later). Indeed, even McAuley's (2015) critique of Bowie's approach accepts that music can provide insights into "non-linguistic or non-conceptual aspects of human existence" unavailable to more traditional philosophical methods (60). However, whilst Bowie endorses music as philosophy *in theory*, I would argue that, in practice, his work frequently relegates the thirty or so music practices/musicians referenced to secondary, illustrative, positions. For instance, in a section concerning "the erosion of traditional forms of temporal order associated with modernity" (187)—notably, how our understandings of time are transformed by the pace of life and change in the "modern" era—Bowie makes (brief) example of the music practice of the saxophonists Charlie Parker and John Coltrane. Both of these musicians are well-known with regard to a propensity for playing large numbers of notes articulated at high speed.[1] "Music exemplifies the question of time," writes Bowie, adding, more specifically, how the "modern" (in this case, post–WW2) style of jazz that is typified by Parker and Coltrane is "unthinkable without the impact of the temporality of urban life"—a temporality that altered our experience of time, thus paving the way for such "new musical possibilities" (188). By using music/musicians in exemplary fashion in this manner, Bowie denies precisely the kind of philosophy of music "in the subjective genitive" he declares his project in support of. In the example made of Parker and Coltrane, the musicians function in a mimetic/imitative, rather than creative, fashion: re-presenting the speed of progress/change of their time, not investigating and/or conceptualising it through their advanced music practice.

It was with these issues in mind—the epistemological problems of applying notions and concepts from one field to another, and the possibility of practising philosophy in a discipline other than that of philosophy—that the field of Performance Philosophy was formed in 2012. As one of its co-founders has stated, a driving concern of this nascent field is to leave the question of the relations between the creative processes of performance and philosophy open to ongoing scrutiny, making for "a deliberate attempt to leave the relationship between the two terms undetermined, but also to imply an unsettling of identities" (Cull Ó Maoilearca 2014, 19). It provides a scholarly "home" for those who identify their work between the disciplines; for those who question the traditional boundaries of what is considered the realm of performance and what is considered the realm of philosophy (Cull Ó Maoilearca 2020, 5). Such openness and interdisciplinarity clearly resonates with my own investigation in the musical-philosophical, and, in similar vein to Cull Ó Maoilearca, I am less concerned with attempting to pin down definitively what the musical-philosophical *is* and more interested in practising it (as a process) via the series of research projects exploring my original concept of Rhythmicity.

At present, music is rather under-represented in the extant literature on Performance Philosophy—at least in comparison to contributions from practitioners in the fields of dance and theatre, for instance. Notable exceptions include Bowie (2015), Assis (2017a), Jude (2019), McAuley (2015), Roden (2019), Rothenberg (2015), Tartaglia (2016), Teixeira and Ferraz (2019), and Tromans and Schmidt (2022). Of these, a venture that would appear to share the most similar concerns to my own in this book and its practice as research projects (i.e., a musical-philosophical undertaking mixing philosophical concepts with music composition and improvised performance) is that of the philosopher and jazz saxophonist, James Tartaglia, and his band Continuum of Selves. Formed in early 2016 in order to record (and subsequently tour) original material for the album, *Jazz-Philosophy Fusion*, Tartaglia's septet performs composed songs that open out into long sections of group and solo improvisations. There are two vocalists in the band, and they are used for different musical-philosophical purposes. The more conventional "jazz vocals" (provided by Jessica Radcliffe) deliver a narrative outlining the basic philosophical problem of each song, while Sonja Morgenstern's "conceptual vocals" are intended to develop the themes of that problem in various emotionally (and musically) expressive directions.[2] Morgenstern's vocals are delivered at the same time that different members of the ensemble engage in improvisation (mostly of a "time/no changes" or "free" nature, but also sometimes including regular, repeating chord sequences).[3] In Tartaglia's (2016) argument, one purpose of these vocals (beyond adding extra emotional content for listeners) is to provide what he calls "non-argumentative effects" in order to influence the improvising musicians, who may (or may not) decide to "react to or emulate their effects" (106).

From my own perspective in my musical-philosophical enquiry, here, Tartaglia's jazz-philosophy fusion is, ironically, most problematic in how it fuses its music and its philosophy. By his own admission, Tartaglia (2016) is sceptical about the possibility of music being able to practice philosophy without the addition of vocals: "By using vocals, a composer can channel the broad and vaguely demarcated conceptual expressiveness of instrumental music into something more conceptually fine-grained" (99). Tartaglia's assertion is not surprising, given his professional background as a philosopher in the analytical tradition, and it concurs with the analytical view that philosophy is a linguistic-conceptual practice of propositional argument. However, in terms of exploring the philosophical potential of music, it is immediately—and, I would argue, terminally—dismissive. If the instrumentalists in Continuum of Selves are limited to practising a quasi-philosophical kind of music-making—that is, taking (some manner of) "influence" from the "conceptual vocals" Morgenstern performs alongside the series of individual and group improvisations in each piece—it raises the question as to whether or not any aspect of the music that is made in the process is anything other than "background dressing" for the linguistic-conceptual components propounded.[4]

One is reminded, from Tartaglia's perspective on the role and usefulness of music to the presentation and concerns of philosophy, of Immanuel Kant's (1987) remarks concerning what he termed the "agreeable" (as opposed to the "fine") arts—for instance, "table-music," which Kant memorably dismisses as "agreeable noise," the function of which is merely to foster "the free flow of conversation between each person and [their] neighbour, without anyone's paying the slightest attention to the music's composition" (173).[5] While an amusing—and welcome (from a gigging musician's perspective!)—critique of what tend, these days, to be known as "background" or "function" music, these remarks also reflect Kant's deeper philosophical attitude as to the hierarchy of words over music in the sense that he considered music to be non-representational, and therefore inferior to writing in terms of a capacity to infer a sense of his famous *noumenon*, or concept of the "thing-in-itself," forever inaccessible to experiential existence or artistic artifice, and best understood in terms of the *noumena*, or "things we can only think" (Pluhar 1987, xxxviii).[6]

Certainly this is a question of great importance to an enquiry such as my own, in which I am seeking to develop/explore a novel concept of "Rhythmicity" as a means of musical-philosophical expression via a marriage of text and sound through the rhythms occasioned by each—and, in particular, the rhythms of interdisciplinarity by which the musical-philosophical can "speak" (or otherwise communicate with the reader/listener) with a singular (though multifaceted) voice. Accordingly, in the next section of this chapter, I turn to the issue of rhythm: its theorisation and use in extant research in music/performing arts and philosophy. I will consider the range of ways in which rhythm might be defined or conceived by way of context for my own account of Rhythmicity: specifically, in terms of music practice, but also more broadly as the passage between disciplines, or as the organisation of processes.

RHYTHM

While rhythm has received widespread study in a diverse range of musics (including, but not limited to, musics from the African continent and the Indian subcontinent), in the more traditional areas of musicology, there has historically been substantially less interest in rhythm than in its more traditional concerns of harmony and counterpoint. Noting, and explicitly setting out to begin the work of making right this deficit in the second half of the twentieth century, Cooper and Meyer (1960) provide a significant early contribution to the literature in terms of their detailed, *gestalt* analysis of rhythmic structures in music composition.[7] In the process of unfolding their analysis, the authors offer a taxonomy of what they consider the basic modes of temporal organisation in music: pulse, metre, rhythm—where the latter is defined as "the way in which one or more unaccented beats are grouped in relation to an accented one" (6). They proceed, from this basis, to differentiate accent and stress—respectively, "the focal point, the nucleus of the rhythm," and "the dynamic intensification of a beat" (8), before moving on to engage in a book-length exploration of various rhythmic groupings, from lower to higher architectonic levels, drawing examples from well-known works in the Western "classical" canon: from J. S. Bach to Stravinsky.[8]

Following in the wake of Cooper and Meyer's pioneering study, a series of theorists have approached and explored our understandings of rhythm from a variety of musical-theoretical standpoints. Attesting to this surge of interest in music's rhythmic aspects in academic thought of the last half-century are the likes of (but not limited to) Arom (1991), Berry (1987), Caplin (2002), Chernoff (1979), Clark and Rehding (2016), Clayton (2000), Hasty (1997), Lerdahl and Jackendoff (1983), Lester (1986), London (2004), Scruton (1997, 2014), Winold (1975), and Yeston (1976). These writers (and others) provide a range of perspectives on the nature and practice of rhythm, making useful contributions to the fields of ethnomusicology, historical musicology, the psychology of music, the philosophy of music—and, in the case of Arom (1991) and Lerdahl and Jackendoff (1983), for instance, the modelling of music in grammatical/linguistic terms.[9]

For this book and its practice as research projects, which investigates how Rhythmicity can express the movements between certain practices of music and philosophy, the most pertinent facets of the extant music research in rhythm reside in the close attention paid to the nuances of its definition and articulation, and to the creative process of its transformation across compositional structures. In particular, I am interested in how we tend to conceptualise the relationship between the play of rhythmic movement and the constrictions—perceived or otherwise—of metric regularity and disciplinary boundary. For Scruton (1997), for example, rhythm is experienced as "a kind of animation": an experience that is "something more than an experience of metrical structure" (35). In contrast, for London (2004), our temporal experience of music is part of the wider natural process of entrainment (a subtype of which he labels metric entrainment), which he defines as "the sympathetic resonance of our attention and motor behaviour to temporal regularities in the environment" (161). And for the participants in the dramatised "dialogue form" of Hamilton et al. (2019), rhythm is scrutinised with regard to its relationship with movement, where the latter is argued as being either metaphorical or literal depending on whether music is considered to be a "strictly sonic art" or one that involves "bodily and visual experience" (17).

These (and other) attempts to understand the rhythmic as other than metrical or metaphorical/literal are common in the literature on rhythm, and have resonances with Massumi's (2002) notion of the rhythmic connectibility of concepts—"the rhythm without the regularity" (20) as discussed in the introduction to this book—and also with Deleuze's work with Guattari. In certain passages in *A Thousand Plateaus*, for instance, they remark: "It is well known that rhythm is not metre or cadence" (Deleuze and Guattari 2004, 345); and "Metre is dogmatic, but rhythm is critical" (346). An interesting exception to this common practice of making a distinction between metre, on the one hand, and rhythm, on the other, is Hasty (1997). As noted by Hulse (2010), Hasty approaches metre from the perspective of the creativity of the listener in experiencing music performance as it unfolds in time; in "his or her capacity to retain and project temporal spans" (Hulse 2010, 29). This act of temporal projection Hasty equates with metre—"projection and metre are one" (Hasty 1997, 91)—making metre just as much an aspect of the uncertainties of lived temporal experience as rhythm. I embrace Hasty's argument in this direction—and, indirectly as a result, his critique of Deleuze and Guattari's (and others') rhythm/metre binarism—and consider Hasty's grounding of metre in rhythm to be an important example of how music research can provide original contributions in Deleuzian terms, in situations where Deleuze's own writings fall short of his philosophical practice of breaking away from restrictive binarisms.

Their rhythm/metre oversights aside, however, Deleuze and Guattari's (2004) notion that rhythm provides a key—or a "transcoding"—to theorising critical movements between different disciplines/milieus is one that offers much to my own enquiry. "There is rhythm," they argue, "whenever there is a transcoded passage from one milieu to another, a communication of milieus" (345). To reiterate the musical-philosophical concerns of this book, I am arguing that a relationship between music and philosophy can be experienced through my concept of Rhythmicity, where the latter is expressed as an interdisciplinary movement drawing together practices from both fields (improvisation, composition, analysis; conceptual apparatus, argument, analysis). This notion invites consideration of extant literature dealing with ways to connect practices and processes across disciplinary (or any) boundaries.

As noted by Michon (2011) and Cheyne et al. (2019), recent years have seen a growing interest among scholars in employing/evolving various concepts of rhythm across a range of disciplinary fields. This comes in the wake of a marked disinterest in the rhythmic that had been the case in much of the twentieth-century scholarship around philosophy, aesthetics, linguistics, and music (as discussed above) (Cheyne et al. 2019, 4).[10] Prior to its curious absence from research concerns, studies focused on, or around, issues of rhythm had a long history dating back to the Ancient Greeks (Heraclitus being perhaps the most famous example, with his interest in flow over stasis), right up until Nietzsche's late-nineteenth-century lectures on rhythm (the "Rhythm Researches of 1870–1872") and Bergson's early-twentieth-century concept of duration (*la durée*) (Cheyne et al. 2019, 1–4). The rejection of Bergson's work that followed his death in the mid-twentieth century, and the widespread appeal of structuralist models of diverse practices, may go some way towards explaining the disappearance of notions of time and the rhythmic in much scholarship before the emergence of the post-structuralist critique (as outlined earlier in this book).

By way of addressing this neglect of time and the rhythmic, Deleuze's early work on Bergson, and the development of his philosophy of process, brings much of interest to rhythm studies. Michon (2011) acknowledges the opportunity, via Deleuze, to "reintroduce temporality, creativity and diversity" in a wide range of research enquiries, enabling a move beyond structuralist/systematic models of practice (human and otherwise) that tend to exclude change/flow/time from consideration.[11] Michon states that rhythm is of central importance in Deleuze and Guattari (2004), and also in Deleuze (1986 and 1989). This is a curious observation, since the term receives minimal entry in the index of *A Thousand Plateaus* (in respect of de/re/territorialisation, predominantly), and none in either of the *Cinema* books. However, given that all three publications are concerned with movement, change, becoming, and time (as is the majority of Deleuze's oeuvre), it is plain that rhythm is indeed implicit (and on occasion explicit) in the conceptual apparatus developed by Deleuze. Michon critiques the Deleuzian approach for its insistence on speed/acceleration/tempo—an approach, he argues, that overlooks the potential of rhythm as a means of theorising the "complex organization of processes."

On this point of how we understand processual organisations of a complex nature, Turetsky (2004) is instructive. Discussing the ways in which different elements can come together to form a "rhythmic assemblage" (of various, and temporal, kinds), he argues that these elements typically arise "independently of one another," prior to becoming "rhythmically organised" (144). Turetsky adds that the elements in such an assemblage do not necessarily need to be inherently connected, in respect of (for instance) either material or cause, as long as they "become coincident" (144). Since the driving concern of my enquiry is to explore a rhythmic-conceptual expression of the musical-philo-sophical, Turetsky's theorisation allows me to consider rhythm in interdisci-plinary, rather than exclusively musical, terms. Turetsky argues that rhythm "becomes expressive" (150), effecting temporal syntheses that bring together "living present" (144), "*a priori* past" (147), and enabling the production of future novelty (151).[12]

Of the potential of rhythmic expressions and their temporal syntheses to undertake musical-philosophical enquiry (or, in his terms discussed previ-ously, the philosophy of music in the subjective genitive), Bowie (2007) offers a useful contribution via Schelling's nineteenth-century *Philosophy of Art*. Expanding on Schiller's conception of rhythm as operating beyond merely its acoustic manifestation, Bowie speaks of rhythm in terms of the "unification of a multiplicity of elements" in which notions of identity/dif-ference are combined in an act of "reflective awareness" (82). He equates this sense of awareness with a Kantian *schematism*, which involves a process of determination "in which objects are intelligible in relation to time" (88). Since such a process relies on our capacity for experiencing and synthesising various elements and moments in time, Bowie posits a link between feeling and cognition at the level of the rhythmic—theorising, as a result, our aware-ness of rhythm as pre- or proto-conceptual (82, 90).

Building on Bowie with regards to the rhythmic basis of the process of conceptualisation, my enquiry seeks to explore and to express Rhythmicity in the interdisciplinary border zone of music and philosophy: the musical-philosophical. I use the term "border" advisedly, since, as Feitosa (2020) points out, a border is more properly understood, not as a barrier between things, or as a fixed limit, but in terms of "agency" and interaction. A border, for Feitosa, is less a "homogeneous line, but much more an irregular zone of mutual communication and incorporation" (4). Accordingly, the relation-ship between the fields of performing arts and philosophy can be thought of as operating at the borders, not the limits, of each (5). The musical-philosophical, then, is a direct expression of these border-zone interactions: a rhythmic quality of interdisciplinarity, existing permanently in between the two fields in question, yet not limited by either of them in that expression of in-between-ness.

As noted by Morris (2017), rhythm is indeed the key to expressing this quality of in-between-ness, establishing, as it does, "the boundaries of when/where one thing ends and another begins" (19). Regarding the process by which rhythm goes about establishing these boundary zones (or borders, to use Feitosa's terminology), Morris suggests that it operates "through qualities of expression and the differences that form between these"—indicating performance as one important practice through which rhythm is able to carry out its territorial pursuits (19).[13] By highlighting Deleuze and Guattari's (2004) notion of de/re/territorialisation with the performing arts ability to "mark out a space, a time, a shared sense or fragmented identity through rhythm" (Morris 2017, 19), the need for a sustained enquiry into a musical-philosophical concept of rhythm/Rhythmicity via a series of practice-research projects is made plain. And it is toward the task of building and expressing such a concept that the remainder of this book is dedicated.

NOTES

1. In the case of John Coltrane, this approach was memorably described by the jazz critic Ira Gitler as "sheets of sound" in his liner notes for Coltrane's 1958 album *Soultrane*.

2. The terms "jazz vocals" and "conceptual vocals" are those used by Tartaglia in the liner notes to the 2016 *Jazz-Philosophy Fusion* album.

3. "Time/no changes" is an improvisational style that came to prominence with the Ornette Coleman Quartet in the late 1950s/early 1960s, and the Miles Davis Second Quintet of the 1960s. As the term implies, the band maintains a regular tempo, but there are no pre-set chord sequences over which to improvise. So-called free improvisation removes even the necessity for a regular tempo.

4. On this question, Tartaglia has himself stated that the philosophy of *Jazz-Philosophy Fusion* is contained solely in the lyrics and spoken text of the songs and not in any of the instrumental playing. This comment was made during a Q&A session prior to a concert given by Continuum of Selves as part of the launch event for the Centre for Performance Philosophy, Surrey University, 16 September 2016.

5. It is useful to note, on this point, the work of Michel Chion (1999) with regard to his notions of "vococentricity" and "aural triage," through which he argues that, in combination with music (or visual art), the vocal/the voice is necessarily privileged for the listener, given that it conveys information, directly (while the other two are less direct, at the very most—according to Chion at least) (3).

6. Arthur Schopenhauer, for his part, notably took the (polar opposite) perspective to Kant on the word/music hierarchy. As Bowie (2007) notes, music, in Schopenhauer's conception, is "the highest form in the hierarchy of the arts," with "tragedy," with its utilisation of words—the written, the vocalised—taking a mere second place to music's much closer connection to what he calls "the Will," or an "endless striving," forever inaccessible to human definition and understanding, "never "finally objectifiable" (197).

7. By way of contrast to Cooper and Meyer's (1960) in-depth analysis of rhythm on different structural levels, in an essay of 1949, Cage defined rhythm "in the structural instance" as simply "relationships between lengths of time" (1978, 64). See chapters

10–11 for a discussion of this approach (and others' approaches) to understanding, and using, rhythm in music composition and performance.

8. Not that either J. S. Bach or Igor Stravinsky could be considered as classicists, of course (Stravinsky's "neo-classical" period aside). "Classical" is used here (and, accordingly, placed in scare quotes) merely to indicate the widespread recognition of such musicians as part of an identifiable canon of composers whose works receive regular performance in concert halls and in recordings by leading orchestras, ensembles, and soloists associated with what is generically known as "classical music"— regardless of the historical period in which it was originally composed.

9. Linguistic modelling is also employed, briefly, by Cooper and Meyer (1960), in their analysis of rhythmic groupings in terms commonly associated with prosody— *iamb*, *anapest*, *trochee*, *dactyl*, and *amphibrach* (6).

10. There are important exceptions to this wider lack of interest in rhythm in the early to mid-twentieth century: Rudolph Laban's *eurhythmics*, and Konstantin Stanislavski's *tempo-rhythm*, being highly influential theories in the fields of dance and theatre, for instance (see Morris 2017, 28; 245–246).

11. In this observation, Michon echoes the arguments of Bourdieu (1977) in respect of the importance of reinstalling time into our theories of practice, as referenced earlier in this book.

12. Note: Turetsky bases these syntheses on Deleuze's (2004a) active and passive syntheses of time. These syntheses are utilised in the analyses of the improvisations undertaken for the first practice as research project of this enquiry (see chapters 3–5).

13. Morris is explicit in recognition of a debt to Deleuze and Guattari on this point, quoting from *A Thousand Plateaus* on de/re/territorialisation as "an act of rhythm" (2004, 348).

Chapter 3

Difference and Repetition via Deleuze and the Deleuzian

My decision to draw on Deleuze's *Difference and Repetition* (2004a) for my first project in practice as research (in chapter 4) is in response to the close association of the main themes of his book (difference, repetition) with the issues relevant to my enquiry (musical-philosophical expression, rhythmic movement between different disciplinary practices), and also considering its place in the Deleuzian canon in terms of its being one of his earliest major contributions to the theorisation of time.[1] Temporality is a primary concern of my investigation of the ways in which diverse articulations can operate in multimodal fashion (through simultaneous listening and reading, and the mixing of the investigative and presentational modes and registers of music and philosophy). As such, Deleuze's conceptualisations of difference (in itself) and repetition (for itself), and his three syntheses of time, provide vital touchstones for articulating the kind of musical-philosophical Rhythmicity I am exploring in this book. Accordingly, in this chapter I provide an overview of, firstly, Deleuze's reformulation of our more commonplace understandings of difference and repetition; and, secondly, extant work in the field of music research that explicitly engages with Deleuze on these matters. Without this background, the introduction of Deleuzian concepts and writings in the first project of chapter 4 might be seen as a sudden, unexpected application of notions from the field of philosophy onto the practices of music. This is not my intention. As indicated prior to this chapter, my project seeks to set up a two-way flow between music and philosophy: to demonstrate, alongside how Deleuze can offer new perspectives on music-making, how practice as research in music contributes to our understandings of Deleuze's philosophy of time.

DELEUZE'S DIFFERENCE AND REPETITION

First published in 1968, Deleuze's *Difference and Repetition* represents what its author described (in his preface to the first edition in the English language) as a first attempt to "do philosophy" of his own design: to build his own conceptual apparatus (2004a, xiii). By differentiating this book from his earlier commentaries on the philosophies of Hume, Nietzsche, Kant, Bergson, and Spinoza (respectively, Deleuze 1991; 1983; 2008; 1988a; and 1990), Deleuze was drawing a distinction between the practice of engaging with the philosophical-conceptual apparatuses found in others' work, and a desire to "speak" (or otherwise express philosophical thought) in one's "own name" (2004a, xiii).

Deleuze's major undertaking, in speaking in his own name in the pages of *Difference and Repetition*, was to construct what Smith (2008) qualifies as a "metaphysics of difference." In this new philosophical outlook, Deleuze turns traditional metaphysics on its head, emancipating difference from its subordination to notions of identity and sameness and attending, instead, to what he conceptualises as "difference in itself" (2004a, xiv). In our common conception, things in the world (objects, people, animals, terms) have distinct identities—personal, and also with regard to species/genera and various other categories. Within these systems of categorisation, things are understood to differ from other things, while retaining their identities outside of their coming into relation with those other things in the world. Colebrook (2002) summarises this concept of difference as representing "the difference between different forms, or the difference from some original model" (123). In such an understanding, difference merely indicates an empirical measurement between distinct things, having no purpose beyond determining what Stagoll (2010a) calls "a relationship with sameness" (75).

For Deleuze (2004a), however, difference affirms the multiple, the creative (67); it is the "free form of difference," or "the different within that difference" (182). To conceptualise life in this manner is to embrace the notion that "prior identity" and "internal resemblance" are not set apart from the process of difference, but are engendered through the creative "play of difference" (in itself) that operates at a level more fundamental than our traditional models grounded in "the world of representation" (372–374). Reconceptualising our understandings of the nature of the world, via Deleuze's metaphysics of difference, requires paying attention to what Stagoll (2010a) terms "the uniqueness of each moment or thing"; to look beyond ideas of sameness and similarity—even in situations where the moments/things in question may share practically identical attributes (from an external or extrinsic perspective, at least)—and focus, instead, on the "particularity or 'singularity' of each individual thing, moment" and so on (75–76). In such singularity lies the creative power of difference in itself, which exists, for Deleuze, "between two repetitions": the "superficial" (external) and the "profound" (internal) (2004a, 358). Deleuzian difference is not the consequence of "an elementary repetition" but is, instead, of a dynamic, asymmetric, and causal nature (the intrinsic cause beneath the external effect); it is the repeating event that expresses itself ever anew, not as a banal iteration indicating only more of the same, *ad infinitum* (358–359). Repetition, then, plays a vital role in Deleuze's metaphysics of difference.

The history of the conception of repetition (either via repetition theory studies, or as intrinsic to a particular music as made and understood—implicitly or otherwise—by a particular culture or artistic movement) is, unsurprisingly, both long and convoluted. As Gendron (2008) notes, the Ancient Greeks were divided in their attitude toward the philosophical importance of repetition, with Plato according it the inferior status of the imitative (i.e., as copy not model) and Aristotle proposing its fundamentality to the very biology of the human itself (16). Moving forward to the nineteenth and early twentieth centuries, where Søren Kierkegaard acknowledged the "impossibility of exact repetition" (McGrath 2018, 152), Sigmund Freud conceptualised repetition in terms of his own developing psychoanalytic theory as an act of repression or resistance—as what Deleuze (2004a) describes as "the unconscious of the free concept, of knowledge or of memory, the unconscious of representation" (16). And into the twenty-first century, cultural theorists such as Fink (2005) have recognised the widespread importance of repetition across a host of human practices, from (so called) high art to (so called) lo-fi pop culture.[2]

Considered in terms of Deleuze's (2004a) own focus on the relations between difference and repetition, the fact that our understandings of difference and its relationship with identity and sameness should be aligned with those of repetition is, of course, not surprising. Since the received wisdom concerning repetition is that the thing that repeats remains the same with each given iteration, this is the logical connection to make. However, the innovation that Deleuze provides (albeit one that he credits to Nietzsche's concept of "eternal return"—see below) is to recast the act of repeating in terms of "discovery and experimentation," "new experiences," and processes of "mutation" (Parr 2010b, 225). Approached in this manner, repetition describes neither linear nor cyclical movement, and obeys no teleology beyond its continual elaboration via the "differences in kind and rhythm" and "divergences and decentrings" that indicate the non-imitative repetitive power internal to its concept (Deleuze 2004a, 365). As Roffe (2005) notes, two of the longstanding conventions/clichés that are overhauled in Deleuze's concept of repetition are the notions that time behaves in either cyclical or linear fashion. In the case of the former, time is understood to obey the circular movement of the narrative of the mythic or the natural, where repetition signifies the (habitual) completion of a prescribed cycle—for instance, the oracle's prophesy or the sun's rising and setting. In the case of the latter, time (via Kant's *Critique of Pure Reason*,[3] in Deleuze's argument) is that which places events in straight succession (as in what is commonly known as a "timeline") rather than the converse, where repeated events themselves are considered to construct the temporal through "the passing of present moments" (Roffe 2005). In a Kantian/linear conception of time, cyclical/habitual understandings of repetition are invalid, given that there is nothing that returns (Roffe 2005). Instead, repetition informs temporal experience by means of a process wherein memory synthesises the present and past via the act of "reminiscence," wherein repetition does not simply refer back from the "present present" to previously lived presents, but, rather, provides "the element in which the present passes and successive presents are telescoped" (Deleuze 2004a, 107). This is repetition as the creation of something new in the memory, since it did not exist prior to its involvement in the reminiscing process of interrelating past and present (Roffe 2005).

To these two perspectives on the conceptualisation of repetition (and time), Deleuze contributes a third. Drawing on Nietzsche in terms of the latter's concept of *eternal return*[4]—the "force of affirmation . . . of the multiple . . . of the different" (Deleuze 2004a, 141)—repetition for itself provides a means of thinking the "creative activity of transformation" that is expressed without teleological goal or object of repetition (Parr 2010b, 225–226). What is in fact repeated, then, from a Deleuzian perspective, is not the same or the identical but "the repetition of difference": that which affirms the "creative difference of life" (Colebrook 2002, 67), or "the full force of difference in and of itself" (Parr 2010b, 226). Nonteleological, singular rather than general, and refusing the symmetry of sameness that is inevitable in models that think its process as the recurrence of the *a priori*, a Deleuzian take on repetition offers the opportunity to conceive every repeated act as an act of beginning afresh. In this manner, the action "to repeat" becomes a means of accentuating, rather than diminishing, "the power of the new and unforeseeable," and to destabilise—through finding innovations where, in prior conceptions, there were mere "routines and clichés"—our assumptions of "habit and convention" (Parr 2010b, 225–226).

DIFFERENCE AND REPETITION AND (DELEUZIAN) MUSIC RESEARCH

That Deleuze's engagement with difference and repetition should have an appeal to researchers in music (and the arts in general) is not difficult to understand. After all, all artists are involved in the ongoing production of new work that is different (in various ways) from their previous outputs, but that also repeats (in various ways) the work they have been undertaking in their own name as artists since they began producing art. However, as the previous summary of Deleuze's difference-in-itself and repetition-for-itself makes apparent, there is more to these concepts than a simple case of difference as "difference from X" or repetition as "repetition of X." And, as a result, there are important consequences for music research, as I explore in what follows.

Being open to a Deleuzian perspective in our understandings of music raises the question, posed by Macarthur and Lochhead (2016), of how best researchers are to discuss "particular musical identities," when these are, via Deleuze, perpetually "in flux or process" (5). As Campbell (2013) stresses, Deleuzian music research must be "difference-based," eschewing notions of "the same, the similar, or the identical," and releasing repetition from its definition as the (nonproductive) reiteration of an "original statement or form" that assumes precedence/priority (163).[5] Thinking in this manner, then, requires an overhaul of certain predominant conceptions of, and in, music-making—such as the tendency to model music in terms of theme and variation.

The conceptual pairing of theme and variation is one of the cornerstones of how we understand the process of making music in a large number of musical genres, in both historical and cultural terms. Jones (2017), for instance, enumerates seven different types of musical variation. Across these seven, certain elements—such as repeated melodic/bass lines (as in *cantus firmus* or *ostinato* techniques), harmonic/formal frameworks, or "note rows" and other precompositional sets used in serial techniques—are either combined with other musical elements that differ from them to various extents and purposes, or are themselves subject to various degrees of transformation. While Jones is focused specifically on Western art music, the theme/variation model—whereby an original "thing," be it a theme/line/form/set, undergoes a range of different processes of variation—can successfully be applied to the way we conceive of a wide range of musical practices across a number of genres. To offer two examples among many possible, we might consider: (1) the common jazz performance practice known as "head/solos/head"—structuring the music according to a format of presenting the theme (typically a well-known piece from the so-called "standard repertoire"), undertaking improvised melodic variations over the repeated harmonic form of that theme, and reiterating the opening theme again to close; or (2) the North Indian classical performance tradition of taking a *raga* theme and developing it, via improvisation, through three stages (*alap, jhor,* and *jhalla*), each utilising different techniques of melodic and rhythmic variation.[6]

The theme/variation model is one of the more predominant ways in which we conceptualise the process of music-making. Campbell (2013), for instance, calls it "one of music's richest concepts" (27). As a result of its prevalence, moving beyond the tendency to think via its terms is no straightforward task. For Hulse (2010), one way in which to adopt a Deleuzian perspective in music research is to embrace the "positive, self-differing movement of musical sound" (26). From such a perspective, Hulse argues, the researcher must attend to repetition—"and *only* to repetition" (35, emphasis in original). The theme/variation model begins from a concept of an original element (melody or bass or harmony or form or set or whatever), to which, or alongside which, any number or kind of variation is then effected. In contrast, a method of attending solely to repetition liberates the process of variation from its assumed subservience to an original element in relation to which it is ever of secondary importance. In so doing, the process of repeating becomes less an instance of reiterating something pre-existent—in however complex and varied ways—and more a unique event of its own genesis (as Deleuze phrases it: repetition *for itself*). As Campbell (2013) puts it, repetition, in the Deleuzian understanding, draws attention to the "laziness in our listening habits": where we often presume more of the same, we must, instead, recognise uniqueness and individuality (34).

There is a correlation, here, with the composer Morton Feldman (2000) on his own use of repetition and variation. Feldman describes his compositional process as a "synthesis" of the two—adding that he often varies certain aspects of whatever it is he is repeating, or varies the repetition itself (185). Either way, this encourages dedicated (and rewarding) listening. To listen to music in terms of the unique and the individual is to experience the complex interrelation of the perpetually different and repeated in that music-making. It is to experience what Hasty (2010) calls music's "novelty or difference in the sense of *unrepeatability*" (2, emphasis in original). Unrepeatability, following Deleuze, does not signal a lack of repetition but, rather, is indicative of that which Holland (2004) labels a process of "internal variation," wherein fundamental differences remain unsettled without the need to be aligned according to any "single uniform essence" (20). Internal rather than external, grounded in difference not sameness, repetition's unrepeatability opens an invitation to consider music-making from the perspective of a process of research enquiry—not simply as an object of that enquiry.

This approach to the function of music-making in music research resonates with MacArthur and Lochhead's (2016) appraisal of "immanent" listening as a "continual openness to the not-yet-known" (9). Attaining, and maintaining, such "continual openness" is not an easy task, of course, given the predominance of conceptions of the same/the identical in our conventional understandings of what we are experiencing when we listen to music—and especially to music that uses repetition as a primary compositional and/or improvisational device. However, while adopting a Deleuzian perspective in music research is problematic in respect of overturning (or, at least, rethinking) long-held models of intelligibility as to the nature and practice of music, the problems encountered, generated, and explored, are to be embraced. As Hulse (2010) puts it, repetition, in the Deleuzian sense, "founds an original problem" (33). And it is to the problems encountered, generated, and explored in my own music-making with a Deleuzian difference and repetition that I turn to in the next chapter and the first project in practice as research.

NOTES

1. As is explored in subsequent chapters of this book, Deleuze repeatedly (though differently) returns to the theorisation of time throughout his career. Notable examples include Deleuze (1988a; 1989; 2004b; 2005).

2. See McGrath (2018) for further discussion on the history of ideas regarding repetition theory—in particular, his chapter 2, "Repetition in Music and Literature."

3. The *Critique of Pure Reason* was first published in the original German in 1781 (with a second edition in 1787). Deleuze (2008) provides an extraordinarily concise summary, and reformulation, of the conceptual apparatus offered by Kant's philosophical critiques—including the above-mentioned *Critique of Pure Reason*, alongside 1788's *Critique of Practical Reason* and 1790's *Critique of Judgment*.

4. Eternal return/recurrence appears multiple times in Nietzsche's oeuvre, including (but not limited to) the works *The Gay Science*, *Thus Spoke Zarathustra*, and *Ecce Homo*—each published in the original German in 1882, 1883–1891, and 1888, respectively. Deleuze (1983b) represents his early-career systematic engagement with Nietzsche's conceptual apparatus—although, as Roffe (2005) notes, Nietzsche remains a major point of reference in almost all of Deleuze's eventual output.

5. It must be acknowledged, of course, that this practice (by Campbell and others) of drawing on Deleuze's concepts in order to offer fresh insights on music is very much in line with the conventional direction of the epistemological relationship between philosophy and "X" (in this case, music). As I have already discussed, this "problem of application" always runs the risk of reducing that which philosophy decides to investigate to the status of a mere object of knowledge, rather than an epistemic practice in its own right. In this book, as argued above and throughout, I am seeking to set up and utilise a more reciprocal relationship between "the musical" and "the philosophical," where both are able to provide original contributions to knowledge in the fields of music and philosophy.

6. This summary of the *raga* performance practice is written following correspondence with the renowned sitarist and composer, Jonathan Mayer, who is a friend and frequent musical collaborator of mine (see http://www.jonathanmayer.co.uk). The summary of the jazz practice of head/solos/head is written from my own experience as a professional jazz musician.

Chapter 4

Improvising Difference and Repetition (Project 1)

On two occasions (in December 2016 and May 2017), I undertook a series of solo-piano improvisations (seven in total) for the purpose of improvising a Deleuzian difference and repetition.[1] In this chapter I explore the music-making processes utilised, with a view to articulating the (Deleuzian) perspectives of the musician-researcher concerned—specifically, an understanding of difference and repetition in terms of the three temporal syntheses theorised in Deleuze (2004a). In keeping with the methodological approach adopted in three practice-as-research projects undertaken for this book, what follows should not be taken as an example of the application of Deleuze's conceptual apparatus to my music-making but, rather, as a deliberate attempt to engender a productive movement between each for the purpose of encouraging the emergence of a musical-philosophical rhythmic quality: Rhythmicity.

At this point, the reader is asked to listen to tracks 1–7 on "shuffle mode" (and on repeat) while reading the analyses that follow. Utilising shuffle mode in listening to the music element of my research, here, is useful in helping evoke a sense of nonsequential/nonhierarchical movement that resonates with the Deleuzian concepts of difference and repetition under discussion.

FIRST MUSICAL-PHILOSOPHICAL ANALYSIS: DELEUZE'S FIRST SYNTHESIS OF TIME

In *Difference and Repetition*, Deleuze (2004a) develops an original conception of time with respect to the interrelations of past, present, and future.[2] Whereas McTaggart's A-theory of time (as noted earlier) understands time as moving from future through present to past (i.e., in sequence, linearly or otherwise), Deleuze, instead, *synthesises* these in three different, though interrelated, temporal processes. By synthesising past, present, and future in

51

this manner—and in maintaining the threefold heterogeneity of the synthe-ses—Deleuze constructs a model of time that is both multiple in nature and fundamentally processual. On this latter point, it can be considered an early achievement of his philosophy of *process* (as discussed in chapter 1); of the former, it is irreducible to a single, homogenous time-for-all-times (which is something I pick up on in chapters 9–11 with regard to Deleuze's "other" temporal model, Chronos-Aion) and is, as a result, grounded in difference. To begin this first analysis, I consider the first of Deleuze's three syntheses, and its relation to my musical-philosophical enquiry via the seven improvisations of my first practice as research project.

With his first synthesis of time, Deleuze (2004a) is concerned with what he refers to as the "living present": a present in which "time is deployed," and through which the past and the future are constituted as its dimensions (91). As such, the living present is self-contained in its temporal process—it "alone exists" (97). The present, then, in this condition of aloneness, should not be thought of as a moment or a point on a line that conceives time as the (spa-tialised) progression from past to future (or future to past). Rather, Deleuze's living present "does not have to go outside itself in order to pass from past to future" (91). However, this self-contained present should not be considered in terms of a never-ending or "perpetual" present since, as Deleuze stresses, it "passes"—and such passing can happen in the plural, as overlapping, con-temporaneous durations (98).

For Deleuze (2004a), the living present is "passive" in its synthesis (91). This is in contrast to the decidedly *active* view of the present as understood by (for instance) Bergson. In *Matter and Memory*, his early *magnum opus*, Bergson (2004)[3] theorises the present as an embodied centre of action/actual-ity (178). Correlating the past with memory (see next section) and the present with perception, Bergson argues that the "*actuality* of our perception thus lies in its *activity*," adding that the present is "*that which is acting*" (74). In his first synthesis, then, Deleuze's (2004a) conceptualisation of the present varies from Bergson's since, as he writes: "Although it is constitutive [of the dimensions of past and future] it is not, for all that, active" (91). The living present is a *subjective* present, for Deleuze (as for Bergson), but the passive synthesis it occasions "occurs *in* the mind" and is not "carried out" by it (91).

Despite their different perspectives on this issue of the activity or passivity of the present, Deleuze (2004a) makes reference (albeit rather discreetly) to Bergson's concept of duration (*la durée*) when he links together his concep-tion of the living present and its passive synthesis with "duration": "this living present or passive synthesis *which is duration*" (92, my emphasis).[4] Duration is a central feature of Bergson's conceptual apparatus, and a major influence on Deleuze's own philosophy of time. For Bergson (2001), time as duration is time as experienced, not as abstracted in our (spatialised) models of its nature. "Has true duration anything to do with space?," he asks, before arguing that "time, understood in the sense of a medium in which we make distinctions and count, is nothing but space . . . pure duration must be something different" (91). Bergson proposes "two possible conceptions of time": one is the more commonly accepted notion of time as something extensive, countable or otherwise measurable in much the same way we measure the dimensions of space; the other is pure duration, or "the form which the succession of our conscious states assumes when our ego lets itself *live*, when it refrains from separating its present state from its former states" (100).

The actively subjective nature of Bergson's conception of the present is clear, here, and (as noted earlier) is a key point on which he and Deleuze differ in respect of their models of present time. On these kinds of conceptual difference, Williams (2011b) makes clear that Deleuze's concepts of time should not be considered "the same as Bergson's . . . they are developments of them" (63).[5] In fact, one could go further and say that Deleuze finds, in Bergson's formulation of the present as an embodied centre of activity, a latent *passivity*—or, more specifically, a passivity that *enables* the temporal activity theorised by Bergson in his conception of the durational present. Williams (2011b) indicates much the same thing—although in terms of what he sees as philosophy's (perhaps more widespread) tendency to set passivity and activity in opposition to one another—when he suggests that Deleuze's first synthesis of time (and his philosophy of time in general) offers "an understanding of life—of all things that become—as activity drawn from passivity" (50).

For Deleuze (2004a), the living present of his first synthesis provides nothing less than the "content and foundation" of time (117). In its passing, this present enables the transformation of not only itself (as a consequence of the cumulative, ongoing experience of time as lived), but also the past and future that endlessly feed into, and from, its process. "This is the paradox of the present," notes Deleuze: "to constitute while passing in the time constituted" (100). And the key mechanism by which the living present as time's foundational content operates is *habit*. "This living present," Deleuze stresses, "rests upon habit" (99). The first synthesis, as a result, is characterised by repetition in the *habitual* sense, whereby the "present is the repeater" of that which repeats, repeatedly (117).[6]

Considered from the perspective of the habitual, the improvisations undertaken for this project relate to one another with regard to the limited set of compositional methods utilised in each. For instance, in all seven, small groups of notes provide the melodic/harmonic qualities of each: for five of the seven (tracks 1, 3, 4, 5, and 6), four notes are utilised; for the other two (tracks 2 and 7), there are three (see figure 4.1).

The question of *which* particular notes to use in each of the improvisations was deliberately left as a matter of decision on the day/at the time—that is,

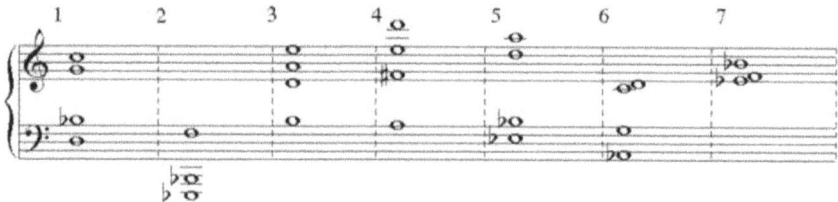

Figure 4.1.

no choices were planned ahead of the performances given. Despite this, it is clear that I favour certain note-combinations/intervals over others. For example (and in order of highest to lowest frequency across the seven), repeated use is made of: the perfect fifth in tracks 2, 3, 4, 5, 6, and 7; the perfect fourth in tracks 1, 3, 4, 6, and 7; the major second in tracks 1, 2, 3, 6, and 7; the minor seventh in tracks 1, 3, and 4; the major seventh in tracks 5 and 6; the minor sixth in tracks 1 and 4; the major sixth in tracks 1 and 4; the sharp fourth in tracks 5 and 6; and the major third in tracks 5 and 6—while single use is also made of the minor third in track 3 (see figure 4.2).

Continuing the theme of the habitual in these improvisations, the manner of articulating these notes/intervals is consistent for each: the damper pedal is depressed throughout; there is a narrow dynamic range (lying, for the most part, between *mp* and *mf*); and a regular pulse is maintained (although with no particular metres becoming predominant for any extended period of time— hence the absence of bar lines in the transcription analyses that follow). In addition, simple rhythmic values are employed: adopting a minimum quantisation of a crotchet in the analysis, each improvisation articulates a series of crotchets, minims, and semibreves (and tied combinations of these)—with extended strings of crotchets being most common across the seven (see figures 4.3 to 4.6).[7]

The decision to apply limitations to the notes/intervals/rhythms/articulations I utilise in each improvisation reflects my long-standing interest in the American Minimalists. In addition, a perhaps less obvious influence comes from the New York School. Of the former, major influences in my music-making/improvising techniques more generally, and especially in terms of the improvisations undertaken for this project, come from Philip Glass, La Monte Young, and Terry Riley; of the latter, Morton Feldman, John Cage, and Earle Brown. As an improviser (and a practitioner-researcher in the musical-philosophical in the context of this enquiry), the ongoing appeal of these musicians' work lies, for me, in how a small amount of musical material and/or compositional direction is utilised in the creation of a diverse array of musical outputs. Glass's *One + One* (1968) stands out as one of the more minimal in terms of performance instruction. In this work, the performer must

Figure 4.2.

differently (and rapidly) combine two rhythmic motifs of (1) a quaver, and (2) two semiquavers and a quaver, at a fast tempo on an amplified table-top (of any description). And yet, it is also one of the more maximal with regard to its improvisational potential in performance. In similar (though differently realised) fashion, Brown's 1952 *Music for Violin Cello, and Piano* and Cage's 1948 *Suite for Toy Piano* are exemplary in terms of conveying a sense of the endlessly mutable potential of small minimal units of rhythmic/melodic material. As Nyman (1999) notes of Brown's piece: as a result of the flexible and (deliberately) arbitrary combination of elements in his compositional process, "all possible assemblages [are] inherently admissible and valid" (56).

In spite of the habitual repetition of a limited set of music-making processes, it is the experience of *difference* engendered as a result of these limits that is most apparent to the listener—and the performer—beyond the (basic) act of repeating. On the surface, this is hardly a radical observation. Plainly, when music is made utilising a deliberately limiting means of production, the ear becomes ever more attuned to the various differences (on larger and smaller scales) between different articulations of repeated material. However,

Figure 4.3.

for Deleuze, it is not the differences *between* that should be attended to in our understandings of difference but, rather (as already highlighted earlier in this book), the differences *in themselves*. As Hulse (2010) argues, from a Deleuzian perspective, musical sounds should be considered in terms of how they differ, not from one another in their spatialised conception, but "from themselves in time" (33). In the case of my seven improvisations, each approaches the articulation of its notes/chords and compositional processes without any overarching teleological consideration. Instead, the repeated articulations of the materials/methods to hand become the primary concern of each improvisation. From this perspective, neither the first nor the last of these articulations, nor any of those in between, hold any lasting hierarchical-sequential importance over any of the others—and the same is true of the relationship between different improvisations.[8]

This lack of teleology, and the close attention paid to the differences inherent in/emergent from (supposedly) "simple" musical materials/methods, again signals the influence of the American Minimalists—in particular, the work of La Monte Young. Consider, for instance, how less teleologically minded a piece of music can be than Young's *Composition 1960 #7*—and

Figure 4.4.

also how immanently concerned with the process of its self-difference in performance. Young's instruction to the performer to play a perfect fifth (the B below middle-C and the F-sharp above) and to hold it "for a long time" introduces a sense of the eternal, in terms of the (potentially, at least) infinite articulation of a basic interval. But it also indicates the endlessly different possibilities/experience of playing and/or listening to that interval as sounded in performance. If there is a teleological aspect to Young's piece—and others of his oeuvre (especially in the sound installations he has been exploring since the early 1990s)—then it is, as Grimshaw (2011) points out, a matter for the listener not the composer, since it is the responsibility of the listener (and the performer, I would add) to "get inside the sound" or to "follow the musical path already laid out" (175). In following that path in its habitual cycling of a basic sound in simple articulation, the familiar can become unfamiliar, and endlessly fascinating in its inherent and emergent expression of difference.

At the level of Deleuze's first synthesis of time, my process of music-making in the set of seven improvisations proceeds by means of such habitual repetition—but, as with the example of Young's and others' use of repetitive process, this is in no way limiting in terms of engendering novelty. As Deleuze (2004a) notes, habit "draws something new from repetition—namely,

Figure 4.5.

difference" (94). In my improvised articulations of sets of notes and compositional strategies, I want to propose that it is the differences internal to those sets that is made apparent via their repeated sounding, not any fundamental sameness. The more the sets are articulated, the more the process of variation itself becomes the "theme" of the improvisations. Accordingly, I would suggest that the "variations" are no longer variations as such but, rather, indicators of the differences-in-themselves at play in the habitual event of their articulation in the living present of performance.

SECOND MUSICAL-PHILOSOPHICAL ANALYSIS: DELEUZE'S SECOND SYNTHESIS OF TIME

What habit and the "living present" are to Deleuze's first synthesis of time, memory and the "pure past" are to the second synthesis. For Deleuze (2004a), memory is "the ground of time," or that which "causes the present to pass, that to which the present and habit belong" (101). In Deleuze's second temporal

Figure 4.6.

synthesis, it is memory that provides a key to the process by which the present both passes and is grounded via a particular conception of the past as "pure."

In our commonplace notions of the relationship between present and past, the past is formed in the wake of the present. Deleuze (2004a) highlights the flaw in such thinking, whereby such a process would, in effect, freeze the present into a temporal state that neither passes nor admits the arrival of another present after its own. As he argues: "If a new present were required for the past to be constituted as past, then the former present would never pass, and the new one would never arrive" (103). In order to resolve this paradox, Deleuze posits a "pure past" that both coexists with *and* preexists "the present that it *was*," but to which it was neither "present" nor formed "after" (103–104). These references to the past in terms of purity and coexistence/preexistence reflect a conceptual debt to Bergson—as I will explain.

In *Bergsonism*, published two years prior to *Difference and Repetition*, Deleuze (1988a) defines Bergson's notion of the "pure past" as "a kind of 'past in general'"—adding that, in its "contemporaneity" with the present, the past in its pure form can be thought of as "*all* our past" (59). From this perspective on the (pure) past's generality and contemporaneity, Bergson (2004)

makes his famous assertion as to the fundamental independence of matter
and memory: that memory (in its pure, unconscious, generalised state) "is
without attachment to the present" (181); that the "materiality" of the present
(in its pure, conscious state as lived) "begets oblivion" (232). In his argument
in support of this assertion, Bergson draws deliberate distinction between the
body's experience of the present as lived, and the past considered as "pure
memory": a disembodied form of memory that "interests no part of my body"
(179). In fact, Bergson insists that there is a "radical" distinction between
actual sensations and pure memory of the order of a difference *in kind* and not
"mere" degree (179).[9] On the basis of this pre- and coexistence of the (pure)
past with the (passing) present, Bergson describes a "radical powerlessness"
of pure memory: "pure from all admixture of sensation," devoid of attachment to the present, and, thus, "consequently unextended" (181).

Deleuze (2004a) takes these formulations and develops his own (though
certainly Bergson-influenced) model of the past in its temporal-conceptual
purity. For Deleuze, such a past is "pure" in the sense that, in spite of its intimate involvement with the passing of one present to another, it itself is devoid
of content and resistant to representation (102–103). This "whole past coexists with *itself*," argues Deleuze (104); though no longer existent, "it insists,
it consists, it *is*"—as the "in-itself of time as the final ground of the passage
of time (103). In this second synthesis, it functions as not merely a dimension
of time (as was its role in the first synthesis), but as "the synthesis of all time
of which the present and the future are only dimensions" (103).

With regard to music considered solely (or purely)[10] as an historical *corpus*
or canonical body of work, Chouvel (2019) uses the Deleuzian-Bergsonian
formulation of the pure past as exemplar of what he calls music's "memory
immemorial"—that is, music understood as being in a condition of being
"frozen in the archetypes of the past" (35). Chouvel's point is to use this conceptual correlation as a way of introducing the importance of Deleuze's third
synthesis of time. However, as a performer, in performance, I experience my
relation to the past of music (or music in its purity of pastness) far more in
relation to its contentless, unlimited (and unlimiting) nature—and certainly
not "frozen." In other words, I understand this lack of content or limit(ation)
as artistic incentive in the most positive, invitingly open creative aspect of the
terms (see below). This contentless, unlimited (pure) past, then, provides a
ground for the temporal process of the first synthesis (the habitual, living present) while, itself, remaining immune to the empirical hallmarks of that which
it grounds—such as to be representable/to have content, or to be defined by
limit or character. As Williams (2011b) makes plain, the pure past, as Deleuze
conceives it, is "not characterised by or limited by a particular set" (62).

In the improvisations undertaken for this project, despite the repetition of a
basic compositional method across all seven (the use of a limited set of notes

and ways in which to articulate those notes), that method is not, itself, reducible to or contained by any, or all, of its instantiations. Accordingly, in relation to the improvisations given, the method that enabled their content is both present and not present. It is present, in terms of engendering the music that is made, but it is also not present, since the music that is made is not its representation. Its effect can be felt in the sense we receive of its process through prolonged listening to the improvisations it occasions. In other words, each improvisation functions as an expression of the method of its making without representing that method in terms of defined content. The method remains "pure" (in the Deleuzian sense), while at the same time being the ground that enables each of the seven improvisations (and, potentially at least, an infinite number of others).

Despite its elusiveness, then, a sense of the pure past can still be grasped—albeit indirectly, via its temporal relations with that which it grounds. In theorising these relations, Deleuze draws on a particular understanding of memory. In terms of the pure past, Deleuze (2004a) argues how memory "invents no less than it remembers" (358). Conceiving memory in this manner moves our understandings of its temporal function beyond that of mere recall, or repetition of "the same," and into consideration of its creative aspect. I use the term "its" deliberately since, following Deleuze, memory is not something that we, ourselves, need to be in possession of "in order for recollection to occur" (Stagoll 2010d, 164). Through its process of creative repetition, memory provides the agency by which the pure past becomes "something new" via repeated acts of self-differentiation (163). Such novelty emerges, then, on account of a relationship between the difference/s occasioned by the mediation of memory, in respect of which, in Deleuze's words, the (pure) past is no less than "repetition itself" (2004a, 117).

Feldman (2000), in discussing the compositional process he developed through working on his 1981 *Triadic Memories*, draws attention to the role of memory in our understandings of music. He explains his deliberate attempt to *disorient* the listener for the purpose of exposing the "illusion" of "functional and directional" harmony utilised, and to use repetition to move beyond any sense of "discernible pattern" (2000, 137–138). For Feldman, the memories evoked for listeners to his piece are reminiscences of older, tonal/triadic harmonic functions (156); the reality of his process of composition, however, is that he was exclusively concerned with combinations of the intervals of the minor second and the major second (155). For my own part, in the seven improvisations undertaken for this first practice as research project, an important aspect of my process of combining intervals is much less a case of prolonging the single chord of each (as represented in the transcription shown in figure 4.1) than that of repeatedly, and differently (and in repeatedly different rhythmic patterns), "sounding out" the intervals in question (as shown in figure 4.2). Where Feldman explores ways to make explicit or problematise the relationship of memory and pattern in *Triadic Memories* (and in other works—such as his six-hour long *String Quartet no. 2* from 1983), in my improvisations I am also interested in exploring how to repeat without repeating. I aim to draw attention to the operations of memory at a level other than that of the (merely or otherwise) habitual, and to embrace memory as a ground for a patterning process beyond that of the (simply or otherwise) repetitive.

To repeat, in terms of process, but not to repeat, in terms of content: that is the relationship of the compositional method to the performances engendered in my non-sequential set of seven improvisations—and also the relationship of the different performances in respect of one another. Each performance is, accordingly, the "repeater" of that which repeats (i.e., that which, as indicated previously, Deleuze called the habitual, "living present" in his first synthesis of time), but not the mechanism by which such repetition (for itself) occurs. To listen, and listen repeatedly, to the performances recorded (in tracks 1–7) is to begin to garner a sense of that mechanism at work via the operations of memory. Memory is being invested, and bolstered, with every performance given, with each improvised articulation of the compositional method within and across those performances. Memory, as such, belongs, not to one or another person, but rather expresses what Gallope (2010) calls "the truly creative nature of memory to our experience . . . the dice throw that affirms the whole of chance with each throw" (84).

However, it is neither the act of throwing the dice, nor the concept of the throw (as affirmation of chance process), that brings about the throw *as event*—that is, as something new and emergent in the world, and in time. In a similar fashion, in the performances undertaken for this project, neither the process of repeating the compositional method by means of improvisation, nor the act of giving that improvisation in performance, get to the heart of the issue of *how* such processes become in the event of their novelty. In order to investigate this particular aspect of creative emergence Deleuze theorised a third temporal synthesis, which I turn to in what follows.

THIRD MUSICAL-PHILOSOPHICAL ANALYSIS: DELEUZE'S THIRD SYNTHESIS OF TIME

In Deleuze's third synthesis of time, it is the future that drives the endlessly repeating play of differences in themselves. For Deleuze (2004a), the "echo" of the presents living and passing, engendered by the pure past as ground of their relation, poses "a persistent question"—the answer to which "always comes from elsewhere" (107). This "elsewhere" is the time of the future, understood not as the continual passing of presents to come but, rather, as that for which the past is brought to pass in order for novelty to emerge. Even though in the second synthesis, the pure past—as "repetition itself" (107)—is posited as that which causes successive presents to pass via the process of memory, it is only with the third synthesis that we reach a sense of what drives such memory-repetition operations, and why.

In its conceptualisation in the third synthesis, the future "is that which is repeated": offering, in that repetition, a key to "the secret of repetition as a whole" (Deleuze 2004a, 117). This key is cut from an understanding of time as a "pure and empty form" (114). Both pure and empty, the future time of the third synthesis drives the process of a profound novelty. As Gallope (2010) puts it, the future, thus conceived, becomes a "force of change," occasioning "the absolutely new in itself (84). As Deleuze (2004a) puts it (in reference to his reformulation of Nietzsche's famous concept), the empty purity of this final synthesis "is there only for the revelation of the formless in the eternal return"—as the endlessly returning "yet-to-come" (114). And from my perspective as a creative artist, such temporal emptiness/purity is essential to the novel potential of that "yet-to-come," lest the future be determined in advance of itself (and creative possibility die with it as a result).

Through my interest in certain musicians and musical works of the New York School and the American Minimalist movement, I have previously engaged with the notion of how music can evoke a sense of the emptiness of the event considered in its temporal purity, or as an "eternal" time beyond the time of its articulation. Of the latter, I am thinking in particular of La Monte Young's "drone" works—such as *The Tortoise, His Dreams and Journeys* (1964–present), *The Second Dream of the High-Tension Line Stepdown Transformer* from *The Four Dreams of China* (1962), and the various situated instantiations of his concept of the *Dream House* that Young has been almost exclusively concentrating on since the early 1990s. Regarding his lifelong exploration of a time that is only hinted at in the event of performance, Young has talked of his interest in "stasis," and "form which allows time . . . to stand still" (Grimshaw 2011, 145). Young utilises the extended drone/s as a means of evoking a sense of this state of timelessness, and conceives of a music that "lasts forever and cannot have begun but is taken up again from time to time" (97).[11] In similar fashion, though via different means, I have in mind the *rhythmic structures without prescribed content* explored in Brown's *December 1952* and Cage's (in)famous *4'33"* of that same year. The score to the former consists solely of thirty-one differently sized horizontal and vertical blocks (Brown calls them "events"), providing performers with a "graphic implication" of what may transpire during performance. Other than a suggestion that the thickness of each block/event can indicate factors such as "relative intensity and/or (where instrumentally applicable) clusters," Brown hands performers majority control of how a performance of *December 1952* will both work and sound.[12] As Nyman (1999) notes, Brown considered his composition to be "devoid of content," since this aspect of its music (i.e., its content) becomes the responsibility of the performer/s and not the composer (69).[13] Through its content-less form, then, Brown's *December 1952* enables a way of experiencing what, earlier, I called the emptiness of the event. For its performers, the score presents a way of structuring the event of performance via a conception of time as that which is to be filled—a time that is overfull with possibility.

As I indicate in chapter 2, as early as 1949, Cage was working with a base definition of rhythm as simply a means of structuring time. In an essay from that year, Cage wrote that "rhythm in the structural instance is relationships of lengths of time," adding, in a footnote, that measure should be considered as "literally measure—nothing more . . . thus permitting the existence of any durations, any amplitude relations (meter, accent), any silences" (1978, 64). For its part, Cage's *4'33"* offers the blankest of rhythmical-structural can-vases in respect of what we are to embrace *as* its musical content in perfor-mance, since no actual prescribed sounds are articulated by the performer/s in any of its three movements (each marked "tacet"). At the same time, it provides the same kind of "overfull" potential I refer to above in respect of *December 1952*, and also that one experiences in the event of improvisation considered in terms of its temporal quality of "anything-can-happen." And while several recorded versions of Cage's work do exist, the most vital ren-dition is ever the one that is, in fact, happening at the very moment that the listener starts to become aware of "the non-existence of silence"—a nonexis-tence that is "not a negation of music but an affirmation of its omnipresence" (Nyman 1999, 26).[14]

From my own experience, to sit at the piano with a view to improvise is to garner a sense of this musical omnipresence in the emptiness/overfullness of time, and the experience of improvising the seven pieces for this project provides no exception. Nothing stretches further in the imagination, or is more keenly felt by the improviser, than the event of the music to follow. It is a "pure" event that, even as soon as the first note is articulated and the performance has (officially) begun, retains its temporal remove from the (actual) event that unfolds. The purity of the pure event is the purity of the future as "empty form" (to reiterate Deleuze's term from above): it is never actualised, but it is intimately involved in the event as actualised. It has no content, but that which is performed cannot be formed without it. The pure event is the ever-undetermined future that coexists with the performance, as the performance itself is determined.

Something *is* determinable about the future, however: that it is indeterminable. This seeming paradox rests on the notion (as noted earlier) that the third synthesis of time produces a "groundlessness, a universal ungrounding which turns upon itself and causes only the yet-to-come to return" (Deleuze 2004a, 114). In the process of this turning/returning, the present and the past no longer operate as the foundation or the ground of time (as they do in the first and second syntheses, respectively). Instead, they become dimensions of the future: the present as "agent," the past as "condition"—but neither return, neither are repeated; only the future returns (113). For the past to function as a condition of the future indicates a change in kind between its operation in the second and the third syntheses, but not a contradiction. The reader will remember that, in the second synthesis, the (pure) past "is repetition itself" (117). In the third synthesis, Deleuze asserts that repetition "is a condition of action before it is a concept of reflection" (113). Repetition repeats difference; in so doing, it occasions the novel before the memorial, the act of the new before its reflection into memory. It is in this manner that, on Deleuze's account, the "autonomy of the product, the independence of the work" is guaranteed, and repeated, (potentially) *ad infinitum* (113).

In each of the seven improvisations undertaken, it is the future that is repeatedly repeated while never being actually actualised. Acting as the agent of this repetition-without-actualisation, the present is itself always already passing into the past (as condition). The pure event, as the event that triggers each new articulation of the limited set of compositional strategies, expresses future temporality as the repetition of emptiness. With each new performance, the compositional method is called upon to provide the ground for an improvisation (as we saw in the analysis surrounding the second synthesis, above). However, it is the emptiness, the groundlessness of the unactualised (pure) future, "which is repeated" (Deleuze 2004a, 117). Not one of the tracks 1–7 captures this emptiness (since it is ever-resistant to representation), yet each manifests a sense of it in the (actual) event of their unfolding in improvised performance.

The improvisations for this project reflect the empty nature of the performance event, destined to repeat that which cannot be fully or exhaustively actualised (the future as pure event), but without which nothing in the performance would ever be actualised. But they also reflect the overfull nature of such events, in the sense that, as they repeat its work (in the living present), their ground is the pure past (as repetition itself), mediated via the process of memory, in relation to which they are yet another passing present enabling the remembering (re-membering) of the past. As such, these improvisations move between Deleuze's three syntheses of time, and are implicated in each by virtue of their ability to bring together the different differences and repeated repetitions. They express difference with the repetition of limited materials;

they repeatedly draw on a set of compositional tools without exhausting its potential; and they echo the emptiness of time in its pure form via the event of improvisation considered as that which repeats without ground (but nevertheless grounds all with its repetition).

In the next chapter, I consider the insights that have emerged from this first project. These are detailed in respect of my evolving concept of Rhythmicity, as well as in terms of Deleuze's concepts of difference and repetition and how they have been practised and transformed during the process of the musical-philosophical enquiry undertaken.

NOTES

1. Tracks 1–5 were recorded at a private location in Birmingham, 16 December 2016. Tracks 6 and 7 were recorded as part of a lecture-recital presentation during the *Music and/as Process* conference at Wolverhampton University, 20 May 2017. The lecture-recital was themed along similar lines to this chapter, and the two improvisations were given as further examples of the compositional method under discussion, here—and, hence, my decision to include them alongside the initial five improvisations from the previous year to make a set of seven.

2. Of course, despite their originality, Deleuze did not create his three syntheses in a vacuum. As discussed later, concepts from the philosophies of Bergson and Nietzsche are important to the context and development of aspects of Deleuze's syntheses of time.

3. As indicated earlier, Bergson's work plays a key role in Deleuze's philosophy of time, in this, his first synthesis, and especially in his second synthesis (as discussed in the next section, below).

4. In a footnote to the paragraph that this quote comes from, Deleuze points to both Bergson's *Time and Free Will* (2001) and *Matter and Memory* (2004) as relevant to his arguments in the main body of the text. In the footnote, Deleuze summaries the dual nature of Bergson's concept of time: "fusion or contraction in the mind, and deployment in space," before noting that contraction "as the essence of duration" is a major focus of the latter of the two Bergson books mentioned, earlier (Deleuze 2004a, 157 fn. 1). I would suggest that Bergson's use of the terms "fusion" or "contraction" in his own philosophy of time is analogous (though not identical) to Deleuze's use of the term "synthesis" in his three syntheses of time.

5. With this remark, Williams is specifically referring to aspects of Deleuze's *second* synthesis of time, but I would argue that the point also holds for these encounters with Bergson's philosophy of time in the first synthesis.

6. Although the present is "the repeater" in Deleuze's first synthesis of time, it is not, however, that which repeats—as is discussed, below, in relation to the third synthesis of time.

7. Two (minor) exceptions are tracks 5 and 7. In the former, there is a short section (2'51"–3'10") employing a "shuffle" or "jazz swing" time-feel; in the latter, repeated use is made of *appoggiatura* grace notes.

8. This is one of the reasons why I indicate the "shuffle play" mode of listening to the tracks, earlier—to disrupt the sense of a pre-planned sequence or temporal hierarchy from the first to the last tracks.

9. As Deleuze (1988a) memorably puts it, recognising, and thinking in terms of, differences of kind and differences of degree is "the Bergsonian leitmotif" (23)—such is its major importance and wide-ranging usage across Bergson's *oeuvre* (from his early works, *Time and Free Will* and *Matter and Memory*, through *Creative Evolution* to the collected essays in *The Creative Mind*). One could also say that Deleuze's own formulations of positive, productive differences continue and develop Bergson's thought in this regard (albeit differently, as noted earlier)—for instance, as differences in themselves (as in *Difference and Repetition*), and as what, from a Bergsonian terminological perspective, we could call differences in kind (for example, the conceptual relations of the virtual and the actual, and those of Chronos and Aion as investigated in chapters 9–11).

10. My use of "purely," here, is deliberately intended to continue the conceptual associations of purity in respect of Bergson and Deleuze, under discussion in this section.

11. Exemplary of his tendency to consider each performance of a given work as a new event of its composition is Young's *The Second Dream of the High-Tension Line Stepdown Transformer* from *The Four Dreams of China*. While originally composed in 1962, in the mid-1980s Young oversaw the recording of a version for four trumpet (with harmon mutes), duly retitled as *The Melodic Version of the Second Dream of the High-Tension Line Stepdown Transformer* and given its own date of composition (1984).

12. The quotes from Brown, here, are taken from the programme notes to the 1964 premiere of *December 1952*. At the time of writing, these notes and a range of resources on Brown's work (including a recording of the 1964 premiere at Darmstadt) are available online at: http://www.ubu.com/sound/brown/html.

13. There is a parallel between Brown's *December 1952* and my work, *The Time Is out of Joint* (composed as part of the third practice as research project for this book), with regard to these issues of empty/content-less compositional structures and the relationship between composer and performer. See chapter 10 for further discussion of Brown's approach to time and compositional structure in the *Folio* collection of 1952 (a collection that included *December 1952*).

14. Silence as a musical and, importantly, a *rhythmic* quality is something I return to in the third and final practice as research project of this enquiry. In chapters 10 and 11, I discuss the primary role of silence in developing one aspect of my concept of Rhythmicity (in what I call a "Rhythmicity of silences") and transforming Deleuze's interconnected concepts of Chronos and Aion as a result.

Chapter 5

Rhythmicity

Difference, Repetition, and the Musical-Philosophical

In exploring my first practice as research project, I have composed chapters 3 and 4 from the following elements: two overviews of the Deleuzian concepts of difference and repetition—the first general, the second concerning the use made of these in music research; seven improvisations, each performing the repetition of a compositional method, differently; and three analyses of these improvisations, interrelating aspects of Deleuze's three syntheses of time with musical-philosophical reflection from the first-person perspective of the improviser in question (myself). With the interrelation of writing and music in a musical-philosophical expression, a rhythmic quality is occasioned: one that works through the differences between, and internal to, the modes of enquiry and presentation utilised. This is the Rhythmicity that I am working to develop, and to conceptualise, in the first practice as research project of this book.

On one level, Deleuze's three syntheses of time offer a way of conceptualising the music-making undertaken, yet they are not allowed to dominate the epistemological balance of music and philosophy in this project on account of the compositional structure employed in chapter 4. Instead, they are utilised as elements in a musical-philosophical mix: Rhythmicity. Via Rhythmicity, the seven improvisations are enabled to offer something new to our understandings of Deleuze's difference and repetition, rather than functioning as mere illustrations of a differing set of repetitions of simple musical material. Given that the audio recordings of these improvisations are a parallel "voice" in the expression of Rhythmicity as a means of exploring Deleuze's difference and repetition, Deleuze's concepts are transformed as a consequence. They cease to find articulation in the written word alone, and, accordingly, the written word of their concept can no longer contain their potential as musical-philosophical expressions.

I will give an example from my own experience of creating, and engaging with, the musical-philosophical expressions of difference and repetition in chapter 4. Each analysis was written while listening to the audio of the seven improvisations (on shuffle play, and therefore looping continuously throughout the writing process). The music-making thus served as ground for each analysis undertaken—though differently in each case. In the three analyses presented in chapter 4, there is no one-to-one correlation attempted (or desired) between specific improvisations and specific analyses. As a result, the improvisations work collectively. In other words, the shared practice of repeating, differently, a set of intervals at the piano brings the seven improvisations together in a shared purpose: to express difference-in-itself and repetition-for-itself—and, through that expression, to transform the concept of each. By virtue of this shared practice and purpose, it is not the mere fact that the intervals are repeatedly varied in rhythm and order that becomes important to the project. Rather, it is the reader-listener's sense of becoming aware of a process of differing and repeating across the seven improvisations that provides a key to the musical-philosophical expression. The improvisations are not so much *enacting* a pair of philosophical concepts as *rephrasing* them. If it is possible to *hear* difference-in-itself, and not only read about it, then it can be heard in the movements *between* the improvisations: when the broader practice of differing intervals and rhythms is heard as other than the particular intervals and rhythms being articulated at a given moment—that is, when it is heard *as process not content*. And the same goes for repetition-for-itself: when the reader-listener's perception of the repetitions of specific intervals and rhythms gives way to a sense of a wider (or more fundamental) repetition: repetition-for-itself, or repetition as process not content. Combine this awareness of process not content (or content giving way to awareness of wider process) with the issues dealt with in the writing of each analysis, and the interference patterns set up in the combination of audio plus writing, writing plus audio, engender a difference-in-itself and a repetition-for-itself that exists beyond the sole dimensions of each (audio, writing)—and ever between.

The music-making undertaken for the first project not only practises difference-in-itself and repetition-for-itself in the movements between and across the seven improvisations, but it also adds something new to our understandings of these Deleuzian concepts. And that fresh insight comes via my concept of Rhythmicity. Rhythmicity, in chapter 4, is expressed in two different (though interrelated and coexistent) "musical-philosophical" movements. The first is cyclical, in its repetition of a set of compositional methods: the reiteration of three or four notes in similar articulation across a group of seven improvisations; the shuffled and (potentially endlessly) repeated presentation of the audio recordings of that group of improvisations; and the looping movements of the musical-philosophical in the chapter 4. The presentational format adopted thus occasions these three differently expressed processes; it becomes the repeater of the difference at the heart of its Rhythmicity: ever open on account of its habitual cycling.

The second musical-philosophical movement (coexistent with the first) operates between the linear and the cyclical; it expresses the asymmetry of its conceptual grounding as musical-philosophical movement. In this manner, the notion of the musical-philosophical grounds its actual expression in similar (though different) fashion to the mechanism by which the "pure" past grounds the passing present in Deleuze's second synthesis of time. As with Deleuze's second synthesis, this grounding/argument both coexists with and preexists that which it grounds (its expression)—hence, the asymmetry at the heart of its movement. This movement is linear in the sense that it describes the "onward" temporal motion of the reader's eye on the page, or their ear for the music as the audio of tracks 1–7 are played one after another (although, ideally, not in numerical sequence). It is cyclical in that it repeatedly loops back in reference to the ground which enables its process/progress (the musical-philosophical). Irreducible to either the linear or the cyclical alone, the motion of this second aspect of Rhythmicity resonates between the modes of its expression. This neither exclusively linear nor cyclical *hyperbolic* movement is echoed in the articulations of the groups of three or four notes utilised in the seven improvisations, since these are perpetually repeated, though differently, despite leading nowhere in particular (other than the eventual end of the performance) in terms of teleology. It is also echoed in the operations of difference and repetition in the writing that runs in parallel with the audio of the improvisations given. The writing moves forward in that its argument is continually added to, though it repeatedly cycles back to the themes of difference and repetition in the process of that argument. Experienced together, the audio and the writing convey to the reader-listener a sense of this second, more elusive, movement of musical-philosophical Rhythmicity—an exaggerated movement, since it cannot be limited to either the linear or the cyclical; non-Euclidean, asymptotic, since neither motions coincide, in spite of being experienced simultaneously.

Alongside a first attempt to build a concept of Rhythmicity, in mixing together the modes of the musical and the philosophical in this opening project of my enquiry, I have also begun to explore the question of how Deleuze's original concepts may receive fresh insight from such a process. I have already referenced, elsewhere in this book, the danger of applying the conceptual apparatus of another's work to one's own (or to others'): the latter has a tendency to be considered as mere example or illustration of the former rather than as a source of thought in itself. Deleuze himself articulates these concerns in relation to his philosophical encounter with the paintings of Francis Bacon (see Deleuze 2005). In interview, he speaks of the twin dangers of the process of melding philosophy and art in the following manner: "either you describe the painting, and then a real painting is no longer necessary . . . Or you fall into indeterminacy, emotional gushing or applied metaphysics" (Deleuze 2007, 183).

The danger of imposing the hierarchy of application (inadvertently or otherwise) is lessened in the parallel presentation of the modes of articulation utilised. While the reader listens, the listener also reads: no one mode of expressing the concerns of this project takes centre stage in relation to its other. And in this deliberate multimodality, something new is added in respect of the practices, and the notions, involved. Rhythmicity, simultaneously expressed across the modes of the musical and the philosophical, provides, in its dual movements of articulation (as outlined previously), a key to thinking difference and repetition other than via the written page. Where Deleuze utilises writing as his primary mode of presentation, the Rhythmicity of musical-philosophical expression allows the expansion of the concepts of difference and repetition past the limits (such that they are) of the textual. And with regard to the music-making concerned, the musical-philosophical provides a means of utilising its practice in terms beyond the registers of the musical, alone. In listening to difference and repetition at the "same" time as reading about difference and repetition (though in different modes), the reader-listener is thus cast "into the volcano" with regard to being forced to encounter the novelty of the event that is Rhythmicity's multimodal, multi-temporal expression of these concepts.[1]

On this point about the encounter (forced or otherwise) between the reader-listener and the multimodality of Rhythmicity, a reference can made to Sauvagnargues (2016) and Assis (2018) on the concept of *modulation* in the work of the philosopher Gilbert Simondon. As Sauvagnargues (2016) details, Simondon influenced certain aspects of Deleuze's thought from *Difference and Repetition* onwards—for example, his concepts of difference, event, becoming, and the Deleuzian-Guattarian concept of haecceity (62; 64–65).[2] For Simondon, modulation provides a way of understanding the process by which seemingly disparate entities can enter into reciprocal communication, resulting in the emergence of something new that cannot be reduced to either of its constituent agents. Simondon gives the example of a brick—or, rather, the process of forming a brick, considered as not simply a case of the mould being *applied* to the clay and "the active form of the mould impress[ing] its form on passive matter [i.e., the clay]" (Sauvagnargues 2016, 69).[3] Instead, Simondon conceives it as a process wherein both parties (the mould and the clay) "enter into a common system, an associated milieu, and together realise an operation of individuation (the brick) through a continuous exchange of information" (69).

Individuation is the process by which a thing becomes defined in its individuality, and Simondon's modulation theorises this act of definition through interrelated notions of *transduction* and *disparation*. Simondonian transduction, argues Sauvagnargues (2016), is "truly an invention in that it provokes a system to enter a new state, an unpredictable change of phase" (16). While the system (and any system thus provoked) is in this unpredictable state, disparation establishes "a *metastable* relation between two orders of different realities that enter into resonance" (64–65). In this manner, disparation is at the same time both "problematic" and "creative" (63). Deleuze (2004a) reflects his Simondonian influence when he describes individuation as emerging from the act of solving a problem, adding how such a process "consists not in suppressing the problem, but in integrating the elements of the disparateness into a state of coupling which ensures its internal resonance" (307). As Assis (2018) notes, transduction, operating via disparation, changes "one type of energy into another, critically leading to new and unexpected individuations, which contain emergent properties that were not predetermined in advance (56). For Assis, Simondon provides a way for us to reimagine "the plane of artistic creation as the material individuation of complex assemblages of forces" (155).

In terms of my own concerns, here, the reader-listener's encounter with Rhythmicity as a multimodal, multitemporal concept is facilitated in a similar way to transduction and modulation *à la* Simondon. The musical-philosophical encounter itself is similarly *problematic*, as a coming together of disparate elements (the audio, the text)—the relation of which can indeed be considered "metastable." As such it is, inevitably, temporally short-lived, since its existence is measured by the duration of the reader-listener's engagement with the media in question. Nonetheless, it lasts long enough to be useful for practical purposes—that is, as part of the concept/conceptual practice of Rhythmicity. The encounter itself can never be predetermined (at least not in its entirety), since the experience of reading the text of the analyses at the same time as listening to the solo improvisations will always be: (1) subjective to the reader-listener in question; and (2) endlessly variant on account of the combination of the shuffled audio tracks and the section of the text being read. Rhythmicity is thus also a *creative* process, mediated in the dimensions of the musical-philosophical, in that it puts in motion an unpredictable engagement of the senses that does not pre-exist its expression.[4]

Through Rhythmicity in this chapter/project, the reader-listener's senses are immersed in experiencing the rhythmic quality of the musical-philosophical explorations of Deleuzian difference and repetition in parallel (though interrelated) fashion. And the insights garnered through such experience are themselves expressed in parallel (though interrelated) fashion. In this manner, the problem of application is addressed beyond the linearity of its hierarchical imposition: the arguments made and explored in the musical and the philosophical modes of this project are repeated, differently, in never less than two, parallel, rhythms of articulation. As a result, the creative (or "differencial") difference at the heart of difference itself is echoed in the impossibility of reducing the investigation to a single mode of dissemination.[5] Likewise, the "hidden" repetition that repeats these differences-in-themselves, yet is itself never actualised, is experienced in the movements of the musical-philosophical: movements which are ever conveyed via that which they place in motion in the experience of the reader-listener. These intimations of Deleuzian difference and repetition are conceived via a developing concept of Rhythmicity, and expressed in the multimodality of the musical-philosophical: in the movements of conceptual resonance and creation with each repeated engagement of the reader-listener, and the repeated difference that such parallel presentation performs.

Given this summary, a new question must now be raised ahead of the next project in this book. That question is: What is yet to be investigated, in light of the musical-philosophical revelations above, in order to further evolve my concept of Rhythmicity and its insights into a Deleuzian philosophy of time (beyond the conceptual pairing of difference and repetition)? While Rhythmicity is developed in this first project alongside consideration of Deleuze's difference and repetition as a means of thinking time via the three syntheses, in conjunction with the seven improvisations played by myself-as-pianist, there remains further exploration to be undertaken in respect of the mechanism by which different practices are able (or enabled) to come together to resonate (though differently) toward a common aim. This common aim is the musical-philosophical expression that lies at the heart of this enquiry: Rhythmicity as explored throughout the practice as research projects of this book. Where the pairing of difference and repetition provided an opportunity to repeat an analysis of my improvisations (three times, differently each time), the process of bringing together the musical and the philosophical involves allowing what is different in each practice to resonate in its own terms. In other words, the act of musical-philosophical expression is, at its heart, an expression of differences: differences that are presented in parallel in the combination of music audio and written text in chapter 4—specifically, what we might consider a combination by *folding*. This act of folding moves the Rhythmicity of the musical-philosophical expression across two different modes of presentation: music audio and written text. The differences between these two modes of presentation are such that one cannot be translated into the other; their differences retain their specificity.

In the next three chapters of this book, and the second practice as research project, I take this initial development of Rhythmicity as the basis for an engagement with these other concepts from Deleuze's philosophical apparatus: concepts reflecting the acts of folding and combining different elements as practised in this first project and its chapters. Continuing the practice of bringing together different modes of research and presentation, I ask the following questions: Given that Deleuze's concepts of the fold and the incompossible are concerned with exploring diverse relations considered apart from the terms of their relation (in the fold), and multiple states of temporal coexistence (in the incompossible), how might a nonhierarchical, musical-philosophical Rhythmicity be further developed through the incorporation of these concepts as elements in the enquiry? And, in so doing, how might the Deleuzian fold and the incompossible in turn be transformed through their investigation, and expression, in the modes of the musical-philosophical? These questions initiate a new practice as research project and the three chapters that now follow.

NOTES

1. I am, here, alluding to Deleuze (2004a) in his call for the reader/researcher to "throw oneself into the volcano" as one means of evoking a sense of experiencing the third synthesis of time in its sheer novelty of event (112). The instruction is, of course, purely metaphorical!

2. Both Deleuze and Guattari's (2004) concept of haecceity, and, crucially, its reformulation by Assis (2018) as the "micro-haecceity," are discussed in relation to my notion of Rhythmicity as a "tonality of time" in the second practice as research project, later.

3. There is a resonance, here, with the epistemological issue of *application* as discussed both earlier, and previously in the book—at least in terms of questioning how we conceive the relations between things other than via perceived hierarchies of importance. This is an issue that is taken up and developed (via Delezue's concepts of the fold and the incompossible) in the second practice as research project, below.

4. On this point of a process of "putting in motion," see chapter 9 with regard to the temporal concept of *kairos* as a coming together of past and future in the present moment of the event of performance, as well as my discussion of the evolution of Rhythmicity via the first practice as research project in the conclusion.

5. I am using the Deleuzian term "differential" here to indicate what Paul Patton, in his translator's preface to Deleuze (2004a) refers to as the creative act of making or becoming different (viii).

Chapter 6

The Fold and the Incompossible
via Deleuze and the Deleuzian

As I have already noted, Deleuze is well known for engaging with the works of other philosophers through his (sometimes radical) reconfigurations of various aspects of their conceptual apparatuses. Of these, it is Deleuze's engagement with Foucault (in Deleuze 2006b) and with Leibniz (in Deleuze 2004b and 2006a) that is most relevant to the concerns of the second practice as research project of this enquiry. This is on account of a shared interest in conceptualising relation as topological transformation (the myriad folds of Leibniz's infinities, the twisting folds of Foucault's ontology of the inside-outside, my multimodal Rhythmicity of the musical-philosophical), and the way in which Leibniz's incompossibilities enfold coexisting temporal states, providing a resonance with my own conception of Rhythmicity as parallel articulation of the musical and the philosophical.

I begin with an overview of the use Deleuze makes of Foucault's and Leibniz's ideas in order to create his own concept of the fold, before moving on to discuss his reformulation of Leibniz's notion of the incompossible.

THE FOLD

More commonplace definitions of "fold" tend to divide between the act of bending something back on itself, mixing two or more elements (such as ingredients) together, or (in the entry under "fold" in the *Oxford English Dictionary*) the "line or crease produced in paper or cloth as the result of folding it." For Deleuze (2006a), however, the fold is the most basic of elements, and is itself "always folded within a fold," the whole process being "divided to infinity" (6). The Deleuzian fold, then, is not an act of folding different things together, but provides, instead, a way of conceptualising things themselves in terms of the fold considered as the "smallest element of the labyrinth" (6). The "things" Deleuze understands in terms of the fold are, most commonly (though not limited to): different forces and powers, types of knowledge, statements and visibilities, life and death, the corporeal folds of the body (in Deleuze 2006b), matter and the soul, the different types of infinity, and the groups of voices and/or instruments that create the neo-Baroque "new harmony" of certain modernist compositions (such as Boulez) in mid-twentieth-century music (in Deleuze 2006a).[1]

As with much of Deleuze's work (alone, and with Guattari), the scope of his enquiry into the fold brings together diverse fields of research, as well as placing all manner of notions/practices in relation in the process.[2] As Deleuze has noted, once one starts looking for them, folds can be found everywhere: "in rocks, rivers, and woods, in organisms, in the head or brain, in souls or thoughts, in what we call the plastic arts" (1995, 156). Where other philosophical understandings of thought, for example, model its process in terms of language (Fodor), logic (Russell), or linguistics (Chomsky), Deleuze offers a move away from such "atomistic" epistemologies (i.e., where things are considered to be knowable through analyses that divide into distinct elements), and prioritises the *process of folding itself* as fundamental. To "think" with the Deleuzian fold is to conceive the epistemological in terms of *relation*. In a project such as mine, folding music and philosophy in three singular expressions (the three practice-as-research projects of this book), to be able to conceptualise the musical-philosophical as fundamental to those expressions is paramount. In other words, the musical-philosophical becomes the primary epistemological condition rather than something that emerges from a process of folding distinct elements. Its concept pre-exists its multimodal expression, although each expression expresses the musical-philosophical uniquely. The fold thus offers a means of adding to (but not "explaining away") the conceptualisation of musical-philosophical Rhythmicity by virtue of the fundamentality of relation in its ontology.

Deleuze's concept of the fold is characterised by its singularity, not its universality (1995, 157). For Deleuze, no two acts of folding are alike, and it is this creative difference (even in repetition) that marks the fold in question as a singular, rather than a general, expression—an expression that "can only get anywhere by varying, branching out, taking new forms" (157).[3] From his singular perspective on the fold, Deleuze theorises an ontology of relation. This relation is not, however, a relation of subject to object—at least not where subject and object are considered in essential, or fixed, terms (see Boundas 2010, 274). It is, instead, an ontological relation grounded in ever-varying perspectives/points of view, rather than in things seen (or otherwise apprehended) by invariable entities standing in distinction from that which they perceive/apprehend. As Deleuze (2006a) argues: "The point of view is not what varies with the subject . . . it is, to the contrary, the condition in which an eventual subject apprehends a variation" (21). This is what Deleuze (in the title of the first chapter of the third section of Deleuze 2006a) refers to as "perception in the folds," since the process that engenders such perceptual apprehension is a process of folding the without within. As O'Sullivan (2010) puts it (with admirable succinctness): "To 'have' is to fold that which is outside inside" (108).

In the last chapter of his book on Foucault, Deleuze (2006b) formulates this ontological relation in the (spatial) terms of the inside and the outside, where "the inside is constituted by the folding of the outside" (98). This is not a hierarchical relation, however, since the two (the inside and the outside) are ever in contact as a consequence of their folding together. Deleuze labels this fold a "topological relation" (98)—thus introducing a sense of movement/change into the ontological model. In his encounter with Leibniz, Deleuze (2006a) theorises such transformation as a process of folding that continues indefinitely rather than finishes: a process wherein that which is expressed "does not exist outside its expressions" (39). Of this particular approach to our understandings of expression, Colebrook (2010) notes how, for Deleuze, expression is not restricted in its creative possibilities: we are enabled to "think a type of relation but not any concluded set of relations" (96). Accordingly, these folded relations are expressed in intensive rather than extensive terms: the fold is primary—we "begin with a relation," not with the two (or more) things that have come together from outside that relation—and its expression has the potential to "unfold itself infinitely" (96).[4]

In my enquiry in this book, investigating a notion of musical-philosophical expression and a novel concept of Rhythmicity, the usefulness of Deleuze's fold, beyond its ontology of relationality, lies in the focus on the creative potential of a given relation over the terms of its relation. Although my project brings together music and philosophy (as disciplines), "the musical" is not solely found in the music, "the philosophical" is not solely found in the philosophy—as I argue earlier (and demonstrate throughout this book). And I am, in the second practice-as-research project that follows in the next chapter, pursuing a means of folding together my music practices and Deleuze's conceptual apparatus in a rhythmic relation, where that relation itself (the musical-philosophical) becomes the primary focus of the folding, and unfolding, that ensues.

THE INCOMPOSSIBLE

According to the *Oxford English Dictionary*, the adjective "compossible"—meaning "compatible or possible in conjunction with another"—is rare in modern-day usage. Likewise, its opposite, "incompossible," has long been replaced in everyday language by, for instance, its synonyms "inconsistent, incompatible" (from the entry under "incompossible" in the *Merriam-Webster Dictionary*). However, each of the terms has more recently received fresh (philosophical) treatment in certain of Deleuze's published works (2004a, 2004b, and 2006a, in particular), as I detail in what follows.

Deleuze's use of the term in/compossible stems from his engagement with the writings of Leibniz. In the *Theodicy* of 1709, and elsewhere in his oeuvre, Leibniz tackles the longstanding philosophical "problem of evil." As Murray (2013) summarises, the problem of evil can be split into two constituent parts: "the underachiever problem" and "the holiness problem." The former argues that, in a world in which evil exists, the notion of God as "knowledgeable, powerful, or good" comes under question; in the latter, God is "implicated in evil," given the level of his "intimate causal entanglements" in all things. Leibniz (1985) proposes a solution to the problem by way of a principle of non-contradiction: "I set no bounds to God's power, since I recognise that it extends *ad maximum, ad omnia*, to all that implies no contradiction; and I set none to his goodness, since it attains to the best, *ad optimum*" (268). As Nicholls (2010) states, for Leibniz, anything that is "bound by the same law, governed by the principle of non-contradiction, belongs to the same world"; Leibniz calls this a "compossible world" (146). The constituent elements of compossible worlds are not subjects and objects, but series of singularities that Leibniz terms "monads." These monads connect on a single existential plane, and, as Deleuze (1995) notes, each monad enfolds the world, albeit differently, by virtue of its relationship to each other monad on the plane of singularities (157).[5] In this manner, noncontradicting monads express a harmoniousness that befits the best of all possible worlds—a "harmonious unity that is preestablished by God" (Nicholls 2010, 145). In the famous biblical example given by Leibniz, the possibility of Adam the nonsinner is conceivable in itself, but is "*incompossible* with the rest of the actualised world" (Smith 2012, 48). Through his notion of the in/compossible, Leibniz moved focus from the either/or of good/evil towards a consideration of how the best possible world is that with the least possible evil and discord. As Burnham (2018) summarises: "The best possible universe does not mean no evil, but that more overall evil is impossible."

In Deleuze's engagement with Leibniz, he questions the equation of the compossible with the non-contradictory and the incompossible with the contradictory. The incompossible "is not reducible to the notion of contradiction," Deleuze argues, but rather, the latter is itself "derived from incompossibility" (2004b, 128). The sinning Adam and the nonsinning Adam are not mutually exclusive, nor are they bound to contradict one another on account of having nothing in common with regard to the original sin. Deleuze resolves this seeming paradox from the perspective of singularities: through only a handful of singular qualities ("to be the first man, to live in a garden, to give birth to a woman from himself"), this "vague Adam" is, for Deleuze, inherently nomadic in expression and common to many worlds (131). On such an understanding, incompossibility is not the principle by which expression across contradictory worlds is forbidden, but provides, instead, as Nicholls (2010) puts it, a notion of "foldable, polychronic temporalities, where incompossibles and compossibles co-exist" (146).[6]

While Leibniz had embraced the notion of an infinite number of possible worlds ("I think there is an infinity of possible ways in which to create the world, according to the different designs which God could form"), the principle of noncontradiction restricted each of those worlds to elements compossible with one another: "the universe is only a certain kind of collection of compossibles; and the actual universe is the collection of all possible existents, that is, of those things that form the richest composite" (as quoted in Look 2013). The incompossible, reformulated via Deleuze, similarly embraces the infinite, though "not only in the totality of possible worlds, *but in each chosen world*" (2004a, 332, my emphasis). In the infinite foldings and unfoldings it engenders, incompossibility implies—not opposition or contradiction—but rather, "divergence" (59). Deleuze describes this multiplicity of distribution, or of divergence considered in affirmative (i.e., not negative/contradictory) terms, as the "play in the creation of the world" (62).

The pertinence of Deleuze's theorisation of the incompossible to my own enquiry revolves around its encouragement of this playfulness, wherein creative processes are unlimited in their temporal foldings-together of that which they hold in relation. The philosophy of time particular to the incompossible is one of multiplicity: multiple temporal states coexisting without contradiction (or in spite of it). In this respect, the incompossible is of a similar tenor to the Deleuzian concept of the fold as summarised above. My decision to bring the two together in the second practice as research project is a recognition of this resonance—but also of my sense such practices have been an important part of certain movements in experimental/improvised music-making for a number of years (as I detail in the next section of this chapter). However, despite such prevalence, neither Deleuze's concept of the fold, nor that of the incompossible, are especially well-known or well-referenced in music practice and/or research to date.[7] It is for this reason that, in the next section of this chapter, I make example of the music of others that I consider to be resonant (albeit implicitly) with important aspects of these Deleuzian concepts.

THE FOLD AND THE INCOMPOSSIBLE IN
RELATION TO EXTANT MUSICAL PRACTICES

As Campbell (2013) notes, despite the fact that tonality has often been assumed to be a definitive and stable entity in music theory and history (and "still by far the most prominent musical system for all kinds of Western music"), its actual nature has been one of constant change and development (77–78).[8] In light of this grounding of tonality in terms of change over stability, the commonplace conceptualisation of the tonal system with regard to the opposition of consonance and dissonance, and the notion of functional harmony, is thus problematised. In the last one hundred years or so, the various atonal, dodecaphonic, serial, and heterophonic experiments in Western music are indicative of this testing of the limits—or indeed, of manifesting "the end" (Assis 2018, 202)—of tonality as previously conceived. For instance, many of the works of the Second Viennese School in the early to mid-twentieth century, and the New York School in the mid- to late twentieth century, are testament to this calling into question of received notions of concordance/discordance.[9]

In terms of the relevance to my own music experience, and the concerns of my second practice as research project, there are certain key examples from the field of improvised music with regard to a similar move toward incompossibility/the fold in creative music-making process—in act, if not specifically in name. In this respect, primary in terms of influence on my own improvising/composing are: the ensemble AMM; Derek Bailey's Company Week events; the Scratch Orchestra; Ornette Coleman's Prime Time ensemble; and Anthony Braxton quartet in the 1980s/early 1990s. Next, I give a brief overview of the aspects of the music-making practices of each of these improvising ensembles/artists that resonate most strongly with the concerns of the project.

AMM were formed in 1965 and have existed with various lineups up to the present day. Their first album, *AMM Music*, was released in 1966 and features the founding members of the group, Eddie Prévost, Keith Rowe, and Lou Gare (who each came from a jazz background), the artist Lawrence Sheaff (who was shortly to cease making music to concentrate on his art projects), and the avant-garde composer, Cornelius Cardew. Cardew had joined AMM to explore an interest in improvisation as a means of making a music he felt he was previously unable to achieve through composing with sounds alone in mind. As quoted in Nyman (1999), Cardew was attracted to the collective process of improvising, explaining: "It's not what it sounds like that interests me, it's what it *is*" (127). Throughout their history, AMM have explored an approach to collective music-making that Prévost, in conversation with Derek

Bailey in 1991, has described as "concurrent commentary: separate voices speaking at the same time, interweaving and interleaving" (Bailey 1992, 129).

Although sharing an interest in the potential of collective improvisation, the impetus behind AMM's experiments and those of Derek Bailey's Company Week events have important differences. Bailey first used the term "Company" to describe his programmed gatherings of improvising musicians in 1976, and they continued on a regular basis into the mid-1990s. In contrast to the regular core of members in AMM (Prévost, Rowe, Gare) with whom others frequently collaborated, Bailey's concern with Company was to encourage what he called "*ad hoc* groupings": a means for pursuing what Watson (2004) describes as Bailey's "critique of the way that once musicians have established ways of working with each other, their music becomes more predictable" (207). "Company Week is a building site," Bailey wrote in a programme note in the early 1990s—"we get together and make something that wasn't there before" (208). This fascination with music made by musicians (and often artists from other disciplinary fields) with little or no familiarity of one another's methods of making continues a theme that was to the fore in Bailey's various activities as an improviser—a theme on which he is explicit in his reflections in Bailey (1992) on the Company Week experiments. "In this kind of playing," Bailey writes, "I had always found the early stages of a group's development the most satisfying, the most stimulating" (133). He describes this concern with the emergence of new music from *ad hoc* combinations as "not some endless search for the perfect combination of musicians, but as a recognition that the shifting process itself provided the perfect foundation for making this kind of music" (134).

Bailey's commitment to organising events in which performers were able to come together to explore the *ad hoc* and the transient was itself predated (by only a few years) by the collective known as the Scratch Orchestra—although, as with the differences between Company Week and the AMM, not necessarily by virtue of the same driving concerns (as is detailed, below). Between 1969 and the mid 1970s, the Scratch Orchestra pursued what (former member) Keith Rowe described in interview in 2001 as "the ethos of collectivity, lack of leadership, lack of centralisation."[10] Another former (and founding) member of the Orchestra, Michael Parsons, has explained how the collective was not interested in producing "monuments and finished works," but rather with the setting "in motion" of various "currents" of practice—where the (simple or otherwise) emergent acts of "doing things together" were granted the same importance as more precomposed/prestructured approaches to organising events of music-making (quoted in Harris 2013, 79). Despite the Orchestra's desire to flatten its hierarchy in favour of such leaderless activity, its most influential member was the composer Cornelius Cardew. This was hardly surprising, considering Cardew's prominence in the

avant-garde/experimental music world at the time of the collective's existence.[11] However, as Cardew (and certain others in the Orchestra) gradually
became explicitly aligned with the politics of the far-Left in the early 1970s,
the divide that began to separate those committed to an overt political cause
and those committed to the collective's activities as a worthwhile activity
in itself led to an ideological split.[12] And this split, ultimately, installed a
hierarchy among members of the Scratch Orchestra that rapidly led to the
disintegration of its ethos of collective heterogeneity.[13] In this respect, the balance of activities of the collective provides a pertinent lesson in terms of the
problem of application (as discussed earlier in this book) in the practice/s of
music alongside other disciplinary fields: in the case of the Scratch Orchestra,
music/art and politics; in the case of my own project, music and philosophy.

Between the late 1970s and the late 1990s, the saxophonist and composer
(and occasional trumpeter and violinist), Ornette Coleman, extended the ideas
of nonhierarchy and collective independence that he had been working on
in a small-group format (for instance, in his celebrated quartet in the 1960s
with trumpeter Don Cherry, bassist Charlie Haden, and often alternating
between drummers Billy Higgins and Ed Blackwell) to a larger ensemble:
his Prime Time band. Coleman called his particular conception of intragroup
equality, "harmolodics." As Rush (2017) summarises, harmolodics is "an
approach that attempts to value each element and each participant equally."
For Coleman, harmony, movement (i.e., rhythm), and melody are equal
components in musical expression (hence the name, har-mo-lodics)—as are
each of the members of a given ensemble. Gone are the older hierarchies of
soloist-plus-rhythm section that had developed in jazz since Louis Armstrong
up to the time of the beboppers of the 1940s and 1950s and the hard bop
players contemporaneous with Coleman's earlier work with his quartet with
Cherry et al. in the late 1950s and early 1960s. With Prime Time (beginning with the 1976 album, *Dancing in Your Head*, and up until the 1995
album, *Tone Dialing*), Coleman explored his conception of harmolodics in
an ensemble consisting of (variously at times) saxophone/trumpet/violin, two
(sometimes three) electric guitars, (often) two electric basses, (sometimes)
keyboards, drums, and tabla/percussion.[14] Each musical voice or element is as
relevant as any of the others in harmolodics, and the resulting (often chaotic)
ensemble sound is testament to Coleman's commitment to this approach to
building a collective expression.

In resonance with Coleman's notions (and those of the others, earlier) of
the value of combining diverse elements in contemporaneous expression in
performance, the various projects that the composer and multireed player,
Anthony Braxton has undertaken in his career to date have often undertaken
similar (though differently driven, and realised) experiments in heterophony.
Exemplary in this regard, is the work he pursued with his celebrated quartet

featuring the pianist Marilyn Crispell, bassist Mark Dresser, and drummer Gerry Hemmingway during the 1980s into the early 1990s. With this band, Braxton established a regular performance practice of having the members of his ensembles play different of his works at the same time. For instance, in conversation with Graham Lock during his tour of England in 1985, Braxton talked of how the quartet were exploring the simultaneous performance of different compositions, or parts of compositions, from his extensive oeuvre. "The quartet music is becoming a platform for all the work I've been doing in the last twenty years," Braxton explains—"Some of the things we're doing now are like a collage of several different works all mashed together to create a dynamic sound space" (Lock 1988, 202). Later in the same interview, Lock asks: "You could have a quartet concert where all four players were simultaneously playing completely independent works?"—to which Braxton replies, "That's exactly where it's going" (203).[15]

For these musicians/collectives, the motivations for pursuing their own particular practice of (what I would call) incompossible foldings were/are, variously: social-cultural concerns, anti-establishment tendencies, the politics of identity, and a desire to work without/flatten the accepted structural hierarchies (musical and otherwise). In these regards, the artistic imperatives at work are not dissimilar to those that motivated Deleuze's philosophical project: a focus on overturning established ways of practice in a given field or fields, and on finding alternative approaches that make little or no distinction between notions of inside or outside (a field, a practice, a role), or received wisdom as to which things can be brought into relation with other things, for instance. As noted previously, the artists referenced above did/do not themselves use the Deleuzian terms of the fold or the incompossible to describe their own creative processes. However, their interest in composing, improvising, or curating music and/or performance events exploring the combination of diverse elements not previously considered harmonious, or consonant, or compossible, puts them in line with my own concerns in the second practice as research project detailed in the next chapter.

NOTES

1. For further discussion of Deleuze's conception of this "new harmony," see chapter 7.

2. In fact, Deleuze's (and Deleuze and Guattari's) philosophical practice can be understood as a process of folding: enfolding elements from a wide range of fields in the making of his (and their) novel concepts.

3. Plainly, there is a conceptual link/continuity, here, in relation to the explorations of Deleuze's concepts of difference and repetition in chapters 3–5.

4. It should be pointed out that, in Deleuze's formulation, the act of unfolding is not the opposite of folding but, rather, "the continuation or the extension of its act" (Deleuze 2006a, 40).

5. See chapter 7 for further discussion on a Deleuzian-Leibnizian understanding of the monad, in its singular aspect.

6. See chapters 7 and 8 for more on these types of coexisting acts of folding in relation to my musical-philosophical project and its central concern with building a concept of Rhythmicity.

7. It should be noted that Castro-Magas (2017) provides an excellent overview of the influence of Deleuze's concept of the fold in the 2007 work *The Pleats of Matter* by the composer Aaron Cassidy. However, while the work itself, and the essay by Castro-Magas, utilise Deleuze with regard to compositional impetus and analytical modelling, the contribution of each in respect of the aim (as in my book) of *transforming* Deleuze's concept as a result of the encounter of the musical and the philosophical, is noticeably absent from either Cassidy's or Castro-Magas's undertaking.

8. Of the assumption of the timeless stability of the tonal system, there are resonances with Leibniz's notion of God having "ordained a pre-established harmony among everything in the universe" (see Burnham 2018).

9. From the Second Viennese School, I am thinking, in particular, of the experiments in atonality undertaken in Schoenberg's *Five Orchestral Pieces*, *Erwartung*, and *Pierrot Lunaire* (the first two from 1909 and the latter from 1912), and Webern's *Six Bagatelles* of 1913. And, in addition, the later works of both composers exploring the twelve-tone/serial technique (for example, Schoenberg's *Variations for Orchestra* from 1928 and the *Piano Concerto* from 1942, and Webern's *Symphony* of 1928 and his *Variations for Piano* from 1936) are exemplary in terms of musical construction via a nontonal/nonhierarchical approach. In terms of the New York School of composers, Cage's notions of "non-harmoniousness" and "interpenetration" pursue a similar interest in problematising consonance/dissonance—in Cage's case, with regard to which things are considered acceptable to be performed alongside which other things. The combined performance of *Concert for Piano and Orchestra* (1957) and *Song Books* (receiving its premiere) in Paris in 1970, and the collaborative project with Lejaren Hiller, *HPSCHD* (1967–1969) for seven amplified harpsichords, fifty-two tape machines, 6,400 slides, and forty films, are examples of Cage's interest in bringing together a wide range of different elements for audience members to experience simultaneously, and in which to immerse themselves.

10. Keith Rowe was both a member of the Scratch Orchestra and, as is noted earlier, a continuing member of AMM. At the time of writing, his 2001 interview with Dan Warburton is available online at: http://www.paristransatlantic.com/magazine/interviews/rowe/html.

11. One only has to consider, for instance, Morton Feldman's assertion (in 1966) as to the central importance of Cardew's ideas and influence in experimental music to follow: "If the new ideas in music are felt today as a movement in England, it's because he [Cardew] acts as a moral force, a moral centre" (quoted in Nyman 1999, 115).

12. As former member, John White, lamented in this respect: "I feel it would have been constructive to ignore what seemed to me to be a stifling obsession with politics in the last days of the Scratch Orchestra and, instead, recollect with delighted nostalgia its early atmosphere of inventiveness and its character as a model for a society in which everyone's talent had an important place." White's comments (on page 40) form part of the programme notes to a twenty-five-year retrospective concert on the activities of the Scratch Orchestra, *25 Years from Scratch*, at the ICA, London, 20 November 1994. These programme notes were previously available to download online via the London Musicians' Collective website; however, since Arts Council England's funding for the LMC was withdrawn in 2008, online copies of the publication would appear (at the time of writing) to be unavailable. The quote, above, is taken from my own PDF copy of the notes downloaded and printed out prior to the organisation's dissolution.

13. As Roger Sutherland is quoted as stating (on page 35) in *25 Years from Scratch* (see previous note for reference details), the Scratch Orchestra was "possibly the most heterogeneous group of people ever to have been united in a common artistic cause."

14. From the 1995 album, *Tone Dialing*, one of the more striking experiments in Coleman's interest in layering different instruments on different rhythmic cycles, and with exploring a group sound that is often far from harmonious in the more traditional sense of ensemble togetherness, is the treatment of the "Prelude" from J. S. Bach's *Cello Suite No. 1* (composed sometime between 1717–1723), simply titled "Bach Prelude" on the album.

15. The set lists for the quartet's concerts during that 1985 tour—as printed in Lock's book—are illustrative of this practice of folding together different compositions in performance. For instance, from the concert in Birmingham: Compositions 69M + 33, 110A + 108B, 60 + 108C + 96, 85 + 108D + 30, 105B + 96, 87 + 108C, and 69H +31 (see Lock 1988, 110–111).

Chapter 7

In the Garden of the
Incompossible (Project 2)

On 26 June 2018, I recorded a series of improvised performances of my composition, *In the Garden of the Incompossible*.[1] I composed the work in November 2017 as a means of investigating aspects of Deleuze's concepts of the fold and the incompossible via music-making, and, in addition, to further evolve my concept of Rhythmicity. What follows is an analysis of the composition and its performances from a musical-philosophical perspective. This analysis is divided into three parts: the first regarding the compositional process, and the latter two regarding the performing process. In each, my writing moves between musical and philosophical concerns and deliberately folds together the two different approaches. This combining of elements that may not more typically be articulated together is undertaken, in part, to reflect the specific interests of this second project (the Deleuzian concepts of the fold and the incompossible), and, in wider context, with regard to the overarching concern of my book to explore musical-philosophical expression by means of a concept of Rhythmicity (of which, see chapter 8).

At this point, the reader is asked to listen to *In the Garden* #1–#6 (in shuffle mode and on repeat) while reading the analyses that follow. Since there is no prescribed sequence from track to track, the shuffle mode is useful in evoking a sense of nonhierarchy between the improvisations concerned (as with the tracks relevant to the first practice as research project in chapter 4). Each is a separate actualisation of the composition in question, and therefore the order of listening to the six tracks needs not be fixed. This method of listening to the music while reading the text provides a way of bringing together the musical and the philosophical—where, as argued earlier, neither are considered particular to the disciplines of music or philosophy alone. Rather, the dynamic, affective, and rhythmic aspects of the practices of both disciplines are enabled to resonate together across the differences between the two fields (as I demonstrate in what follows). In the case of this chapter, this approach allows the reader-listener to experience the act of folding together elements relevant to the concerns of the second practice as research project, rather than encountering them separately.

FIRST MUSICAL-PHILOSOPHICAL ANALYSIS: THE COMPOSITIONAL PROCESS

In *The Fold: Leibniz and the Baroque* (2006a), Deleuze draws on the short story, "The Garden of Forking Paths," by Jorge Luís Borges as an example of the coexistence of incompossibles and compossibles. Borges's text refers to a labyrinthine garden created by the (fictional) "philosopher-architect" Ts'ui Pên—a labyrinth in which converging and diverging routes through the garden combine to form what Deleuze memorably describes as "a webbing of time embracing all possibilities" (70). Deleuze's reformulation of Leibniz's thought embraces such in/compossibilities as part of "the same motley world"—one in which "divergent series are endlessly tracing bifurcating paths" (92).

In composing *In the Garden of the Incompossible* (for solo-piano impro- viser), I continued my practice of working with simple, well-known musi- cal elements developed through the first practice as research project of my enquiry, but this time focusing on the interrelation of basic chords instead of basic intervals.[2] In this second project, I began by forming a set of all major and minor triads having the same note (I chose an F#) as either root, minor/ major third, or perfect fifth (see figure 7.1).

Since there are six basic triads fulfilling these criteria, I then produced a score consisting of all 30 possible combinations of these triads in pairs of two. I arranged these in a grid on the page of the score, with the chord for use by the right hand at the top of each pairing, the chord for the left hand at the bottom (see figure 7.2). The precise manner of articulating the triads is left to the performer, as is the decision whether or not to use closed or open voicings (which is why I chose to present a grid of chord symbols rather than writing the triads in staff notation).[3] In addition, I set no prescribed route through the score, the performer having free reign in how they move from chord-pair to chord-pair in the actualisation of its musical material—navigating the laby- rinth of "compossible" and "incompossible" harmonies in the process.

There are, of course, many instances of composers utilising various forms of grids in their compositional process. Notable examples from the twen- tieth century are: Feldman, in his use of graph-paper and other forms of grid structure in the *Projection* series (1950–1951), the *Intersection* series (1951=1953), and *The King of Denmark* (1964)[4]; Cage, in his use of overlaid/ overlapped transparencies incorporating grids in the likes of *Fontana Mix* (1958), *Solo for Piano* from the *Concert for Piano and Orchestra* (1958),

Figure 7.1.

Music Walk (1958), *Theatre Piece* (1960)[5]; Boulez, in his attempts to expand dodecaphonic and serial techniques in *Sonatine* (1946) and *Structure 1a* (1952)[6]; and Glenn Branca, in his early works (prior to his adoption of standard musical notation) including *Symphony No. 6: Devil Choirs at the Gates of Heaven* (1989).[7]

As Gottschalk (2016) notes, examples of composers in more recent years who make use of grids in their compositional process include the composers Michael Pisaro (from the Wandelweiser collective) and Bryn Harrison and the artist/composer Chiyono Szlavnics. For Pisaro and Harrison, grids provide a way of blurring the experience of musical time—although by differing means. Gottschalk refers to Pisaro's use of stopwatches as an external means of maintaining a temporal grid while "the performer is allowed to lose time knowing that it is being kept for [them]" (138), while Harrison notates rhythms onto grids that are then "stretched or contracted to create subtly shifting rhythmic relationships between instruments over time" (139). Szlavnics, on the other hand, begins by drawing shapes by hand which she then transforms into a score via superimposing horizontal and vertical grids determining various musical parameters (98–99).

| D | B | Bm | D$^{\#}$m | F$^{\#}$m | F$^{\#}$ |
| F$^{\#}$ | D | B | Bm | D$^{\#}$m | F$^{\#}$m |

| B | Bm | D$^{\#}$m | F$^{\#}$m | F$^{\#}$ | D |
| F$^{\#}$ | D | B | Bm | D$^{\#}$m | F$^{\#}$m |

| Bm | D$^{\#}$m | F$^{\#}$m | F$^{\#}$ | D | B |
| F$^{\#}$ | D | B | Bm | D$^{\#}$m | F$^{\#}$m |

| D$^{\#}$m | F$^{\#}$m | F$^{\#}$ | D | B | Bm |
| F$^{\#}$ | D | B | Bm | D$^{\#}$m | F$^{\#}$m |

| F$^{\#}$m | F$^{\#}$ | D | B | Bm | D$^{\#}$m |
| F$^{\#}$ | D | B | Bm | D$^{\#}$m | F$^{\#}$m |

Figure 7.2.

While these composers have utilised grids in a fascinating variety of different ways, the closest resonance with the particular manner in which I instruct the performer to move around the grid/score to *In the Garden* is provided by Larry Austin's work *art is self-alteration is Cage is...* (1981 . . . –1983). Composed in dedication to his friend John Cage, Austin produced a grid of what he calls a "uni-word omniostic," or "all possible arrangements of the letters of one word . . . CAGE."[8] The work is to be performed by four quartets of either double basses, celli, or combinations thereof. Each performer moves through the score, spelling out the letters C-A-G-E by moving either horizontally, vertically, or diagonally according to their inclination. Contained within each letter on the score/grid are four notes played on the open strings of the bass/cello, which are tuned to the pitches C, A, G, and E (but in different combinations on each instrument). The piece is over once all sixteen performers have played through the score a total of sixteen times.

Rather than using single notes (as in Austin's composition) or intervals (as in the improvisations I undertook for chapter 4's first practice as research project), in *In the Garden* I am, as indicated earlier, using basic major and minor triads. In so doing, I am deliberately drawing on listeners' familiarity with these well-known chords (to Western musical sensibilities, at least).[9] Certain of the scored combinations of the triads produce an overall harmony that is in line with more traditional music theory ideals of (what I am calling, using Deleuzian-Leibnizian terminology) compossibility. For instance, the Bm/D combination on the second line down, second column from the left (see figure 7.2), could be notated with the chord symbol D6—hardly an unfamiliar harmonic sound in the history of music, Western and otherwise. However, even though both chords have two out of three notes in common, this is not a guarantee of the compossibility of their combination. Consider the chord combination of F#/F#m at the far right of the first line as a counterexample. Both chords have two out of three notes in common, the same as with the Bm/D combination. The difference in compossibility between the two stems from the harmonic relationship of the third notes of each pair. The A and B notes in the former combination sound together with more consonance (the interval of a major second/major ninth) than the A and A# notes in the latter (the interval of a minor second/minor ninth). By way of contrast, in the mirror image of the F#/F#m pairing—that is, the F#m/F# combination at the far left of the bottom line—the interval occasioned by the A# and A sounds more consonant/compossible by comparison (enharmonically describing a major seventh).

Borges' "Garden of Forking Paths" appeals to Deleuze in that all possible paths through its labyrinth are chosen (by Borges's protagonist) at the same time. Deleuze (2006a) equates this act with the notion of God bringing into existence "all compossible worlds at once instead of choosing one of them, the best" (71). In support of these (seemingly paradoxical) acts in a "game without rules," Deleuze argues for incompossibility as "an original relation, distinct from impossibility or contradiction" (71). Resonating with this perspective, my score for *In the Garden* presents the full range of possible combinations of two basic triads sharing a minimum of one note, a maximum of two, with no regard for the "rules of the game" in terms of more traditional attitudes to tonal compossibility. In surveying the field of pairs of chords to be folded into one another (see figure 7.2), one is made aware of the "new harmony" occasioned by the combining of triads according to shared elements rather than older notions of key and tonality, concordance and discordance.[10] This new harmony is concerned, not with ideas of what is or is not compossible but, rather, with incompossibility as the ground by means of which such combinations relate on the page. As a result, the fact that all of the chord pairs displayed are (by default) considered possible, opens an invitation for repeated exploration of the various paths one can take through the "garden" of the incompossible, where no one path is considered superior or more compossible than any of its others. In the tonality of *In the Garden*, incompossibility is the ground of all that it enfolds through its possible worlds of composition—its Rhythmicity of multiple temporal coexistence.

Given, then, that *In the Garden* is not prescriptive of anything other than the pairing of major and minor triads that share at least one note in common, the compositional-editorial decision of which triad pairs are in/compossible, and also which of these pairs are in/compossible with which other triad pairs, is removed for the performer. As noted in Campbell (2013), Arnold Schoenberg considered the major-minor system to be "a historical product that is subject to change . . . only one of an indefinite number of possibilities" (77). In performance, the performer of *In the Garden* is free to move around the grid of major/minor chord pairings as they choose. While moving in time "in the garden," the (more traditional) hierarchy of tonal compossibles and incompossibles is suspended, and the performer is, instead, presented with a grid of possible combinations. These combinations each share a common note or notes, equally grounded incompossibly as a productive, creative potential for music-making—a tonality of incompossibility and folding; a Rhythmicity mediated in time via composition and performance. And it is to the performance-making concerns of *In the Garden* that I now turn the reader's attention in what follows.

SECOND MUSICAL-PHILOSOPHICAL ANALYSIS: THE PERFORMING PROCESS (1)

In my capacity as the performer of the work, faced with the grid of two-chord combinations that constitutes the totality of the score of *In the Garden of the Incompossible* (figure 7.2), I began by considering two performance-making factors: how I might go about articulating the harmonies indicated, and how I might trace a path through the "garden" (i.e., the grid of chord-pairs) in question. Regarding the first of these concerns, I decided to continue my practice of utilising the damper pedal to a significant extent (as I had done in the improvisations for the first practice as research project). On account of the sustaining of the sounds of each chord into one another in this manner, the listener is better able to hear the harmonic relationships in each chord-pair than if the damper pedal had not been used—although I approached the act of articulating the chords together in different ways in each of the six performances given.

For instance, in *In the Garden #1*, with the damper pedal depressed throughout, I articulate each chord in open voicings, beginning with my right hand followed by my left, where the timing of the placement of the left-hand chord and that of the next right-hand chord that succeeds it (and so on) is left open, not fixed to a set tempo (see figure 7.3).

Adopting a similar approach, in *In the Garden #6* I alternate again between hands (this time using closed voicings), beginning at first with my right hand, then joining with my left before moving on to the next chord-pair—but this time beginning with my left hand and then joining with my right. After this mirror-image alternation, the right hand starts the articulation of the chord-pair again and the pattern repeats (see figure 7.4). Despite the similarity of approach, a major difference between the two performances lies in the introduction of a continuous pulse (though not a set time signature) throughout the latter.

In addition to these means of articulating the material, in both *In the Garden #2* and *In the Garden #4*, I arpeggiate the notes of the two chords (again making extensive use of the damper pedal) in two different manners. In the former, I begin each time with the lowest note of the left-hand chord

Figure 7.3.

Figure 7.4.

followed by the second and then the third, followed by those of the right-hand in the same order, using open voicings for both chords. I maintain the same rhythm for all of the arpeggios articulated (see figure 7.5).

With the latter, *In the Garden #4*, I use both hands to make a (closed-voiced) mirror-inversion of the order of notes in each, starting each time with the lowest of the left-hand notes followed by the highest of the right-hand's, then the second of the left's and the second of the right's, and concluding the arpeggiation of each chord-pairing with the third of the left's and the first of the right-hand's. As with *#2*, I employ a consistent rhythm throughout *#4* (although different to that utilised in *#2*), varying it only slightly for seven of the twenty-seven iterations of the arpeggio (see figure 7.6).

In contrast to these four performances (*#1* and *#6*, *#2* and *#4*), in *In the Garden #3* and *In the Garden #5*, I play both chords in each pairing at the same time—again with the damper pedal depressed throughout the performances. In the former, I adopt a steady pulse (though, as with *#6*, not a set time signature) (see figure 7.7).

Figure 7.5.

In the latter, *In the Garden #5*, I play without fixed tempo, sounding out the left/right-hand chord-pairs in free tempo, though in unison (see figure 7.8). In both performances, I use closed voicings.

As with the improvisations in the first practice as research project in chapter 4, the rhythms utilised in these performances are not complicated. In each of the six renditions of *In the Garden*, I deliberately keep the note values simple: crotchets (in *#2*, *#3*, and *#6*), *a tempo* semibreves (in *#1* and *#5*), or combinations of these with quavers (in *#4*). A further point of note is the use made (or not) of repetition. For instance, in the two performances where I alternate between hands (*#1* and *#6*), in the former of the two each chord-pair receives only a single iteration, whereas in the latter the number of iterations of each chord-pair varies between four and twenty-five. In similar fashion, in the arpeggiated renditions (*#2* and *#4*) the chord-pairs in the latter are played a single time each, while those of the former are repeated between four and eleven times. Lastly, in the performances where both chords of each pair are sounded at the same time (*#3* and *#5*), the number of repetitions of each chord-pair varies between fifteen and forty-two in the former and single iterations in the latter.

Figure 7.6.

Despite the fact that, on paper and in transcription, the major/minor triads in each pair are identifiable as distinct entities (a "D," a "D#m," etc.), in performance these distinctions become less relevant when the two chords are sounded/folded together. The chord-pairs in question operate as expressions of a harmonic "world" they bring into existence by means of the fold. These different acts of folding explored in the improvised performances give rise to a series of *monads*—to use the term Deleuze (2006a) borrows from Leibniz's conceptual apparatus. As Deleuze writes of monads: "they include an entire world that does not exist outside of them" (157). Developing Leibniz's original conception of the monad to fit his own notion of a "new harmony" grounded in incompossibility (rather than Leibniz's compossible selection regarding "the best of all possible worlds"), Deleuze theorises a monad that is "in tune with" divergence/dissonance and, thus, perpetrates an act of openness to the incompossible through which the privileges of rank and relation are dissolved (157). Running parallel to this notion, none of the chord-pairs/monads in *In the Garden* are harmonically or structurally more important than any of the others; each expresses the tonality of the novel

Figure 7.7.

harmonic world of the composition in *singular* fashion—"To be actualised is also to be *expressed*" (Deleuze 2004b, 127; emphasis in original). It is, of course, impossible to exhaust *all* of the possible harmonic movements of the score-labyrinth (even in a multitracked recording superimposing multiple pianos), given that there are an infinite number of ways the performer can negotiate the twists and turns of the pathway through the "garden"—especially since there is no limit on how long the piece is played, or how many movements are made in the course of a performance. However, the articulation of any of the monads/chord-pairs on the score constitutes an expression of the composition in singular terms, where each is intimately related to all expressions possible (echoing the protagonist's seemingly paradoxical choosing of all possible paths in Borges's tale of coexisting worlds referenced here). With the movement from chord-pair to chord-pair around the grid of the score, the incompossible tonality of the composition is expressed again and again by this act of folding two chords together as one monad, following by yet another act of folding two chords together as one monad, and so on. And it is to the ways in which I articulated this movement between monads that I turn attention to in what follows.

Figure 7.8.

THIRD MUSICAL-PHILOSOPHICAL ANALYSIS:
THE PERFORMING PROCESS (2)

Of the second of my two performance-making concerns (i.e., how to go about navigating through the grid of chord-pairs in the score), I chose to adopt a method of moving from one pair to another by steps in either horizontal or vertical directions. This approach is similar to Austin's directions to the performers in his homage to Cage discussed earlier—although there is no predetermined number of moves in the case of my own composition. Beginning anywhere on the grid, I moved my gaze either up or down, left or right, as I articulated the chord-pairs in question in various ways (as discussed in the section above). For example, in *In the Garden #1*, I begin in the top left-hand corner (a vestige, perhaps, of the traditional manner of reading scores in Western music), before moving down to the chord-pair below (B over F#) and then through twenty-two more of the chord-pairs in the manner indicated in figure 7.9.[11]

I complete the movement around/folding of the chord-pairs/monads of the score by returning to the first chord-pair articulated (top left). This return to the opening chord-pair was not on account of any stipulation in the performance directions (for instance, for the performer to finish in the same location

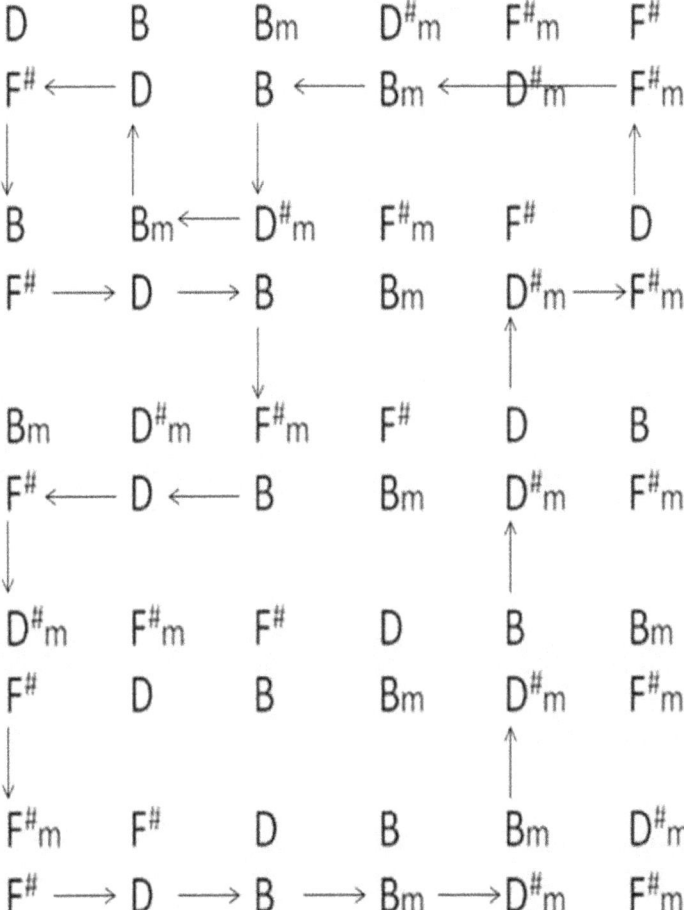

Figure 7.9.

where they start), and other of the performances given of the composition do not follow this logic—or path. For instance, consider the particular path traced through the "garden" of chord-pairs/monads in *In the Garden #3*: starting with the chord-pair third from the top right (D#m over Bm). Here I begin the movement/folding by moving right (to F#m over D#m) and then meander around the score in the manner described in figure 7.10, before concluding the performance with the chord-pair second from the bottom right.[12]

Since there is no indication in the score regarding any particular duration of time for which the performer is to move around the grid of chord-pairs, or how many movements are to be made, the potential for a performance of *In the Garden* to continue indefinitely is certainly implicit in its composition. However, it is more by means of the irregularity of the twists and turns of

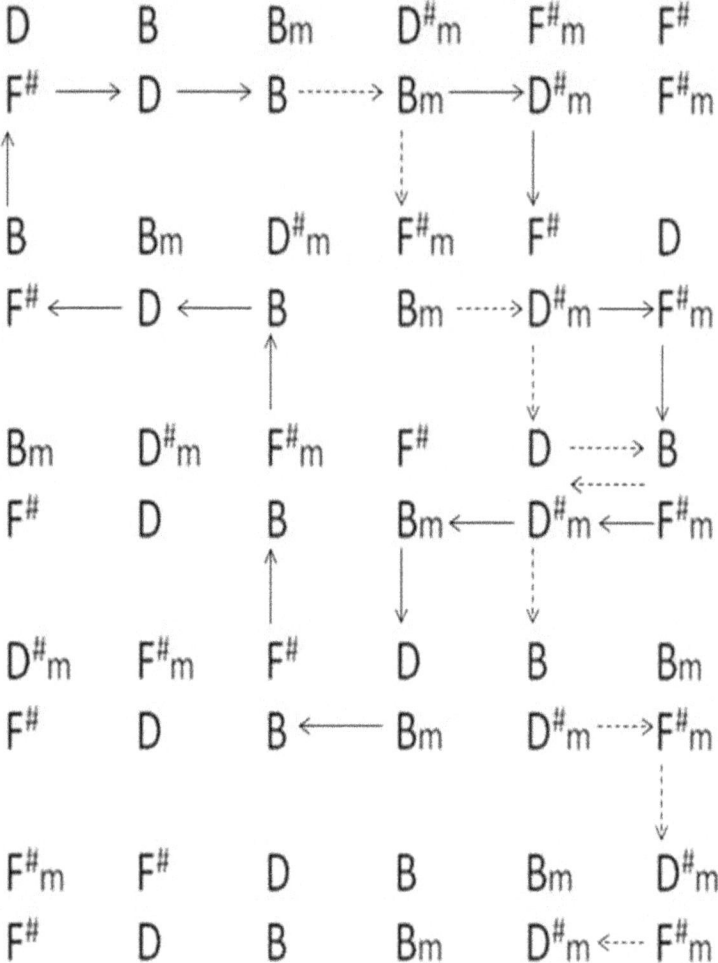

Figure 7.10.

the movements around the score that a sense of an infinite process of unfolding via folding is evoked. The walk through the garden is really a meander,
a walk without destination; a tonality eluding all defining sense of tonal
fixedness—a tonality expressive of multiple, coexisting, enfolded times. For
the performer, and for the listener, to be inside this operation of folding chord
into chord/chord-pair into chord-pair is to experience the infinite unfolding
in terms of the finite.[13] For Deleuze (2006b), such operations are performed
by means of "the fold of the infinite, or the constant folds of finitude which
curve the outside and constitute the inside" (80). The inside, thus conceived,
is "an operation of the outside," or its fold (81). While an infinitely long

performance of *In the Garden* obviously remains outside actual performance practicalities, each (finite) performance contains—within itself, via the movements of folding in and between chord-pairs—fold upon fold in unique expression of the composition in its infinite aspect.

In this manner, finite, irregular movements are able to evoke a sense of the infinite, despite being unable, durationally speaking, to actualise its indefinite extendibility (without, as noted, being given an unlimited amount of time). For instance, both the wide variation in the number of times the chord-pairs are sounded in the six performances of *In the Garden*—ranging between single iterations (in *#1*, *#4*, and *#5*), and a maximum of forty-two (in *#2*)—and the nonsequence of the movement between repetitions (for instance, see figure 7.4 with regard to the asymmetry of repeats in *In the Garden #6*: 7, 15, 11, 16, 5, 14, 6, 13, 8, 12 . . .), are reflective of my intention for the performance of each chord-pair/monad to constitute a unique expression of the composition, while also relating to those others around them in equally singular manner. As Deleuze (2006a) writes: "Singularities proper to each monad are extended as far as the singularities of others," adding how each monad "thus expresses the entire world, but obscurely and dimly because it is finite and the world is infinite" (98)—the "world," in the case of *In the Garden* being the score of the composition (in its infinite capacity for folding and unfolding in performance).

The singular qualities of the chord-pairs/monads that converge around the note F# in the grid-score of *In the Garden*, articulated by means of the various, and irregular, movements in each of the performances *#1* to *#6*, express the infinite possibilities of their world according to the simple, variously enacted process of folding chord into chord/chord-pair into chord-pair. As Deleuze (2004b) writes: "A world already envelops an infinite system of singularities selected through convergence" (126). And through this world of singular qualities weaves the curve of the infinite outside—not as the polar opposite of the inside movements that constitute its expression in actual performance, but as it's coperformed: an outside-inside, or an inside oriented toward the perspective of an outside to which it is intimately related by means of the fold, in the garden of the incompossible.

NOTES

1. The recordings were made at the University of Surrey (UK).

2. As discussed in chapter 4, in the first project of this enquiry I utilised common harmonic intervals and simple rhythms in undertaking the improvisations recorded in tracks 1–7.

3. Closed voicing is a term indicating that a given chord is articulated within the span of a single octave. In an open voicing, the chord in question is articulated beyond the span of one octave.

4. See Welsh (1996) for a detailed analysis of Feldman's use of a grid-structure in the first of the *Projection* series, *Projection 1* (1950).

5. See Pritchett (1993) for a comprehensive overview of the different periods of Cage's work, including details of his experiments using grids (during the late 1950s and early 1960s, in particular).

6. See Campbell (2010, 160–161) for analysis of Boulez's utilisation of a rhythmic grid to determine pitch choices in the transition sections of his early serial work *Sonatine* from 1946. See Williams (2016, 48–49) for analysis of the grid used to determine compositional elements of pitch, duration, and attack in Boulez's 1952 *Structures 1a*.

7. Kyle Gann, in his online article from 2010, "Getting off the Assembly Line," includes an image of part of Branca's score to *Symphony No. 6* (1989) on graph paper. At the time of writing, Gann's article can be accessed at the following address: http://www.artsjournal.com/postclassic/2010/01/getting_off_the_assembly_line.html.

8. Taken from the sleeve notes to album *A Chance Operation: The John Cage Tribute* (Koch International Classics, 1993), featuring compositions and performances from a variety of artists inspired by Cage's artistic process and legacy. The sleeve notes also reproduce the score of Austin's work.

9. I acknowledge, here, that perception of tonality is a culturally specific issue—hence my reference to music sensibilities in the West, and to the history and development of Western music more generally. The composer, Helmut Lachenmann's seeming equation of tonality and tradition, as noted in Assis (2018, 234), bears further testimony to this cultural perspective on the concept of tonality. See Assis (2018) and Lachenmann (2004) for more on this issue of the close relationship between music and the cultural tradition in which it is made.

10. My use of the term "new harmony," here, is a deliberate reference to the title of the last chapter of *The Fold* ("The New Harmony")—a reference that is developed further later.

11. Also notated in figure 7.9 is the mistake I made in jumping two steps instead of one from the chord-pair at top right towards the end of the performance.

12. To avoid confusion, as soon as the movement around the score happens to return to the same chord-pair I begin the performance with (D#m over Bm) I have indicated the movement that follows (and to the finish of the performance from there on) with dotted-line arrows.

13. As noted in chapter 6, for Deleuze (2006a), unfolding is not the opposite of folding but is, rather, the continuation/extension of its process (40).

Chapter 8

Rhythmicity

The Fold, the Incompossible, and the Musical-Philosophical

In chapter 5, Rhythmicity was conceived with regard to two movements of the musical-philosophical: the cyclical and the hyperbolic (as unbound to either music or philosophy considered in solely disciplinary terms). These simultaneous, temporal movements were expressed in the interrelation of writing and audio in the musical-philosophical analyses of the performances, and the music-making practices utilised in undertaking those performances. As a result, Deleuze's difference and repetition were rephrased in terms of the musical-philosophical—that is, in multimodal form, where their concept was moved beyond its original formulation (in/as text) and into the Rhythmicity engendered by the cyclical and hyperbolic movements of the interrelations of the modes of expression utilised in the first practice as research project of this enquiry.

In the second practice as research project, Rhythmicity has been developed in two key ways. The first of these relates to the specific admixture of the sections and modes (writing, audio) of the chapter itself and the intensity of the musical-philosophical expression occasioned. The second development comes via the patterns of temporal relation between notes and chords played in the left and right hands during my solo-piano renditions of *In the Garden*, and also in the movements around the score of the work enacted in the six performances, understood in terms of the what I am calling the "tonality" of their musical-philosophical expressions of incompossibility and folding. Both developments provide insights into the Deleuzian concepts engaged with.

Of the first of these developments of Rhythmicity, the different sections of chapter 6 function as the seemingly incompossible "outsides" of the second practice as research project that are subsequently "folded in" as part of *In the Garden*—and also with regard to the overall composition of chapters 6 and 7 considered in relation. I use the phrase "seemingly incompossible" on account of it not being commonplace to bring together such diverse topics as Deleuzian-Leibnizian incompossibility, Deleuzian-Foucauldian-Leibnizian folding, and the music practices of free improvisers such as AMM, the Scratch Orchestra, Derek Bailey's Company, Ornette Coleman's Prime Time, and Anthony Braxton's 1980s/1990s quartet in the same body of text (chapter 6). By deliberately positioning these two sections one after the other, I am encouraging the reader to experience a sense of rapid movement: the sudden change between diverse fields of knowledge in the move between the sections of that chapter. This structural feature of the text's composition is designed to evoke an intense rhythmic quality (Rhythmicity)—one that sets the ground for the faster musical-philosophical *tempi* of interdisciplinary inter-relation that occurs in chapter 7. In addition, in chapter 7, the multiple acts of musical-philosophical folding undertaken are not, of course, performed solely in the registers of the writing; the audio and transcribed components of its composition add extra dimensions to the mix, making its Rhythmicity a deliberately multimodal expression. The musical and the philosophical become intensive qualities (of affect, of rhythm, of dynamic), unrestricted to disciplinary notions of music and philosophy as separate fields of practice. The musical-philosophical unites these intensities in a multimodal experience for the reader-listener, and a multimodal expression for the concepts of the fold and the incompossible.

Of the second development of Rhythmicity, this second practice as research project has shown how incompossibility and folding might contrib-ute to our understanding of the music practices utilised—that is, the uses of arpeggiation, simultaneity, and alternation of the score's compound chords in the improvisations given. At the same time, it has also shown how such practices can offer new insights into the Deleuzian concepts selected. These musical-philosophical insights collectively produce a tonality born of incom-possibility and folding: a tonality of Rhythmicity. This tonality is engendered from a single note: the F-sharp chosen as pivot for all of the compound triads that populate "the garden" of the score. This F-sharp functions, not as a tonal centre (the composition is not "in" any particular key), but as a means of finding one's way through the labyrinth: it is found in the middle of every chord-pair articulated and provides the thread that traces the unique path trod-den by each performance. It is the incompossible at the heart of the fold, or the fold *as* the incompossible; but, first and foremost, it is the tonality of these as expressed via Rhythmicity.

Through this conceptualised tonality of Rhythmicity, I have explored a musical-philosophical folding of in/compossible elements in the relations between the notes/chords played in both hands, and also in the movements articulated around the score of *In the Garden*, in the six improvised performances given. In these improvisations, Deleuze's concepts are not approached with a view to illustrating or otherwise representing the fold/the incompossible, but, rather, to consider what Rhythmicity can add to our understandings of these. As I argue in chapter 7, the various acts of folding the in/compossible notes of each chord-pair, through arpeggiation, simultaneity, or alternation, and of the folding of in/compossible chord-pair to chord-pair in the movements around the score give rise to multiple, potentially unlimited, expressions of *In the Garden*. This coexistence of an infinite number of instantiations of the composition is itself expressed via a rhythmic quality that is *intensive* in nature, its ever-going process of fold-upon-fold-within-fold-between-fold having neither beginning nor end but an eternal middle—an inside-outside that pulses never in the singular, always in the plural. There is not one single path through "the garden," since each act of folding chords and notes expresses not only the choice made at the time but also the possible choices *not* made this particular time. Deleuze (2004b) writes of bifurcating paths, but it is ever, rather, a *multifurcation*—a multiple splitting of possible choices that, in itself, moves nowhere and everywhere at the same time/s. It is this intensive, ever-changing rhythmic quality that drives every act of folding, that grounds the in/compossible in an eternal multifurcating best-and-worst-of-all-possible-worlds, and which I am here calling Rhythmicity.

The notion of Rhythmicity as a multifurcating tonality of time finds a certain correlation in what Assis (2018) has called "micro-haecceities." Assis describes the micro-haecceity as "a temporal radicalisation of the concept" of Deleuze and Guattari's *haecceity* (Assis 2018, 149). In *A Thousand Plateaus*, Deleuze and Guattari (2004) conceive the haecceity as an alternative to conceptions of the individual as separate from its surroundings: "Climate, wind, season, hour are not of another nature than the things, animals, or people that populate them" (290). They propose assemblages of haecceities (a term they borrow from Duns Scotus's thirteenth-century notion of *haecceitas*, or "thisness") in place of individual subjects in situation or setting (289). Assis takes this concept and appropriates it as the micro-haecceity. Where Deleuze and Guattari's haecceity has the tone of a leisurely contemplation of assembled things (human, nonhuman) in relation in a given event—"a day, a season, a year, *a life*" (289)—Assis's microhaecceities reflect more accurately the experience of a musician charged with the act of performing, right here, right now. Microhaecceities are temporally unstable, unpredictable singularities which the performer is required to negotiate as part of "the unavoidable urgency and imperative sequentially of the here-and-now [of performance]" (2018, 149).

Through microhaecceities, Assis is seeking to conceptualise the temporal singularity of the event of performance, where the making of art is conceived as "generating and enhancing heterogeneous tensions that produce the conditions of their own (transient) resolutions" (149). With my conception of Rhythmicity as tonality of time, I am interested in creating a multifurcated experience of temporality, where incompossibility grounds the ever-restless movement of major and minor triads folded (potentially) *ad infinitum*. Where Assis draws our attention to the emergent nature of music performance considered as a "metastable horizon" of "pre-individual and impersonal tensions" (138), Rhythmicity expresses the time-sense of such metastability considered in tonal terms. The tonality in question is not tonality in respect of any particular theoretical system; it is, instead, a tonality born of movement: the folded movements around the score of *In the Garden*. This movement expresses time in its unfolding and ephemeral state: the time of just-beginning, of never-quite-establishing. The correlation with Assis's microhaecceities is on account of our similar concerns with examining temporal emergence from the perspective of the performer—and, in the case of this chapter, the listener/analyst. As Deleuze (2005) asserts, one task of the musician is to "render time sensible in itself" (45). Music renders the temporal audible, and Rhythmicity renders the musical-philosophical *experienceable* (i.e., via the experience of simultaneously reading text and listening to audio). And, in the case of the second practice as research project, that musical-philosophical rendering has a tonality: of time.

As with the first practice as research project in this enquiry, the process of researching and writing up this second project has indicated further areas for investigation. In the second project, Deleuze's concepts of the fold and the incompossible have provided ample resources for the transformation of Rhythmicity from a movement of difference and repetition to a movement via the folding of incompossibles. This movement, in turn, has helped transform understanding of the original concepts themselves—not least by means of the music-making and the analytical practices undertaken in chapter 7, examining the fold and the incompossible from the perspectives of the composition and performance. This analytical move between the work of composition and the work of performance introduces a temporality into the enquiry that is a development on the temporality of the improvisations and analyses undertaken in the first practice as research project (chapter 4). Through the folding together of incompossible elements (the music audio, the written text, the temporalities of composition and of performance), I engender a temporality that is transferred to the presentation of the fold and the incompossible by means of the musical-philosophical expression I am practising in this enquiry—marking it distinct from Deleuze's original presentation of the concepts. The temporalities of the analyses, combined with the temporalities of the acts of composition and performance, present a time-sense that transforms the fold and the incompossible. Such a time-sense introduces into these concepts a dual temporality: a chronology, and a "timeless" time. The sense of the chronological is evoked by the start-to-finish progression of experiencing the audio tracks in whatever order they are played by the reader-listener, and in the way the writing traces a step-by-step chronological order into the times of composition and performance. The sense of timelessness is evoked through the collation of these acts of the analytical and the composed and performed, operating "after the event" of my experiences of having composed, performed, and analysed the musical-philosophical expressions in question. In these ways, timelessness and chronology are bound together as part and parcel of the practice of making the music and analysing it after the event—sometimes in (relative) silence, sometimes in midst of the process of performance.

Accordingly, the next (and final) practice as project of this enquiry will take this relation of the chronological and the timeless and moves it into a deeper consideration of subjectivity in time with respect to the composer, performer, and listener. Through the performance and analysis of a new composition interrogating Deleuze's concepts of "Chronos" and "Aion" (selected for their conceptual relation of temporalities of the chronological and the timeless), the impetus for the third project follow these main avenues of enquiry: How might Rhythmicity be expressed in terms of composer, performer, and listener experiences of the time/s of composing, performing, and listening? And what can silence, considered as more than the mere absence of sound, offer our understandings of the interactions of the time/s of composing, performing, and listening? Finally, I will consider how Deleuze's Chronos and Aion might themselves be differently understood through their investigation/ expression in the modes of the musical-philosophical. My enquiry into these further research questions forms the basis for the third practice as research project and the focus of chapters 9–11.

Chapter 9

Deleuze and Chronos and Aion

In *The Logic of Sense* (originally published in French in 1969), Deleuze (2004b) makes use of two terms borrowed from the Stoic movement in philosophy.[1] These are "Chronos" and "Aion," which Deleuze utilises to build a theory of time that moves beyond linear notions of past-present-future. In this respect (i.e., theorising time as other than a simple movement from past to the present to future), Deleuze is, with *The Logic of Sense*, retreading ground he had previously explored in *Difference and Repetition* (first published only a year before *The Logic of Sense*). This retreading is deliberate. Deleuze retreads the steps toward a different philosophy of time for reasons of Event: his notion of Event as *Eventum Tantum*, or "the Event for all events" (2004b, 75).[2] Where, in *Difference and Repetition*, he elaborates a theory of time via the three syntheses (as I have already explored), in *The Logic of Sense* Deleuze begins anew in order to set up a resonance between two, not three, perspectives on the temporal: that of Chronos, and that of Aion.

By constructing this new philosophy of time by means of two (interrelated) concepts, Deleuze is potentially falling foul of the kind of conceptual dualism that Badiou (2000), Žižek (2004), Hallward (2006), and Mullarkey (2006) have criticised. In addition, there is the spectre of a charge of conceptual inconsistency, given that his previous publication, *Difference and Repetition*, sets up, in seeming stark contrast, a tripartite philosophy of time (the three syntheses) as opposed to *The Logic of Sense*'s bipartite temporal model. So, how compatible are these models; how should we understand the relationship between them? Of the first of these charges (dualism), it is plain that, in *Difference and Repetition*'s three syntheses of time, Deleuze immediately sidesteps the potential dangers of theorising time (or anything else) in terms of two opposing states or positions. With the pairing of Chronos and Aion in *The Logic of Sense*, it would seem that Deleuze is adopting a somewhat less flexible approach to theorising the complexities of the temporal in (presumably) reducing its operations to either one or the other (of Chronos or of Aion). Of the latter charge (inconsistency), it is true that Deleuze would appear to have changed his mind quite radically about the operations of time in the (very) short amount of time between the publication of *Difference and Repetition* and *The Logic of Sense*. As a result, one could be forgiven for thinking that neither of Deleuze's two books provide a workable philosophy of time given that each would seem to claim to have arrived at a complete system on its own terms, a system that is undermined as soon as its rival system is considered (i.e., when the two books are compared). In other words, the two theories of time, considered together, do not seem to cohere or make a philosophical whole. However, as Williams (2013) quite correctly points out: with regard to philosophical systems, "Whole and complete do not mean the same thing" (153). While Deleuze is providing a *complete* philosophical system detailing the processes at work in each one of the three syntheses of time (in *Difference and Repetition*), none of these should be considered as *whole* in terms of standing alone as an explanation in itself of the operations of time. The importance of the three syntheses is that they must be considered in *relation* to each other. The same is true of the processes at work in Chronos and in Aion (as we shall see in what follows). Chronos and Aion each present a complete system of temporal process, but each system is inherently open to its other—requires it in order to cohere on its own terms as well as those of its other/s.

Williams's defence of Deleuze thus applies equally to both of the accusations levelled earlier (of dualism and of inconsistency). *Difference and Repetition* presents a complete philosophical system in respect of time, but this does not make it irrelevant to consider time from a different perspective, as Deleuze does in *The Logic of Sense*. And of the latter philosophy of time, at this point I provide an overview of Deleuze's concepts of Chronos and Aion (and, ultimately, their relation) as detailed in *The Logic of Sense*, beginning first with Chronos.

CHRONOS AND THE LIVING PRESENT

In *The Logic of Sense*, Deleuze theorises Chronos as the time of life as lived in the present moment. "Chronos," he writes, "is the present which alone exists" (2004b, 89). In its solitary existence, the present, in Chronos time, consists of "bodies which act and are acted upon" (8). It is thus bound up with corporeality and the causal interactions of all living things. Here, Deleuze shows his Spinozan influence in terms of the affect of bodies upon bodies. Spinoza developed his concept of affect in relation to bodies in his *Ethics* (published posthumously in 1667). Deleuze published two books on Spinoza, *Expressionism in Philosophy: Spinoza* in 1968, and *Spinoza: Practical Philosophy*—the latter first published in shorter form in 1970, and then later in an expanded edition in 1981. He also drew on Spinoza's philosophy in other of his books—for instance, in *A Thousand Plateaus*, *What Is Philosophy?* (both of these written together with Guattari), and in conversation in the *Negotiations* collection. Of Spinozan affect and the body, Deleuze (1988b) writes: "a body affects other bodies, or is affected by other bodies; it is this capacity for affecting and being affected that also defines a body in its individuality" (123). The corporeality and the causal interactions of all living things in relation to Chronos time, as indicated above, thus owes a clear debt to the notion of Spinozan affect, with the addition of an explicit temporal quality—that of the Chronic.

As Deleuze argues: "the temporal extension which accompanies the act" in Chronos time is populated with causes not effects—"causes in relation to each other and for each other" (2004b, 7). Effects belong to the incorporeal realm of Aion (of which, see later); causes, for their part, inhere in mixtures of bodies and "quantitative and qualitative states of affairs: the dimensions of an ensemble" (8). Chronos thus appeals to our sense that time is something that can be qualified and quantified (measured by one or other means—such as the chronology of the clock, or the regular pulse of "crotchet equals 120" in music notation). In these respects, time is qualified, as in our lived experiences of its passing, and quantified, as in the measuring out of beats and bars in music on the page of the (traditional) score and in the performance of such, or via the seconds/minutes/hours of our various chronometers.

For Deleuze (2004b), the past and the future indicate the direction of temporal flow in relation to the living present. In the lived experience of Chronic time, "presents follow one another inside partial worlds or partial systems" (89). There is a resonance, here, with the concept of the incompossible. As discussed in chapters 6–8, incompossibility theorises multiple, partial, possible worlds composing a (new) harmony that permits seemingly paradoxical yet simultaneous states of existence (for instance: the Adam who does and does not eat the apple; the myriad possible performances of the score of *In the Garden of the Incompossible*). Chronos introduces a sense of the *subjective* into such abstraction. As Williams (2011b) notes, in respect of these partial worlds or systems, our experiences of present time in Chronos "are lived differently according to the limits set for them" (156). In the field of music and the performing arts, there are many examples of such limits: for instance, the durations imposed on performance events themselves (such as the start and finish times of a particular performance); the sections/subdivisions that take place/are marked out within the structure of a given piece/performance; and also, the length of one's career (and the various episodes within a life in music/performance). These limits create what Williams refers to as "bounded" presents, through which each present is related to other presents by virtue of "an operation of inclusion [that] is also a transformation" (156).

Through such operations, presents are able to incorporate past and future into yet greater presents to which they are made relative. "There is always a more vast present which absorbs the past and the future," argues Deleuze, continuing: "Thus, the relativity of past and future with respect to the present entails a relativity of presents themselves, in relation to each other" (2004b, 186). In Chronos time, then, there are not three temporal dimensions that follow on from one another in linear series (past, then present, and then future). Rather, the dimensions of the past and the future are always relative to the present as lived, which is itself continually transformed and incorporated in relation to other presents as lived, in an unending process of temporal becoming that is ever unfolding in the moments of its existing as a plurality of "nows."

At this point in the chapter, I turn the reader's attention to Chronos's companion concept in Deleuze's philosophy of time from *Logic of Sense*: Aion.

AION AND THE EVENT

With Aion, Deleuze moved into temporal conception beyond that of endlessly enveloping presents in lived experience. While Chronos time is the realm of measures, causes, living presents and the interactions of bodies, Aion time is incorporeal; its realm is not that of existences and causes, but of infinitives and effects—and of the Event. Aion is conceptually bound up with Deleuze's notion of the incorporeal Event. To give the well-known example, it is not that there are these things, trees, that turn green following the winter, nor is it that such trees are now green in the summer—since, as Stagoll (2010c) notes, both of these perspectives suggest that trees have a permanent essence that is now changing or changed (90). Rather, the incorporeal Event is encapsulated in *the tree greens*, the dynamic effect that is the Event as actualised, which Deleuze expresses in the form of an infinitive: "the tree greens" (2004b, 8).

It is useful to note, here, the difference between the fact of *a* tree going green and Deleuze's conception of *the tree greens*. The distinction is important because it highlights the difference between the physical act of a tree turning green in the summer and the Aionic process of *the tree greens*— where the latter is considered in relation to the (virtual) plane of the incorporeal Event, not the (corporeal, actualised) event. Such effects and infinitives, writes Deleuze (2004b), are not of the time of the living present (Chronos) but belong to "the unlimited Aion," in which they inhere rather than exist (8). A further example of this temporal distinction offered by Deleuze is the incorporeality of the wound: "my wound existed before me, I was born to embody it" (169).[3] As with *the tree greens*, in which the tree and the act of greening are united *as* process (in contrast to their differentiation into a tree, and an act of going green, or a condition of being green), Deleuze's conception of the wound is likewise concerned with the coming together of (for instance) flesh and knife in the wound considered *as* Event (on the plane of Aion). Such an Event is impersonal, existing before (and after—see later) its actualisation in the process that is the knife-meets-flesh of a given wounding. Of the coming together of both these temporalities (the Event of Aion and the event of Chronos), Deleuze argues that every event is "double and impersonal in its double" (172). This doubling is on account of the double nature of Aion and Chronos in respect of the Event/event, and of the wound considered as "the living trace and the scar of all wounds" (170).[4] This latter (the "scar of all wounds") is the wound in its Aionic aspect: impersonal, incorporeal; a double of the actualised (and Chronic) "living trace" of the act of wounding.

Whether in terms of the-tree-greens, or the wound as knife-meets-flesh, or other examples of processes considered in their incorporeal aspect, each event is "adequate to the entire Aion," according to Deleuze. Each event "communicates with all others, and they all form one and the same Event . . . the Event for all events" (2004b, 74–75). Therefore, individual events are singular in their instantiation as events in the world, yet are also bound to all other possible events, past and future. Accordingly, in its nature as other-temporal companion to the lived actualisations of Chronos time, Deleuze conceptualises Aion as "an empty and unfolded form of time" (75). As with Chronos time's resonance with the coexisting partial worlds of lived experience as present (as noted above), Aion time, here, demonstrates a link with the experiments of the last chapter with the concept and practice of folding. However, with Aion, unfolding is not a case of continuing or extending the act of folding (as it is in Deleuze's concept of the fold). Rather, in Aion time, it is a way of interrelating the temporalities of the past and the future on a plane of unfolding emptiness. Aion time is not grounded in an ever-present plurality of presents (as in Chronos time), since, Deleuze argues, it is both that which has already happened *and* that which is yet to come. It is the past-future, endlessly subdividing the present "however small it may be, stretching it out over their empty line" (72).

In chapter 4, I drew on Deleuze's three syntheses of time, as presented in *Difference and Repetition*, as part of my analyses of the music-making undertaken. This emptiness Deleuze writes of in respect of Aion time (as quoted previously) bears striking resemblance to "time as a pure and empty form" as theorised by Deleuze in the third of his three syntheses (2004a, 114). Where the two conceptions differ, however, is in the relationship between past and future in Aion time. In time as theorised in the third synthesis (in *Difference and Repetition*), it is the future that is paramount; present and past are mere dimensions of the future, processes for its continual rejuvenation, and the repetition that is at heart a repetition (for itself) of difference (in itself) is that of the future-to-come. In Aion time, Deleuze theorises not only a conception of the future (however detailed and convoluted the third synthesis's inter-relations with past and present may be), but of the past-future. I exploit this (subtle but important) difference between the third synthesis and Aion as part of transforming Deleuze's Chronos-Aion by musical-philosophical means in my third practice as research project (as I explore in chapter 10). But first, it is important to consider Chronos and Aion as dynamic relation—a task to which I now turn, in summary.

CHRONOS-AION IN RELATION IN THE EVENT

Despite the usefulness of writing about Chronos and Aion in (relative) separation for clarity, the logic of Deleuze's philosophy of time—in terms of Chronos and Aion—is never that of the "either/or." In other words, it is never a case of either Chronos or Aion; it is always foremost about the relationship between the two. As Williams (2013) notes: "Chronos and Aion are con-nected through determinations which mean that they cannot be separated"—adding, further, that the two are "connected not in one or two simple ways, but as multiple processes on each side of time and between them" (154). The "sides" of time of which Williams writes are like two sides of the same coin; each is determined by the other through the impossible-to-separate relation between Chronos and Aion as the double aspect of time: Chronos-Aion.

This double-aspect relation of Chronos-Aion is a relation founded in the event. Events thus express two time senses, different in nature and operation but in no way incompatible with one another. In one sense, Chronos expresses events in accordance with movements and measurements, through which their duration is limited by "acting bodies and its incorporation in a state of affairs" (Deleuze 2004b, 73). In another sense, Aion expresses events purely in respect of their relation to *other* events. Deleuze theories this relation of event to event in terms of the Event (capital "E"), or what he also calls the "*Eventum tantum* for all contraries, which communicates with itself through its own distance and resonates across all of its disjuncts" (201).

This is not quite as bizarre a notion as might first appear, since, although the event as realised in performance is both unique and invested in the actual as performed, it is also ever aloof of such particular instances of happen-stance. This latter state of affairs reflects the time of the event as the time of Aion, wherein all events are considered on account of their empty, incor-poreal aspect. Of such incorporeality, it is the shock of the new that remains ever fresh: nothing of this aspect has, after all, been materially invested in the (corporeal) event as it happens. As the Event, it has both already hap-pened and is yet to come, *ad infinitum*, on the ever-stretching plane of Aionic past-future as theorised by Deleuze. As Stagoll (2010c) argues: "Events carry no determinate outcome, but only new possibilities, representing a moment at which new forces might be brought to bear" (91).

In respect of the uniqueness of this "moment" and its endless possibilities, the Chronos-Aion dynamic intersects with a notion of temporality in terms of *kairos*. Kairos is a temporal concept utilised by Coessens (2014), Coessens and Östersjö (2014b), Coessens et al. (2014), and Assis (2018), in their theorisations of the event of performance and the role of the performer within that event. From the Greek, meaning "the opportune and decisive moment" (from the entry under "Kairos" in the *Merriam-Webster Dictionary*), kairos was originally conceived in relation to the Ancient Greek notion that each decision, analysis, judgment, must be made in accordance with the conditions particular to the situation or case in hand—as part of the art of the rhetorician, for instance (Coessens 2014, 65).[5] For the practitioner-researcher in music, kairos gives name to that which Assis (2018) calls "the inescapable here-and-now of the event" (208); for Coessens and Östersjö (2014b), it is the moment in which "a question and possible answers conflate, a moment of urgent decision" (327). In situations of such urgency (the event of performance, for example), the decisions and actions of the performer are made in accordance with their experience and expertise, their personal and professional history of similar situations in the past. Kairos, in these circumstances implies what Coessens (2014) calls "the coming together of 'knowing how' and 'knowing when'" (66).

For the performer, then, what transpires in each performance is unique, and such uniqueness cannot be predetermined in advance. The expert performer brings to the event their panoply of skills, honed over the course of their profession, and not every tactic will be suitable, not every technique will be needed. It is a matter for experimentation, and an ability to "look further ahead and back in the development of the ongoing performance" (Coessens et al. 2014, 356–357). In this manner, kairos draws together past and future in the (extremely) present moment of performer-decision. In terms of the Chronos-Aion relation, kairos's funnelling of past and future time into the urgency of the present moment resonates with the (seemingly paradoxical) nature of the Event as both empty *and* overfull.[6]

The implications of the Chronic-Aionic relation are a subject that is returned to in what follows, but this state of coexisting emptiness/fullness is indicated by Deleuze (2004b) when he writes of "the movement wherein the event implies something excessive in relation to its actualisation" (191). This movement describes something *extra* to the actualisations in the living present of Chronos time: "the present of the Aion . . . the present of the pure operation, not of the incorporation" (192). This is no contradiction of what has been previously argued of Aion (that its temporality is that of the past-future); rather, it highlights the close relationship that is fundamental to

Chronos-Aion. As the enveloping presents of Chronos are lived as a multitude of nows, it is the "labyrinthine" line of Aion that "perverts the present into inhering future and past" (189).

This "labyrinthine" nature of the Aionic highlights another connection between the Chronos-Aion conception of time process and that of the labyrinth of folded incompossibles in the previous project. In that second practice as research project (chapters 6–8), it is the multifarious, multifurcating, incompossible worlds of folds within folds, folding and unfolding to infinity, that is brought into musical-philosophical relation with Rhythmicity (for the purpose of transforming all parties in the process). In the next chapter and its description of the third practice as research project (via my conception of a line-cycle movement of Rhythmicity), it is the Chronic present that is folded into the past-future by means of the Aionic as a disembodied, incorporeal line: "the labyrinth of the unique line, straight and without thickness" (Deleuze 2004b, 74).

The (incorporeal) present of Aion and the (corporeal) present of Chronos are two interconnected processes of time. The former is a ghostly partner that ever shadows the latter, which, for its own part, requires this Aionic spectre to haunt its living presents in order to facilitate the dissolution of those presents into past-future eternality—in order for them to have happened, and to facilitate their happening yet to come. In this (dynamic) manner, Chronos-Aion expresses Deleuze's philosophy of time in *The Logic of Sense* in a different way to the three syntheses of *Difference and Repetition*, yet attendant to a similar degree of interconnectedness (rather than simple linearity of past-present-future) in the relations between temporalities—in the case of Chronos-Aion, the living present(s) and the eternal line of the past-future.

Following these summaries of Chronos, Aion, and the relation of Chronos-Aion, in the next chapter I turn attention to my project to explore ways to transform Chronos-Aion via musical-philosophical enquiry and my evolving concept of Rhythmicity, providing two analyses of the work undertaken for this purpose.

NOTES

1. The Stoics flourished between the third century BCE and the second century CE in the Hellenic and Roman eras. The founder of the school of Stoicism was Zeno of Citium, who began lecturing from the Arcade ("stoa," hence the naming of the movement as "Stoicism") of the marketplace in Athens around 300 BCE. A key later Stoic of the Roman era was Marcus Aurelius (121–180 CE). For a useful summary of the philosophy of the Stoics, see Barnes (2005, 595–596). It is interesting to note how, with regard to Deleuze's use of Chronos and Aion as supposedly Stoical concepts,

Sellars (2007) points out that the Stoics themselves made little or no mention of these terms. As with his reconfiguration of the work of other philosophers (as noted earlier in this book), it would seem apparent that with a "Stoical" theory of time, Deleuze is also, once again, impressing his own philosophical project into the words and notions of others. As Sellars notes, Deleuze's reading of Stoic philosophy in respect of what would become his concepts of Aion and Chronos draws on the writings of Chrysippus and Marcus Aurelius—philosophers who, although considered as Stoic, are separated by almost five hundred years (2007, 204). The notion of an explicitly *Stoical* philosophy of time, considered in dual terms (such as Aion and Chronos), therefore owes much to the nuances of Deleuze's own particular reading. Given that it is *Deleuze's* own particular usage of the terms Chronos and Aion that I am primarily involved in exploring in this chapter and the following two, the argument concerning whether or not Deleuze's Aion-Chronos philosophy of time is truly related to a Stoic understanding of time remains a footnote to my main argument.

2. The term "Event" is capitalised here, and often (but, somewhat confusing, not always) in Deleuze's writing, to distinguish its concept from the more everyday use of the term, and also from the use Deleuze makes of it in relation to Chronos (see, for instance, the sections on Aion, and on the relationship between Aion and Chronos in Deleuze's philosophy of time, that follow).

3. Deleuze, here, is quoting from the writings of Joe Bousquet, as indicated in the notes to the chapter, "Twenty-First Series of the Event," in *The Logic of Sense* (2004b, 175 n.1).

4. See the next section for more on the relation of Aion and Chronos.

5. I am put in mind, here, of Bourdieu's (1977) description of the "virtuoso" whose "art of living" is such that their actions in a given situation "play on all the resources inherent in the ambiguities and uncertainties" of the situation in its specificity, resulting in an outcome considered appropriate by all (8).

6. On this point about the emptiness/overfullness of the process of art-making, there is a resonance with Deleuze's (2005) remarks concerning how the artist (in this instance, the painter) is faced with a canvas that is far from blank, but is, rather, full of clichés and givens even before the paint has touched the painting. The artist, writes Deleuze, "does not have to cover a blank surface, but rather [has] to empty it out" (61). Similarly, in the essay that concludes *Spinoza: Practical Philosophy*, Deleuze notes: "One never commences; one never has a *tabula rasa*; one slips in, enters in the middle; one takes up or lays down rhythms" (1988b, 123).

Chapter 10

The Time Is out of Joint (Project 3)

In the third practice-as-research project, I build on the prior projects and conceptions in previous chapters in two ways. Firstly, I rephrase the expression of Rhythmicity with regard to what I call a temporal "line-cycle," in the interrelated subjective trinity of composer-me, performer-me, and listener-me. Secondly, I develop it according to what I describe as a "Rhythmicity of silences": a musical-philosophical movement which forms an integral part of the process of the act of sounding out the composition in question (*The Time Is out of Joint*, written and performed for this third project). While the first project conceived Rhythmicity in terms of cyclical and hyperbolic movements of the musical-philosophical, the third project experiments with its expression via the tripartite perspective of myself as composer-performer-listener. As I will demonstrate, this three-sided formulation describes a temporality experienced not in linear or cyclical terms, but as a line-cycle time sense that cannot be reduced to any one of the subjective temporal perspectives alone.

I provide two analyses of this project, each written from different perspectives. The first is written from the perspective of the composer-me and the second, from the perspectives of the performer-me and the listener-me.[1] As Cage famously and provocatively asked, in an essay of 1955: "Composing's one thing, performing's another, listening's a third. What can they have to do with one another?" (1978: 15).[2] In the case of this third project, I am taking this problematising of the relation among the modes of musical expression in a different direction: that of the musical-philosophical. As noted previously, the musical-philosophical is my primary method of investigation in this practice as research enquiry and is a means of bringing something new to certain of Deleuze's concepts. Where Cage posed his question in terms of composing, performing, and listening, I am utilising the terms and perspectives of what I call the composer-me, the performer-me, and the listener-me—where the listener-me is both active in the act of performance in the first instance, and also in listening back as part of the process of analysing and writing this chapter. These three perspectives operate as modes of the musical-philosophical analyses: sometimes alone, sometimes in combination with one another, but ever in relation. They are three different though interlinked perspectives on my enquiry into Deleuze's Chronic-Aionic philosophy of time. These perspectives are interwoven with the other modes of this enquiry: more traditional scholarship in the form of writing about and around the musical and philosophical issues raised, and the music practice itself.

The analyses are focused on the issue of how Rhythmicity can be expressed in terms of composer, performer, and listener: specifically, the experiences of composing, performing, and listening from my own perspectives as composer-me, performer-me, and listener-me. The role of silence as a music-making tool is interrogated, as is its function in the processes of composing, performing, and listening (both in the act of music-making, and after the event, in analysis).

FIRST MUSICAL-PHILOSOPHICAL ANALYSIS: THE COMPOSER-ME AND CHRONOS-AION

I composed *The Time Is out of Joint* in December 2018.[3] The score for the work consists of three lines of text, which read as follows: "Count to ten (silently) / Play, while counting to ten (silently) / Repeat this process a number of times" (see figure 10.1). How fast or slow the count is made is left to the discretion of the performer (in the recordings made for this chapter, I counted at a relatively slow speed, averaging between one and three seconds in length). How many times the process of counting and then playing is repeated is, as indicated in the score, also a matter of performer decision. All matters of musical articulation are left open to the performer, and there are no suggestions made as to what the performer is to play in each "Play" section, only that they should play (while silently counting to ten).

These three lines of instruction function as what, in the early 1960s, the composer Cornelius Cardew called a "basic score": a deliberately vague set of directions indicating suggestions toward "any realisation" (Harris 2013, 28). Such scores also bear relation to what the Scratch Orchestra, in its "Draft Constitution" of 1969, defined as "Improvisation Rites: short, mainly verbal instructions . . . serving as catalysts or lubricants, introducing . . . the smallest practical measure of stimulation or restraint" (Nyman 1999, 132). Deceptively simple, scores of this type enable the performer to enter into the process of music-making on a level beyond that of the technical articulation of the notes on the page.[4]

Aside from the instruction to silently count to ten and then to play (while silently counting to ten) and then to repeat the process (however many times), my role as composer of *The Time Is out of Joint* is primarily that of the

COUNT TO TEN (SILENTLY)

PLAY, WHILE COUNTING TO TEN (SILENTLY)

REPEAT THIS PROCESS A NUMBER OF TIMES

Figure 10.1.

designer of a temporal structure. This structure provides a means of measuring out the time of performance in two distinct sections (and two distinct, though interrelated temporalities—of which, see later). In this sense, the composition resonates with Cage's experiments in "formalistic control": empty structures, devised by arithmetic means (typically in terms of proportions nested within proportions), in which sounds and silences have the freedom to form relations between themselves (Nyman 1999, 33). (Cage's *4'33"* is surely the purest example of this compositional practice.) By utilising this formalistic process (which I discuss further later in the chapter), Cage was able to go about the business of composing his works without the need to retain full control over how the music would actually sound in performance. This was Cage's solution to the issue of composer-performer-listener hierarchical relations, in terms of creative control, that was explored by him and certain of his contemporaries in the mid-twentieth century (see next).[5]

Of Cage's contemporaries, others of the New York School also tackled this issue in their own manner. Feldman, for instance, in his early work in the 1950s employs a graphic notation indeterminate of its performance in all but the succession of its sounds (see Nyman 1999, 53). Earle Brown, on the other hand, in his flexible attitude to the performance of time in his mid-twentieth century works, prescribes details of pitch, dynamics, and grouping between notes, but leaves the issue of specific rhythmic placement open to the performer (see Nyman 1999, 57; and later). More recently, Wandelweiser's Peter Ablinger, in his *Sitting and Hearing* works (a series the composer began in 1995), has taken this practice a stage further, focusing on blurring the distinction between performer and listener in various ways. For example, in his *Listening Piece in Four Parts* of 2001 (part of the *Sitting and Hearing* series), Ablinger problematises this distinction by means of providing a score specifying arrangements of chairs in particular locations (for example, wind farms, beaches, parking lots) by means of which the listener performs the work (Rutherford-Johnson 2017, 70). In these pieces, no musical content is prescribed; only the form of the work (as seating arrangement in whatever given space) is determined in advance. The listener becomes the performer and the performer the listener. As Ablinger himself stresses in respect of these works: "not the sound, but the listening is the piece."[6]

The Time Is out of Joint, in its compositional structure, expresses a similar lack of concern with the actual contents of its performance; only that they be delivered to a silent count of ten, alternating sections of playing and sections of silence (as much as we can talk of silence in the post-Cage era, of course—see later). The structure enables the making of the music but not the notes played—only their successive durations (and even these not metronomically measured, but loosely counted). The composer-me hands express control of the music-as-performed to the performer (in the case of this third project, the performer-me—of which, see next). Where Ablinger points to the act of listening as the ultimate articulation of his piece (merging performer and listener in the process), the composer-me in *The Time Is out of Joint* is giving ultimate articulation of the piece, beyond the basic rhythm of alternation set up in the two sections of the composition, to both performer and listener (where listener is considered both as the listener-me and the listener more generally speaking)—while at the same time retaining an important role in musical-philosophical terms, as I will now detail.

THE COMPOSER-ME AND RHYTHMICITY: CONTROL/INTERRUPTION AND THE LINE-CYCLE

The composer-me, in the basic structuring of the score of *The Time Is out of Joint*, reformulates the likes of Ablinger's conflation of listener and performer, and Cage et al.'s granting of more creative/compositional flexibility to the performer, according to two (interlinked) practices: control and interruption. Of the first of these, I employ a Cageian disinterest in fixing in advance the actual contents of the music as performed and heard. My control over the music, as the composer of the work, is limited to specifying that two sections, each measured to a silent ten-count, alternate for as long as the piece lasts, and that, in the second of these sections (the "Play" section that follows the "Silence" section), the performer plays something, anything, according to her or his judgment. Of the second of these practices, interruption, the composer-me installs a mechanism through which the performer and the listener are repeatedly reminded of the structure of the work as a whole, regardless of what is actually unfolding in musical terms at the point at which the ten-count is reached. That structure is born of alternation—alternation by means of interruption—which stresses the incessant pulse of its section-to-section rhythm until the conclusion of the performance.

No matter the musical material performed or experienced, these techniques of control and interruption, embedded in both the score of the work and in any of its instantiations, enable the composer-me to instigate a relationship with performer and listener that provides fresh insight with regard to Deleuze's Chronos-Aion conceptual pairing. For instance, while the relative regularity of the (silent) count-to-ten process installs a measure of control by means of interruption in the music's unfolding that cannot but be noticed (as time goes by) by the listener, and cannot but be obeyed (throughout the performance) by the performer, the temporal quality invoked is not exclusively that of Chronos—nor that Aion. In the musical-philosophical terms I am exploring, control/interruption should be considered not as power from above or outside (i.e., the perceived authoritative nature of the composer as prime figure in the power-hierarchy of the composer-performer, and composer-performer-listener, relationship), but as a continual push-and-pull dynamic expressed as a rhythmic quality: a Rhythmicity of control/interruption, casting new light on the Chronos-Aion relationship in the process.

By framing control/interruption as a function of Rhythmicity, the tendency towards chrono-logical regularity that marks the Chronic pole of the Chronos-Aion relation is repeatedly destabilised on account of the relative freedom granted the performer in their performance of the "Play" sections—and vice versa. Counting to ten in silence is one thing; counting to ten in silence while also playing the piano is quite another (as I explore later in this analysis). The composer-me sets up this (limited) level of freedom in the performance of the piece in order to explore and rethink the temporalities of Chronos and Aion in terms of Chronos-Aion, adding something new as a result: control/interruption as a rhythmic relation between composer and performer, with listeners having their own unique experiences of this aspect of Rhythmicity in the event of encountering the work in performance.

In *The Time Is out of Joint*, control/interruption is experienced as the steady progress of the rhythmic structural device of ten-count after ten-count (and so on until the end of the piece). Each lived present envelops that of its predecessors and is itself enveloped at the conclusion of its own ten-count. This

is an enveloping process scored on the page of the work as composition—
and in rhythm, considered in its purely structural form. In this sense, such
rhythm-as-structure has an important historical predecessor in the compositional process of John Cage (as alluded to earlier). As Feldman has written
of the use of rhythmic structure in the early works of his friend, and mentor:
for Cage, rhythm, in this structural sense, occupies the role of "what harmony
may have been for Beethoven," corresponding with the latter's "sense of
scale" (Feldman 2000, 145). As Nyman (1999) notes: for Cage, in his early
compositions, the usefulness of rhythm was less a case of rhythms considered as "individual rhythmic patterns," and much more a case of rhythm "as
structure"—a structure "as hospitable to non-musical sounds, noises, as it
was to those of conventional scales and instruments," since "nothing about
the structure was determined by the materials which were to occur in it . . .
so that it could be as well expressed by the absence of these materials as by
their presence" (32).

Such rhythmic-structural aspect, in the score of *The Time Is out of Joint*,
is manifest in processes of control/interruption that operate, not in one or the
other time of Chronos or Aion, but in Chronos-Aion time considered in/as
relation (and something more besides, as I will explain shortly). The movements of control/interruption are conveyed in the compositional-structural
detail as presented on the page, and express the work as a performance of the
most basic rhythm of all: the alternation of two elements (in this case, the two
sections of the piece).[7] Control/interruption, in this sense, obeys neither the
cyclical nature of Deleuze's Chronos as living present, nor the eternal dual-
ity of Deleuze's Aionic past-future linearity, but instead expresses a rhythm
of alternation that is neither exclusively linear nor cyclical in its process. By
alternating sections of silence and sound, counted (silently) according to the
variable pacing of the performer of the work, the process of control/interrup-
tion instigated by the composer-me creates a rhythm that elucidates the less-
obviously-Chronic aspect of Chronos and the less-obviously-Aionic aspect
of Aion. By this, I mean that the compositional control/interruption process
of *The Time Is out of Joint* highlights, simultaneously, a line generated via
alternation and a cyclical process born of linearity that is a fresh development
of Deleuze's original account of Chronos and Aion (and their relation).

Via the compositional structure of *The Time Is out of Joint*, the scoring of
silence/sound/repeat provides a line-cycle that is not only a matter of music,
but also of the philosophy of time—that is, it is a musical-philosophical
expression. This line-cycle expresses Chronos-Aion in terms of the sense of
linearity that comes with prolonged alternation, and in the sense of cycling
that such linearity-by-alternation affects in time(s). As Hemment (2004)
notes, in experiencing music that is deliberately reductive in its composition, a complication of Aion and Chronos manifests "in a kind of temporal

minimalism that is productive of a surface-affect, where nuance and inflec-
tion are heard *because of* a reduction of indeterminacy on another level"
(86). While Hemment is writing, specifically, about the "four to the floor"
electronic drum-machine beats of disco and house music, the similarity to
the perpetually alternating linear-cyclical rhythm generated, and sustained,
by the two alternating sections of *The Time Is out of Joint*, is plain. The
"nuances and inflections" (to borrow Hemment's terms) that are made apparent in the work undertaken by the composer-me are related, not to theorising the disco/house scene and its musical processes in Deleuzian terms, but
to transforming Deleuze's Chronos-Aion by musical-philosophical means.
Through its incessant alternations without prescribed content (save the most
basic: silence/sound), *The Time Is out of Joint* brings structure to the fore of
the music-making (in quasi-Cageian fashion, as discussed previously). In
bringing this structure to the fore, the composer-me expresses Chronos-Aion
as other than either the line or the cycle of time—even in relation (as in
Deleuze). This transformation is achieved through the expression of the
process of control/interruption as a line-cycle that refuses to be theorised as
either linear or cyclical, Aionic or Chronic. Instead, *The Time Is out of Joint*
sets up a Rhythmicity that embraces both Chronos and Aion—and, crucially,
adds something new: a rhythmic quality expressing a movement continually
forwards and backwards at the same time; a rhythmic quality expressing the
most basic cycle in the form of a line that never moves yet cannot *but* move
(via alternation). This Rhythmicity is manifest in the score of *The Time Is
out of Joint* considered in terms of its directive to move the music in these
linear-cyclical directions simultaneously.

I now turn to a musical-philosophical analysis from the perspective of the
performer-me and the listener-me in respect of the performance of *The Time
Is out of Joint* undertaken for this project. It is at this point that the reader
should listen to the audio track *The Time Is out of Joint* before reading further
in the text.

SECOND MUSICAL-PHILOSOPHICAL
ANALYSIS: THE PERFORMER-ME, THE
LISTENER-ME, AND CHRONOS-AION

This performance of *The Time Is out of Joint* consists of thirty-five iterations
of the two-section form of the work.[8] The first of these iterations (see figure
10.2), from some point after the very beginning of the track to around 0'50,"
is a good example of how much can be conveyed in the short time allowed by
the silent ten-count of the "Play" section of the piece. I use the phrase "from
some point after the very beginning of the track," here, to indicate that the

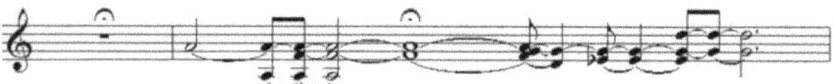

Figure 10.2.

audio recording begins, not with the start of the performance proper—that is, the first, silent, section of the composition—but with the sounds of the process of seating myself at the piano and settling myself before commencing the performance.

The control imposed by the composer-me, in the form of the time-limit of ten, instigates a constraint that is only felt (by the performer-me and the listener-me) at the point of the section's abrupt conclusion. When the notes of the piano finally announce themselves after around thirty-six seconds of silence (merging the boundary between preperformance and the first section of the work), the sense of beginning, of the beginning of something larger, of longer duration, is readily apparent to the listener-me. The performer-me plays the opening three notes (beginning at around 0'36"). These lead, after a brief pause on the third note, into three more, in response. These latter three conclude with a single, upwards-reaching fourth note that suggests, to the listener-me, that a development from the first two phrases is about to happen, or could have happened, if only the ten-count had not been reached so soon. This interruption robs the improvisation of its continuation, its extension in time, and the evolution of its musical material. All that the listener (and the performer) is left with is an absence, a loss that is pregnant with possibility. Chronology, in this instance, is the arbiter without mercy, via the inevitable ten-count that brings the improvisation to an end and signals the next section of silence at the top of the form of the work. There is not enough time to ponder much of what could have been played in response to these seven notes of an opening; their end is final and the mini-piece dies a premature death suffocated by silence—which in turn indicates the beginning of the second improvisation on the "Play" section that follows close on the former's heels.

The second "Play" section is quite a different beast from its immediate predecessor (see figure 10.3). After around fifteen seconds of silence, its initial notes begin at around the 1'06" mark and fizzle out at around 1'19." They spell out an angular line in single notes, some tied over others, the whole improvisation bristling with an intensity of rhythm that seems, to the listener-me, to already be aware of its limited time to flower as music. This urgency communicates through the flurries of crushed-in grace notes that surround the more prominent notes, the latter of which begin to convey a melodic fragment that, as with the first improvisation discussed above, could easily have led to many more developments of the musical material had the ten-count not delivered its ultimatum via the strictest measure: this now must end, regardless.

Figure 10.3.

This alternating rhythm of "interruption of silence by the notes of the piano/interruption of the notes of the piano by silence" stamps (as discussed in the first analysis earlier), the composer-me's control across the entire body of the performance, and in each of the individual iterations of the form of the piece. But, for the performer-me, this control is less a case of domination by another than it is an opportunity to control the content of what little is left for me to express. For the listener-me, listening back after the event of performance, the interludes from silence that the "Play" sections provide bring with them an intensity on account of brevity that makes every note, every chord, every rhythm, all the more vital as a result. When you realise that nothing you are hearing will last beyond a silent ten-count, the ears tend to be more receptive to what is actually being played in those sections of sound-making (at least in the experience of the listener-me).

In the fourth of the thirty-five iterations of the form of *The Time Is out of Joint* (see figure 10.4), this sense of a knowing take on the power of brevity begins to come to the fore in the music-making of the performer-me. I begin to play, after a silence of around fourteen seconds (1'47" to 2'01," when the "Play" section starts), a short sequence of two-note chords. These develop (albeit very temporarily) through a succession of dyads at various intervals: a perfect fifth, a minor ninth, a flattened fifth, another minor ninth, a major seventh, another major seventh, a major tenth, a major seventh, and finally a major sixth. This last two-note chord is played staccato, in contrast to the other eight that precede it. The improvisation could easily have concluded on the eighth chord, held for the remaining numbers of the ten-count.

However, by articulating the ninth of the nine chords in a staccato fashion, the performer-me is making manifest the interruption of one expression of time by another: the free flow of the music as made up to that point (in this fourth iteration of the form) coming into contact with time counted as the chronological. That staccato chord falls on the "ten" of the silent ten-count, and provides, for the listener (including the listener-me), an indication that the time of performance is being divided up according to pre-scribed formal, rather than improvised, reasons. If the performance were an improvisation alone, it is unlikely the performer-me would choose to impose such a punishing, relentless system of continually interrupting the music as it unfolds in performance. That is the doing of the composer-me, and the performer-me—not to mention the listener-me, both during and after the event of performance—feels that interruption in the most affecting way, each time the section of silence is returned to: the end of another attempt at beginning a lasting musical expression. The chrono-logical wins out again, and the silence/sound rhythm of creation and destruction continues unabated, perpetually impassive as to what has come before, or what will follow.

There is a resonance here, with the "moment form" concept of the German modernist composer Karlheinz Stockhausen. As part of a series of lectures given in the early 1970s, Stockhausen speaks of his interest in music that practices "[e]xtreme concentration . . . a development in terms of a particular organisation of notes, and not as a fragment of a larger development" (Stockhausen 1989, 60). Stockhausen imagines a music that is not conceived with a sense of homogeneity that is then developed in various ways to introduce musical interest. Instead, he presents a series of moments of "Now! Now! Now! Now! Now!," which Stockhausen conceives of as "completely separate instants"—where the question of how much each instant (or "Now!") may or may not be related to its predecessors and successors is brought to the fore of the musical experience (67). Of particular interest are the types of moment that Stockhausen describes in terms of strength and weakness: strong moments are extremely self-contained, being "neutral" moments that "give nothing and take nothing"; weak moments, on the other hand, have much in

Figure 10.4.

common with "what has happened before and what is to follow," and are most susceptible to influence by stronger moments (70).

While *The Time Is out of Joint* is not conceived in terms of "strong" and "weak" moments (being designed to explore and transform Deleuze's Chronos-Aion, specifically), the temporal play of influence between, and independence of, its alternating sections as the performance unfolds sets up a Rhythmicity that expresses a similar dynamic to Stockhausen's concerns as described above. The sixth iteration of *The Time Is out of Joint* (see figure 10.5), beginning around 2'57" with twenty seconds of silence, and continuing until around 3'41," provides a good example of this. In terms of such notions of self-containment and independence of articulation in respect of its thirty-four others, the listener-me is particularly struck by a sense of the performer-me seemingly having "all the time in the world" to make the music that transpires in the mere twenty-four seconds that elapse during the ten-count of the "Play" section. The notes of a ten-note melody are harmonised by a total of six chords—the last of which concludes the harmonisation with a flattened-twelfth, then leaves the last of the ten notes of the melody briefly sustained alone before making way for the ensuing silence of the next section/first section again. Of the six iterations up to this point of the performance, this sixth one seems, to the ears of the listener-me, to best embody the possibility of making a coherent musical statement in the short time allocated the performer-me in each repeat of the piece's form. In the briefness of its musical development to the (silent) count of ten, the unhurried phrasing of the melody-and-chords of the sixth iteration performs a rhythm of life that remains unconcerned with the imminent cessation that awaits it at the count of ten. In this sense, the sixth iteration is a reflection of the human experience and expression of life within the temporal play of Chronos-Aion. The performer-me makes the music of this iteration within the living present, knowing that this present will, inevitably, be subsumed by another, but

Figure 10.5.

also knowing that while there remains time enough, all that is required is the power of having that time (or times) to exist, if only fleetingly. Such is the intensity of experiencing the dynamic of Chronos-Aion, away from its literal expression via words on the page (by Deleuze or whoever else).

Of the transformation of Deleuze's Chronos-Aion by means of the iterations of this performance of *The Time Is out of Joint*, the ninth and sixteenth repeats of the form are instructive. Where Deleuze is tied to the language and terminology of his professional practice (philosophy, in its more traditional definition of presenting concepts through writing), these two brief instances of music-making provide the opportunity to take Chronos-Aion beyond the word and the page and into the dimensions of the musical-philosophical. In the first of these two, the ninth iteration (from around 5'08" to around 5'52"), introduces an understated, four-note melody lasting only eighteen seconds (see figure 10.6). Following roughly twenty-six seconds of contemplative silence, the performer-me begins the "Play" section at around 5'34" with an upward-moving whole-tone (from G above middle C to A). There is a delay as the second of the two notes is sustained for around seven seconds, then a pause of around a second or two of silence before the final two notes are presented: the last but one moving the melody down a major sixth (to middle C), and the last one back up a major sixth (to A above middle C) to end the phrase on the same note as the second of the four-note line. This plaintive melody, from the perspective of the listener-me, achieves more than the sum of its few parts in that it encapsulates the overall form of the composition itself in the manner of a microcosm, mixing silence and sound and looping back to conclude, not with a conclusion, but with a return (to a prior note in the melodic line). In this way, Chronos-Aion is explored by means of a musical gesture: to begin from silence (as with all the iterations of the form in the performance), to contrast that silence with a note, another note, then returning, briefly, to silence, then another note, and then another, completing the gesture with a loop to its halfway mark.

In Chronos time, we are ever in the middle, ever in the between-zone where the living present continually loops back on itself, engendering fresh presents in a tight circle without beginning or end. In Aion time, the event (in this case, an event of performance) is ever already happened or yet to happen (Deleuze's *Eventum Tantum*, as discussed in chapter 9). In the two considered in relation, Chronos-Aion plays forever somewhere between these dual conceptions of time. In this ninth iteration (as with each of its others)

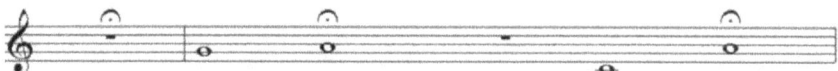

Figure 10.6.

of the form of *The Time Is out of Joint*, the question of when the iteration begins, and when it ends, are impossible to answer for the listener (and even the listener-me, who instead is confined to approximating the moment at which iterations start and conclude). The performer-me knew during the performance, of course, but after the event no such surety is possible. The temporality of Chronos-Aion, despite the chrono-logical ideals found toward the Chronos pole of the relation, is, in practice, experienced as vague and subjective in terms of our determinations of its measure. There is a correlation, here, with what Earle Brown refers to (in the composer's notes to his *Folio* of 1952) as time considered as the "actual dimension in which music exists when performed," a dimension that Brown describes as "by nature an infinitely divisible continuum" that remains untied to any system of measurement by metric or other means (Nyman 1999, 57).[9] This time of the vague and the subjective aspect of performance, unmeasurable with any degree of exactitude, also impresses upon the more Aionic tendencies of Chronos-Aion, transforming them in the process. Where Deleuze's Aion is impersonal in its eternity of simultaneous past-future expansion, in the Chronos-Aion relation I am investigating the mixing of the modes of the temporal saturates the plane of Chronos-Aion, making the act of performing an iteration of *The Time Is out of Joint* a perpetually joint endeavour of the Chronic and the Aionic.

Through such musical-philosophical practice as the ninth iteration of *The Time Is out of Joint*, this Chronic-Aionic joint endeavour is demonstrated as operating by means of a Rhythmicity of control and interruption. Despite giving the appearance (at least on paper) of a perpetual, fluid process of self-creation, the process of endlessly birthing Chronic presents on the Aionic plane of past-future stretching *ad infinitum* expresses itself more in terms of reciprocity: of the Chronic acting in Aionic fashion, and vice versa. The four notes of melody in the ninth iteration demonstrate this temporal-modal reciprocity in their construction, employing brevity while evoking longevity: they revolve on themselves, expressing both the closed-circuit of a temporary musical loop and that same act of looping as a process stretching simultaneously into past and future. This musical-philosophical act performs, not a mere illustration or representation of Chronos-Aion, but rather, transforms our understandings of Chronos-Aion as a result of its expression—its expression via a Rhythmicity of temporal reciprocity, both controlling and interrupting that expression as articulated by the performer-me.

This insight into Chronos-Aion time via a reciprocal Rhythmicity of control/interruption is similarly available through the music practice of the sixteenth iteration of *The Time Is out of Joint*—albeit by different means (see figure 10.7). The silence of section one starts around the 10'14" mark, with the "Play" section beginning at around 10'36" and continuing to around

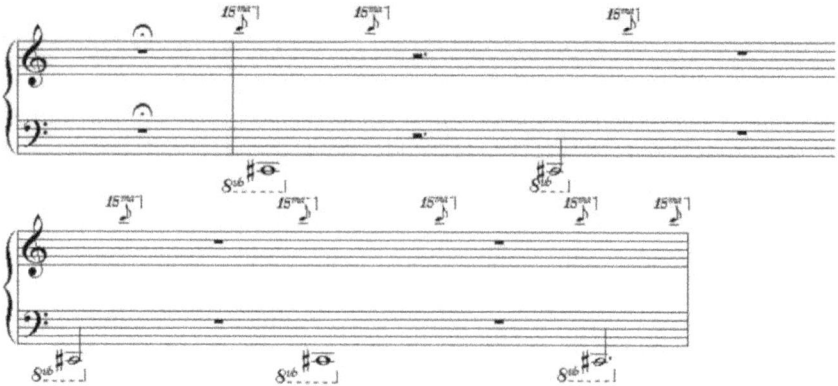

Figure 10.7.

10'53." This improvisation of approximately seventeen seconds explores the simultaneously circular and linear nature of Chronos-Aion by means of setting up a pattern of alternation between two notes at the extreme registers of the piano. These are articulated in a rhythm of short-long duration: a quick movement from high note (the uppermost B-natural on the piano keyboard) to low note (the lowermost C-sharp), the former acting as a very brief grace note, the latter being held for between one and two seconds in the five instances articulated in the "Play" section. Of this short-long rhythm, there are two variants in the iteration under analysis: the first, fourth, and fifth instances of this rhythmic figure describe a pattern of high-note/low-note/high-note; the second and third instances describe a low-note/high-note pattern. In so doing, the performer-me provides for the listener (and the listener-me) a means of measuring out the time of the "Play" section of the iteration—not by the chrono-logic of fixed metre but, rather, by a rhythm that straddles the divide between strict tempo and human temporality of expression.

This rhythmic "straddling" of temporal strictness and a more subjective approach to the expression of time takes an important step towards integrating (or moving beyond) the differences of opinion as to how to compose (with) time in the work of Feldman and the aforementioned Stockhausen. In discussing the differences between his own approach to musical time and that of Stockhausen's, Feldman argued that Stockhausen "wanted it measured, he wanted time measured out, and I wanted time felt, a more subjective feeling for time, you see" (Feldman 2000, 177). While Feldman and Stockhausen, in this reported exchange, take polar stances on the issue of time and its relation to music-making, the approach to performing in and with time/s in *The Time Is out of Joint* alternates between both, ever in the middle of measure and nonmeasure. Through these two patterns of alternation, the listener-me experiences the rhythms of interruption and control that dominate the temporal modes of Chronos and Aion. These rhythms do not articulate the obedient tick-tock of clock time, nor do they fit the general assumption that Chronos chimes with the chronological quantification and qualification of time (as described in the overview of Deleuze's concept of Chronos in chapter 9). Instead, they explore a different sense of how time is articulated and experienced through performance: the performer-me sets up the lopsided short-long and short-long-short phrases of this particular iteration of the piece as a means of making measure without measure. In other words, the listener-me hears the pulse of time in the rhythmic phrasing of these two notes (in two- or three-note patterns) and identifies a practice of measuring time, but not one that imposes regularity from without. Its time is self-made, emerging out from the articulations of these two or three notes acting as rhythm and measure of their own, albeit temporary, existence: a Rhythmicity, marked as all the more temporary on account of the inevitable, enveloping silence that precedes and succeeds its brief flowering as music.

NOTES

1. Mirroring my multimodal practice in the previous two projects, I draw on an audio recording made during the project as part of my musical-philosophical analysis. In the case of this particular chapter, the recording of a performance of *The Time Is Out of Joint* is utilised in the second musical-philosophical analysis (undertaken from the perspectives of the performer-me and the listener-me).

2. In the performing undertaken for this particular project, improvisation is a primary tool of music-making. Performing, in Cage's sense, is therefore related to improvising in the mode of performance of the music made in my third practice as research project.

3. The title comes from a line in Shakespeare's *The Tragedy of Hamlet*, at the moment when Hamlet is confronted by the ghost of his father, who asks him to avenge his murder by Claudius. Hamlet, who now realises that things are not as they should be or once were in the world, says: "The time is out of joint: O cursed spite, / That ever I was born to set it right!" (act I, scene 5). The line is also a favourite of Deleuze's, who draws on it in *Kant's Critical Philosophy* and *Difference and Repetition* (Deleuze 2008 and 2004a, respectively). In both books, Deleuze uses the Hamlet quote to convey a sense of time as "an empty and pure form" (2004a, 111)—a "Kantian reversal," through which time is "no longer related to the movement which it measures" (2008, vii). Beyond the "joints" (Latin: *cardo*) which hold time in place to the cardinal points through which movements are measured, Deleuze explores the fresh definition of time that Kant was forced to undertake in his *Critique of Pure Reason* (see Deleuze 2008) and theorises his third synthesis of time (in *Difference and Repetition*—see chapters 4–5, earlier). Both of these takes on time bear relation to Deleuze's concept of Aion. For my own part, the title reflects the focus on temporal

practices of interruption and novelty that I explore in this project, drawing Deleuze' Aion-Chronos pairing into the enquiry in the process (see later).

4. Of course, any assertion that the performer is merely the technical articulator of the composer's work is readily contestable—see, for instance, Cook (2001) for a comprehensive account of the (traditional) musicological bias toward notions of the composer/composition as the focus of creativity in music practice, and the case for expanding such focus to include the creative role of the performer in the making of music. I would add that the need for this expansion of focus is required even, or perhaps especially, when approaching the most detailed notations of, for instance, the modernist scores of Boulez, or the "new complexity" works of Ferneyhough, and the relationship between score and performance in the music of Anthony Braxton. But the point of my remark, here, is to explicate the major role of the performer in creating the music of *The Time Is Out of Joint* as performed, with the composer's role being limited to providing a structure for that music-making, not the notes as played.

5. As quoted earlier in this chapter, in a 1955 essay, Cage posed the question: "Composing's one thing, performing's another, listening's a third. What can they have to do with one another?" (Cage 1978, 15).

6. At the time of writing, Ablinger's website has a page dedicated to the *Seeing and Hearing* series, available online at the following address: https://ablinger.mur.at/docu01.html.

7. Simons (2019) defines this kind of basic rhythm as a "monorhythm": a repeatable, typically repeated pattern consisting solely of "sounds and silences, which may be of different relative lengths or durations, where some of the sounds may be more accented than others" (69–70). While there is nothing simple or monotonous about the content of the sections of *The Time Is Out of Joint* in performance, its compositional structure can certainly be said to be monorhythmic in this particular sense.

8. The performance was recorded at a private location in the West Midlands (UK), 8 January 2019.

9. A key composition in Brown's *Folio* collection is *December 1952*, which I discuss in chapter 4 in relation to its content-less rhythmic structure and the "empty form" of Deleuze's third synthesis of time.

Chapter 11

Rhythmicity

Chronos, Aion, and the Musical-Philosophical

So far in this book, Rhythmicity has undergone development in a number of directions. In the first practice as research project, it was conceived and practised as a multimodal movement of the musical-philosophical interrelating audio and text and expressing itself via improvised music-making and writing by means of what I termed cyclical and hyperbolic rhythms of composition and reader-listener engagement. Its encounter with Deleuze's difference and repetition was mediated via consideration of his three syntheses of time, which formed an apparatus for the three analyses of the improvisations undertaken—analyses which, in turn, allowed for a two-way process of transformation between the Deleuzian concepts and my concept of Rhythmicity. Accordingly, Deleuze's concepts were rephrased in terms of the musical-philosophical and the movements of Rhythmicity in the dimensions of the cyclical and the hyperbolic.

Building on my first experiment in a concept of Rhythmicity, in the second practice as research project, Rhythmicity's musical-philosophical movements were intensified. The fold was utilised both as a concept and as a method of chapter and sectional construction, and, together with the incompossible, was utilised as a way of practising a Rhythmicity of labyrinthine movements. These movements are implicit in the score of *In the Garden of the Incompossible*, manifest in the improvised performances given, and practised in the analyses undertaken from the perspectives of the composing and performing processes. Where the first project utilised Deleuze's three syntheses of time as an apparatus for initiating musical-philosophical analysis, the second project instead used these music-making processes as an apparatus for reframing Deleuze's fold and incompossible. Rhythmicity was again articulated in musical-philosophical terms, but this time evolved by considering such terms as intensive and coextensive in their relation. In other words, while the first project built its musical-philosophical Rhythmicity in cyclical and neither linear nor cyclical movements between audio and text, the second project shifted the focus to how the musical and the philosophical can be considered (and practised) as intensive qualities irreducible to either music or philosophy (as distinct disciplinary fields), and, in the musical-philosophical, as a multifurcating movement expressing a temporality of simultaneity—a temporality that moves everywhere and nowhere at the same time(s). Infinitely folded, incompossible Rhythmicity: coextensively multifurcating interrelations without end; a tonality of time without tonal or temporal (or disciplinary) centre; a composition (in score and chapters) of compound harmonies, articulated (in music and writing) via arpeggiations, alternations, and simultaneities. Rhythmicity, in the second practice as research project, is the movement that traces infinite paths through a multiverse of (incom)possible musical-philosophical connections.

In what follows, I detail the development of Rhythmicity in the third practice as research project, in terms of how it has developed from the insights garnered in these previous two projects, and also with regard to how it provides fresh understanding of the Deleuzian concepts concerned, the music practices utilised, and the philosophy of time more generally considered.

RHYTHMICITY AND THE LINE-CYCLE THEORISATION OF TIME: IMPLICATIONS FOR CHRONOS-AION AND THE COMPOSER/ PERFORMER/LISTENER RELATIONSHIP

As noted previously, there is a resonance between these latest experiments in time and those detailed in the first practice as research project. The resonance is with regard to linear/cyclical expression in respect of the musical-philosophical in my practice as research. The first of these movements is cyclical in nature: the repetition of a set of compositional methods—in the music-making (crafted from three or four notes in similar articulation across seven improvisations), in the interplay between the audio and the textual elements, and in the switching between concerns of the music practices and philosophical concepts in the analyses. The second movement of Rhythmicity in the first project is neither exclusively linear nor cyclical but, rather, expresses both a line-like motion (the movement of the reader's eye on the page of the text, and the ear as the reader listens, at the same time as reading, to the tracks of the piano improvisations), and a cycle-like motion—the repeated looping back from musical concerns to the musical-philosophical ground (which enables the enquiry) in the references made to it in the text of the analyses. In the first project, I labelled this motion in terms of the hyperbolic: an exaggerated movement—exaggerated in respect of its not being able to be restricted to solely linear or cyclical motions; a non-Euclidean, asymptotic, movement wherein the motions of the not-solely-linear and not-solely-cyclical never once coincide, despite being simultaneous expression of Rhythmicity.

In the third project, however, this movement is developed in a new direction. This new rhythmical-conceptual movement is different to the cyclical and hyperbolic movements of the textual-audio multimodality of chapter 4 in that its concept is that of Rhythmicity as a *tripartite* perspective of a *line-cycle* time-sense. As Guerlac (2006) warns: "When we figure time as a line, or a circle, time stops moving. We inadvertently turn time into space" (1). With a three-sided aspect on a temporal movement that is neither linear nor cyclical but both at the same time (and in triple perspective), Rhythmicity in my third practice-as-research project thus avoids making the mistake of effecting this translation of the temporal into the spatial. The line-cycle never ceases moving to be frozen in (spatialised) time, since the indivisible three-sided perspective of composer-me, performer-me, and listener-me, expresses a simultaneously Chronic-Aionic movement in the modes of the musical-philosophical. Accordingly, the line-cycle of Rhythmicity does more than fuse Chronos and Aion or (simply or otherwise) illustrate Deleuze's Chronos-Aion in musical form: it transforms Deleuze's concept by means of its new movement in and of time. In moving in this novel way, Rhythmicity as line-cycle expresses a temporality grounded directly in the musical-philosophical. In other words, Rhythmicity is (as argued throughout this book) neither solely a musical movement nor a philosophical one, but a musical-philosophical one.

Where Deleuze writes of the Chronos side of Chronos-Aion as existing in the living present (with past and future as relative dimensions within that unending present, rather than distinct times on their own account), *The Time Is out of Joint* transforms this formulation to focus on a *future* temporal perspective on the Chronic-Aionic time of the work's composition (as I will explain). As discussed earlier, Deleuze argues that, in Chronos time, "presents follow one another inside partial worlds or partial systems" (2004b, 89). From the perspective of the composer-me, for instance, in respect of *The Time Is out of Joint*, it is not so much a case of existing in partial worlds, or systems, than it is an act of *composing* those worlds (conceived as the events of performance of the work). The act of composing can indeed be framed according to Deleuze's conception of the living present of Chronos, with each period of time spent working on a given piece of music becoming enveloped in the wider "moment" of its composition—that is, the living present of the process of composing the work over (however long, however discontinuous) a period of time. However, the work itself is designed to engender unlimited expressions of the living present of its performance; such is the role of the composition in relation to all possible performances of it that may arise. So, in the case of *The Time Is out of Joint*, the composer-me was less concerned with Chronic time considered as the time of writing the work than with Chronos-Aion time as the time of all future-possible performances to come (and now of course, on writing the analyses in this and the previous chapter, with performances past as well as to come). In this respect, Chronos (as much as it can, or should, be considered alone) operates in a future-tense capacity—albeit a future-tense that anticipates (though does not prescribe, except in alternating compositional structure) the living presents of the performances that will follow.

From the (musical-philosophical) perspective of the composer-me, this future aspect is a nuance that is missing in Deleuze's approach to the time of Chronos. Rather than being ever in the moment, in the now, the composer-me attends most acutely to the futurity of performance. Chronos, in this respect, does indeed encapsulate a present time, but it is, via my conception of Chronos-Aion, the present-to-come. As Deleuze notes in his original conception, Chronos time draws the past and the future into its expression of the living present, but these remain subsidiary to the living present that enfolds all presents within itself as an ongoing, never-ending, process. In contrast to this, in the act of writing *The Time Is out of Joint*, the composer-me composed the present of the future (of performance) as an ever-alternating rhythm of silence and sound, repeating a structure without pre-written content *ad infinitum* (in theory, at least, if not in practice, on account of the inevitable temporal constraints of live performance events). In so doing, Chronos becomes the measuring of time according to a Chronic-Aionic conception of what will follow, not what is happening at the time of action (of composing the work). Such measure operates by interruption in the act of alternation, with the composer-me controlling the process ever in advance of the performances to come. The rhythm thus set up is chrono-logical in the sense of marking time (and making time) via measure, and the relation of composer to performer and listener is permanently tied to this Chronic-Aionic composition of silent ten-counts through two alternating sections predestined on the page (of the score), but not in the content of the music as actually played.

Such problematisation of the relation between composer, performer, and listener in *The Time Is out of Joint*—by means of control and interruption—is explicitly linked to my own practices in this latest project/chapter. Neither the composer-me, performer-me, nor the listener-me can be expressly separated from its others in these practices, even though it is part of the analysis to write from each different perspective/s in turn. Contrast this with the situation regarding Cage, Brown, Feldman, and Ablinger, who remain solely the composers of their respective works, despite their interest in problematising the role of the composer, performer, and listener in their composition processes.

Each of the analyses in chapter 10, although titled with regard to, and focused on, each perspective in turn or in relation (for instance, "composer-me," performer-me and listener-me"), also draws on the other or others untitled. (It is for this reason that the section on the composer-me, for example, also makes reference to the performer and listener of the work, albeit from the perspective of the work of the composer in question.) The tripartite relations between these three shift in focus and perspective in each of the subsections of the analyses undertaken, bringing fresh perspectives on Deleuze's Chronos and Aion in the process.

To continue this examination of the insights afforded by the third project, I now turn to silence: its role in the music practice and its part in the musical-philosophical expression that is the Rhythmicity of Chronos-Aion conceptualised in the third practice as research project and its attendant chapters.

THE "RHYTHMICITY OF SILENCES" AND CHRONOS-AION

With regard to the importance of silence in our understandings of the experience of music-making (for performer and listener), Spitzer (2019) notes that "silences, like sounds, have a lived duration"—adding how "any sophisticated concept of rhythm should not be deaf to their phenomenological nuances" (122). In *The Time Is out of Joint*, silence performs a dual role, operating as both ground and shroud. Silence grounds and shrouds the work as a whole: the piece begins with a period of silence (the first section of the score) that itself emerges mysteriously (since the count is made in silence) from a longer period of silence—the preperformance setup and preamble before the performance of *The Time Is out of Joint* begins officially (with the silent ten-count). How to know when *The Time Is out of Joint* has begun proper? The listener, for instance, has no idea about when the step is taken by the performer to begin counting to ten in silence, thus triggering the beginning of the piece and the first step in an endless alternation of silence and sound that marks the primary rhythmic structure (and the Rhythmicity) of the work. Of the twenty or so seconds of silence that open the audio recording *The Time Is out of Joint* before the first notes are heard from the piano, who can say at which point the performer-me began the silent ten-count? Listening back while undertaking this analysis, the listener (me or otherwise) can only guess as to when the performer initiated the first section of the piece, and also at what speed the subsequent ten-counts were paced in each of the piece's sections as the work unfolds in the performances given. The chronology of numbers of seconds that one is able to define (after the event, via the recordings) for each section is only a mere indicator in the direction of this silently executed count, not, of course, its ultimate measure.

The opening section of the work deliberately blurs the temporal boundaries of before and after; as a result, the time of performance and the time of preperformance are indistinguishable, since they are both qualified by silence (or the absence of anything being played). Only the performer knows that the performance has, in fact, begun. There is a resonance, here, with the performance practice of the improvising guitarist Derek Bailey, in respect of this blurring of the times of performance and of preperformance. Bailey was well known for masking the exact beginnings of his performances by merging the various acts of on-stage preparation (tuning his guitar, fixing the volume and EQ on his amp, taking a sip of a drink, etc.) with the actual starting point of his improvisations.[1] In this manner, the audience/listener is unaware of precisely when the music has, in fact, begun. The effect is similar to that of the opening section of silence in *The Time Is out of Joint*: the point at which one becomes aware that the performance is underway is always sometime after its actual beginning.

This uncertainty as to when the performance begins proper introduces a dynamic into the unfolding of the work that provides useful insight, via Rhythmicity, into the Chronos-Aion relation. Silence, for the performer-me and the listener-me, both during the act of performing *The Time Is out of Joint* and in listening back for the purposes of analysis, takes on the form of an active process in the music-making (and musical-philosophical enquiry), rather than (simply or otherwise) being considered as the absence of musical sound. For instance, during the act of counting in silence while silence is being observed (in the first of the two sections of the score), the performer-me experiences something akin to what the composer Jürg Frey (a member of the Wandelweiser collective) has defined as silence "which is omnipresent and exists only because sound exists" (Rutherford-Johnson 2017, 69).[2] In articulating the requirements of the score of *The Time Is out of Joint*, the performer-me engages with silence on two levels: one, where silence is considered as a coperformer in actualising the first of the two sections of the work; and two, where silence is the medium through which the privately experienced ten-count is undertaken. Of the first of these: allowing silence to play the role of co-performer of the piece is a profound experience for the performer-me—a giving-over of control as well as a rare opportunity to become more of a listener/audience member in one's own performance. Even in the act of playing (in the "Play" sections of the work), the presence of silence looms large—in both the task of counting silently to ten, and in the realisation that, once the ten-count is reached, the return of the "Silence" section is, each time, inevitable. In such instances, the performer-me experiences the making of music as less an act of making sound than that of temporarily populating (one form of) silence, mediated by (another form of) silence. Interestingly, both the Wandelweiser composer Michael Pisaro and the improvising guitarist Keith Rowe have spoken of a similar attitude to silence and its relationship to sound. In discussing a composition of his for solo oboe, Rowe describes the notes played by the oboe as "an articulation of a version of silence. What I think I've always been doing is making silence audible" (Olewnick 2018, 369). Pisaro, for his part, talks about the experience of silence as "not the cessation of sound" but as "a different sound, one with more density than those sounds made by instruments" (Gottschalk 2016, 29).

In terms of Chronos-Aion, mediated through my concept of Rhythmicity, the musical population of silence experienced by the performer-me contributes something new to both our understandings of Deleuze's philosophy of time (in his conception of Chronos and Aion), and to the musical conception of time in its relation to silence. While (as noted earlier) the listener is ever unaware of the point at which the performer begins the silent count that initiates the piece, the performer-me is, of course, fundamentally aware of this act of beginning, in the event of performance. While everyone but the performer exists in a state of unawareness of this beginning of the time of outset of the music, the performer-me has the unique experience (denied even the composer-me) of moving from one quality of silence to another quality of silence, thereby occasioning the event of music proper. The first quality of silence is silence considered in its general sense: the silence that is all around us all of the time, while we ignore its presence to get on with whatever is to hand. Of course, this silence is never completely silent, but, in terms of the actualisation of the event of performance, it is a certain quality of silence that we all know and understand. The second silence is a musical silence, far more personal to performer and listener alike (though differently, given that the performer knows the pace of the ten-count, while the listener can only guess). In the case of *The Time Is out of Joint*, then, these qualities of silence express a form of Rhythmicity that moves, not from sound to silence (as I have already explored previously), but between different conceptions of silence, different experiences of silence for the performer-me and the listener-me (and the listener in general). And this "Rhythmicity of silences" transforms Deleuze's Chronos-Aion, with the act of counting to ten (in silence), both while observing silence (in the first section) and while playing the piano (in the second), introducing the Chronic at the heart of the Aionic—and vice versa. In a 1971 lecture on his *Momente* work (as discussed earlier), Stockhausen argued that "Silence is the result of the concept of duration: to deal with duration means to break the flow of time, and that produces silence" (1989, 66). While Stockhausen talks of the production of silence as stemming from the measuring of time by means of composing with durations (an approach that has a strong resonance with the work of John Cage as discussed earlier—in concept, if not in practice), I am talking, here, instead, of silence in the plural (silences) as the means by which the music of *The Time Is out of Joint* is both expressed and experienced—and through which the duration of the alternating sections of the work and their silent counts sets up a Rhythmicity, adding something new to our conceptions of the temporal (and the silent).

By way of useful example of this plurality of temporal silences (and their attendant Rhythmicity), the twenty-seventh and twenty-eighth iterations of *The Time Is out of Joint*, in the performance given for this project, are instructive when considered together. The twenty-seventh iteration (see figure 11.1) begins at around 18'23," with the second "Play" section coming in at 18'46" and continuing to 19'08."

This is followed by around twenty-four seconds of silence that mark the first section of the twenty-eighth iteration (see figure 11.2), with its second section beginning at 19'33" and finishing at 19'56." Chronologically speaking, these two iterations are quite similar: their first sections are around twenty-three and twenty-four seconds in length, respectively; their second sections are, respectively, around twenty-two and twenty-three seconds in length. In terms of musical material, they are similar in that they each articulate a series of sustained chords in subdued tone. The twenty-seventh iteration is different to its successor, given that its series of chords are occasionally arpeggiated, and the performer-me adds in a few melodic figures in the left-hand toward the end of the iteration. By contrast, the chords of the twenty-eighth iteration are articulated without arpeggio or additional melodic figure. However, what unites the two iterations more than their chordal approach (or the similarity of the time-lengths of each of their sections measured in seconds) is the movement between their approaches to the population of silence(s) as discussed earlier.

More than any other potential pairings of the other thirty-five iterations that follow on, one from another after the opening iteration, this particular pair stands out most strongly from the others to the listener-me, in terms of expressing something crucial about the Rhythmicity of silences particular to the act of performing *The Time Is out of Joint*. While each iteration stands in relative isolation of its others, in respect of its self-contained musical

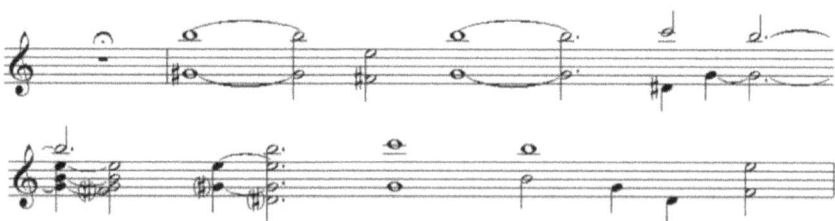

Figure 11.1.

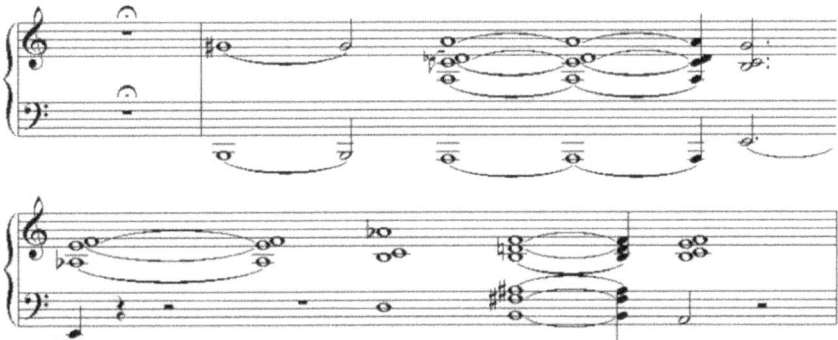

Figure 11.2.

material and development (similar to aspects of Stockhausen's moment form, as discussed previously), there is, to the ears of the listener-me, a connection between the twenty-seventh and twenty-eighth iterations that makes them less the latest in a long series of iterations that act of unique worlds of temporal disjointedness (e.g., this iteration, and this iteration, and now this iteration, and so on), and more an expression of the kind of temporal continuity that can exist, seemingly paradoxically, *because of* such disjointedness—as I will explain.

Temporal disjointedness lies at the heart of my third practice-as-research project for this enquiry ("the time is out of joint," after all, as the composition's title announces). But there is a disjointedness across the temporal modes of the Chronic and the Aionic that operates differently to notions of Chronos and Aion considered solely via Deleuze's philosophy of time in *Logic of Sense*. By this, I mean that the time-feel that is experienced by the listener-me—in the movement between the twenty-seventh and twenty-eighth iterations in particular—is experienced as a continuous rhythmic quality. This is not a continuity of rhythm that duplicates the articulations of one iteration to those of another, or continues a flow that one begins and the second takes up once again (even though both iterations repeat the alternating structure of the composition itself, have sections of similar length, measured in seconds, and also employ similar musical devices to make the music of the "Play" sections of each). Instead, I hear a movement of form that expresses itself precisely *by means of* the disjointedness of the alternations that are grounded, at heart, by my specific conception of the silences at work in the performance in question (in this regard, the listener-me benefits from having also been the performer of the piece). The silences that operate between the four, alternating sections of the twenty-seventh and twenty-eighth iterations perform a secret rhythm: a Rhythmicity that finds Chronos in Aion, Aion in Chronos, ever articulating both in relation, through the multilevel silences that beat (silently) at the heart of the work. Because of the similarity of these two iterations, articulated back-to-back in a performance of a total of thirty-five iterations, the Rhythmicity to which I am referring is both all the more apparent and all the more hidden. It is apparent on the level of what remains to be heard of its process on the audio recording of the performance given: the musical material referred to above. It is hidden on the level of that whichever eludes capture by means of audio recording, but which can be attested to and analysed through the "secret" input of the practitioner themselves. In the case of this piece, and these iterations, it is the Rhythmicity of the silent ten-count across sections of "Silence" and "Play," bringing secret continuity by means of apparent discontinuity.

As I consider the role of silence/s in this project, the three aspects of myself as music practitioner—that is, composer, performer, listener—are connected by means of the Rhythmicity of silences that threads through this project. The composer-me composes the rhythm of the silences that give the work its central character. The performer-me performs the rhythm of the silences, but personally (by means of the silent ten-count) and therefore in relative secret. The listener-me hears the silences and begins to get a sense of their rhythms of alternation as the performance unfolds. Rhythm, and the Rhythmicity of the project, thus gives connection to the disjointedness of the temporal modes at play in the practice (as research) undertaken. The time is out of joint, and the silences play their part in articulating the rhythm of the work at the secret heart of the musical-philosophical enquiry: yet another, and vital, aspect of the Rhythmicity of *The Time Is out of Joint*.

NOTES

1. See Peters (2017, 224) for further example of Bailey's preperformance habits and behaviour in this regard.

2. Frey's definition of, and interest in, silence chimes with a general focus on silence and/as musical material demonstrated by most if not all members of the Wandelweiser collective. Rutherford-Johnson (2017) usefully sums this fascination and focus up as the "denial of the idea of silence as a fixed condition" (68).

Conclusion

This book has brought together research in a variety of practices: my own music-making in solo-piano improvised performance and composition; certain of the concepts of the philosopher, Gilles Deleuze (the pairs difference and repetition, the fold and the incompossible, and Chronos and Aion); and scholarship in music and philosophy relevant to the concerns of the enquiry in the context of each of its three practice as research projects and their attendant chapters. Over the course of my enquiry, I utilised a set of methods in order to explore my notion that the musical-philosophical can bring something new to our understandings of the philosophy of time of Gilles Deleuze. As discussed in the introduction, these methods were as follows: first-person reflections on/ analyses of my practices of improvisation and composition; the interrelation of these reflections/analyses with aspects of Deleuze's conceptual apparatus (i.e., the three pairs of concepts engaged with); and the musical-philosophical as a means of bringing all these together in a multimodal expression. I gave that multimodal expression the name of Rhythmicity, and this book has sought to establish Rhythmicity as a concept of the musical-philosophical—in this instance, by means of intermixing my own music practice with certain Deleuzian concepts. However, this does not mean that Rhythmicity need be restricted to solely those concepts and practices (as I will argue).

In what follows, I consider Rhythmicity through the prism of its development and practice in this book, as a means of casting light on how it has been explored in the chapters and practice as research projects. I also reflect on the implications that my enquiry may have for research in the fields of Deleuze studies (and, in particular, his philosophy of time and wider implications for theories of time more generally considered), practice as research in music, studies in experimental music (including its overlap with musicians working in improvisation), and Performance Philosophy.

RHYTHMICITY AND THE DELEUZIAN

As I discuss at the outset of this book, there are a relatively small (but by no means insignificant) number of music researchers, either in practice as research or in more traditional academic modes of research, who utilise aspects of the philosophy of Deleuze in their work. This work often takes the form of drawing on Deleuze's concepts as a means to understand music practice in new or different ways—an approach exemplified by (though not restricted to) the collections edited by Buchanan and Swiboda (2004), and Hulse and Nesbitt (2010). In other uses of Deleuze—in the collections edited by Assis and Giudici (2017, 2019), for instance—music practice takes on a more active role in the research (i.e., not solely as object of the Deleuzian research), given the practice as research/artistic research approach of the enquiries in question.

While there is clearly a usefulness to understanding music practice by means of different concepts and fresh perspectives, plus a growing desire on the part of practitioner-researchers in music to utilise Deleuze's work in their own, the *nature* of the relationship between music practice and Deleuze's philosophy is open to extended and (necessarily) ongoing enquiry.[1] From the perspective of this investigation, the relationship between a series of Deleuze's conceptual pairs (difference and repetition, the fold and the incompossible, and Chronos and Aion) and my own solo-piano practice in improvisation and composition is interrogated and explored—albeit in different ways in the three practice as research projects, as per the requirements of each. Despite these differing approaches to the question of the nature of the relationship between music practice and Deleuze's philosophy, the concept through which I choose to express that relationship across the chapters and projects—and to connect its various trajectories—is Rhythmicity. Rhythmicity is thus, in this book, my conception of the rhythmic process at the heart of the nature of musical-philosophical expression.

In all three projects, the nature of the musical-philosophical is explored and expressed by means of *composition*. By composition, here, I do not mean strictly musical composition; instead, I am referring to the composition of the projects' attendant chapters themselves. The chapters in question (chapters 4, 7, and 10) use an amalgam of audio, writing, and transcription in their compositions. The nature of each amalgam is particular to the concepts and practices in question and, hence, to the Rhythmicity of the musical-philosophical relationship each practice as research project seeks to elucidate. The composition and the content of chapters 4, 7, and 10, in turn, provide a way of offering fresh insights into the Deleuzian concepts chosen for enquiry: insights that would otherwise be unavailable via other means of research, given the uniqueness of each project (as I detail in what follows). These insights are certainly a key way in which my enquiry provides fresh perspective to the field of Deleuze studies. In addition, the approach I have taken to investigating and, as a result, transforming these concepts of Deleuze's, has consistently been mindful of the problem of application—where application is understood as the process wherein one field or practice epistemologically subsumes another field/practice by way of dominating (directly or more subtly) our understandings of the latter field/practice through use of the former's terms and perspectives alone. As discussed earlier, this is a way in which my book makes a contribution to Performance Philosophy—the field in which the problem has been perhaps most widely debated in recent years (see, for example, Cull Ó Maoilearca 2014; 2020).

RHYTHMICITY: INSIGHTS

Across the chapters of this book, there are implications for Deleuze studies—in particular, his philosophy of time, and our understandings of the nature of time in more general terms—as well as for practice as research in music, the study of experimental and improvised musics, and the field of Performance Philosophy. In each of the three projects, I used Deleuze's concepts as points of departure for the music-making undertaken, and this chimes with the work of Assis and others (as I outline earlier). My enquiry thus stands alongside the experiments of the few examples of music research that takes Deleuze, not as a means to theorise itself but, instead, as a method in the *making* of that music. This highlights the nascence of such approaches to Deleuze in music and music research at the time of writing—hence, the value of an enquiry such as mine. My use of improvisation in the making of experimental music is, of course, hardly a new direction the practice or study of either discipline. However, I contend that the use to which I put that improvisation—as one in a set of methods to investigate and transform certain of Deleuze's concepts—is more novel. As with my use of composition, performance, audio, and writing, my utilisation of improvisation is focused on the task in hand (the Deleuzian musical-philosophical enquiry) rather than the (simple or otherwise) act of improvising for the sake of improvising—as noble an art as that is in itself, of course.

Throughout the practice-as-research projects of this book, Deleuze's concepts have been used as compositional elements in the development of Rhythmicity—that is, they have been utilised rather than applied. This strategy was part of a two-way process of affect and transformation between Deleuze's philosophy of time and my own musical-philosophical book, with important implications for both (and related fields)—as I will now detail.

The composition and development of Rhythmicity offers three unique perspectives on how we understand and experience time. Since rhythm inheres in time (time being its medium of expression), the interdisciplinary rhythms set up by the composition of each chapter (and articulated by the contents) provide a means of modelling and experiencing time in ways other than in Deleuze's (and others') philosophy of time. In all three projects, the reader-listener is invited to experience a musical-philosophical mix interrelating audio and writing and transcription in different ways. The expression of Rhythmicity in the first project describes time as both a cyclical and hyperbolic movement. Deleuze's three-part synthesis of (1) the living present, (2) the past as ground by which the present passes, and (3) the pure and empty form of the future is rephrased accordingly. Where Deleuze's original conception stresses the synthetic (rather than serial or successive) nature of the relations of past, present, and future, Rhythmicity offers, instead, a means of putting *motion* into this synthesis (cyclical and hyperbolic movements to be precise), thus moving its conceptualisation outside the dimensions of the written word and into the realm of the musical-philosophical.[2] For instance, there is a difference in itself that is particular to each of the seven improvisations recorded for the first practice-as-research project, and a repetition for itself. They each differ internally in respect of each being a set of perpetually varying combinations of (three or four) notes with no original theme—or, I suggest in chapter 4, articulations by which the process of variation itself becomes the theme of the improvisations. These articulations repeat for themselves, having no particular start or finish in terms of the teleology of their musical statement; their acts of repetition are for the sake of repetition alone—a repetition that becomes more and more apparent as the improvisations unfold (as single tracks, and in whichever order the shuffle mode plays them for the listener). These are not illustrations of Deleuze's concepts, they are *rearticulations* of them. And they are not articulated alone: the combination of audio and writing in the analyses provided introduces the cyclical and hyperbolic movements noted earlier. Such motion dislocates Deleuze's temporal syntheses and expresses them between the disciplines of music and philosophy. This dislocation means that the concepts themselves cannot be isolated in either the writing or the audio, but ever in between: as the musical-philosophical, describing a constantly cycling motion without settling on either of the terms of its relation. In addition, the musical-philosophical is the ground of its own becoming as greater than the sum of its parts; it is an exaggerated motion beyond the confines of musical or philosophical presentation alone (hence, hyperbolic), but one that indicates the possibility of "the musical" and "the philosophical" as intensive qualities unrestricted to solely music or philosophy (considered in disciplinary terms).

Rhythmicity, in its musical-philosophical expression, offers, in the first project, a way of rethinking the nature of time in two simultaneous movements: the cyclical and the hyperbolic. Thinking time in terms of the cyclical has, of course, a long history in many philosophies and musics of the world: in Buddhist, Hindu, Jainist, and Ancient Egyptian religions, and also in Pythagorean and Stoic thought (and, in more modern times, the eternal return as conceptualised by Nietzsche); and in the rhythmic cycles of Indian, African, Javanese and Balinese (gamelan), African, and (more recently) jazz, blues, rock 'n' roll, Minimalist, and disco/house (and other popular electronic musics). But expressing the cyclical in relation with a hyperbolic movement is something different. And it is a move beyond Deleuze's syntheses and their fragmentary perspective on the convolutions of the temporal ("Time [for Deleuze] is radically fragmentary", as Williams (2011,", 51) notes). A cycle interwoven with a hyperbola adds a convolution to the experience of the Rhythmicity of the first project that transforms our perspective on temporal relation—in this case between the acts of reading and listening, but with implications for how we might understand other multimodal interactions in and of time. Ways in which alternative interdisciplinary and/or multimodal projects could be developed would be for others to explore, but it is my contention that Rhythmicity provides a useful example of at least one way (or set of ways) in which such a project might be conceived and realised.

The second practice as research project offers a second mix of the musical and the philosophical, leading to a new multimodal expression and a fresh perspective on time. Aside from intensifying the (folded) juxtaposition of writing about the Deleuzian concepts (the fold and the incompossible) and the music-making undertaken (a series of improvised performances of the score of my composition, *In the Garden of the Incompossible*), I introduce a "tonality" of the musical-philosophical in its exploration of the temporal. This tonality, as argued in chapter 8, is not a tonality in the purely musical sense; its tonality engenders a "new harmony" of music and philosophy that provides multiple perspectives on (incom)possible ways to move through a labyrinth of compound chords (the score of the work). The "thread" that traces each performed path through the maze is the note F-sharp. The choice of F-sharp was purely arbitrary; it merely functions as a link between the thirty compound chords that populate the score as temporal labyrinth. The tonality that each tracing evokes is a tonality of multiplicity: performances of the composition, and its unique take on time, present, with each movement through the maze, one folding of the compound chords (which are themselves foldings of in/compossible chords) among an infinity of possible ways in which its particular "garden of the in/compossible" can be traversed.

Our experience of time is not without tone or tenor, but to conceive it as a tonality might be considered a useful nuance in our understanding of the

temporal—in other words, as a potentially novel way of conceiving and practising time. The tonality of time, as experienced in the act of meandering (in
performance) through the harmonic "garden" of *In the Garden*, establishes
a temporality without beginning or end: a time-sense that has only multiple
possible existences and avenues of travel. This time-sense has a tonality,
and a temporality, of the ever in-between: between the two chords in each
compound, between the writing and the audio, as the musical-philosophical.
A theory of time that posits multiple coexisting temporalities is, of course,
nothing new. There are the many polyrhythmic and polytemporal experiments in twentieth and twenty-first century music. For instance (and certainly
not exclusively): Igor Stravinsky in his 1913 *The Rite of Spring*; Olivier
Messiaen's rhythmic/temporal conceptions and compositions of the 1940s
and later; Elliott Carter's string quartets of the 1950s and 1970s; the compositional and improvisational collages of the Scratch Orchestra (in the late 1960s
and early 1970s) and Anthony Braxton since the 1960s to the present day;
the looping, changing, and cross-phasing patterns of Steve Reich and Philip
Glass (especially in their earlier work in the 1960s and 1970s); Wandelweiser
since the 1990s; and beyond. Conceptions of multiple coexisting temporalities also have similarities with the B-theory of time coined by McTaggart at
the start of the twentieth century, and with the space-time models established
in the work of Einstein et al. around the same time (both of which are referenced in the introduction to this book). Of these, B-theory and space-time/
four-dimensional models portray time in objective terms only; subjective
experience showing only an epistemological lack in respect of our knowledge
of the future compared to that of the past. In contrast, Deleuze's models of
time emphasise process over the objective or subjective, and his concepts of
the fold and the incompossible continue this emphasis on a process philosophy of time: multiple, enfolded, synthetic.

   Distinct from these temporal models (B-theory and space-time synchronic-
ities; Deleuze's processes in synthesis), the tonality of time conceived by and
expressed via the Rhythmicity of the second practice as research project/*In
the Garden* is forever in the middle of things without itself having a distinct
middle. By this, I mean that there is no beginning or end to the score-labyrinth
of *In the Garden*, but there is a tonality without tonal centre; there is no
beginning or end to the time-sense of my second project's labyrinthine
Rhythmicity, but there is a temporality without temporal centre. Folding these
two qualities of time and tonality, the musical-philosophical presents the
reader-listener with a path through both, in which no single journey can ever
completely encapsulate either, but where each journey is a unique expression
of that which it cannot fully inscribe. The development of Rhythmicity thus
offers the Deleuzian and other temporal models a potentially new way of
conceptualising time: in terms of a (new) tonality—that is, not in the purely

musical sense, but in a musical-philosophical sense as demonstrated in the second project.

In each of the three projects, the uniqueness of each movement of Rhythmicity, as experienced by the reader-listener, introduces the issue of subjectivity into the heart of the attendant conceptualisation of time. This is a matter explicitly explored in the third project (chapter 10), but one that is also implicit in the expression of Rhythmicity in the first and second projects (given that Rhythmicity's time-sense is also uniquely experienced by the reader-listener in engaging with the chapters' composition). In chapter 10, subjectivity is intimately bound up with what I call a "tripartite line-cycle" expression of Rhythmicity: interweaving temporal perspectives on the third project's new work, *The Time Is out of Joint*, in terms of the composer-me, the performer-me, and the listener-me. The (three-voiced) line-cycle is a new development of the musical-philosophical movement of Rhythmicity. It is neither linear nor cyclical but, unlike the hyperbolic motion of the second movement of Rhythmicity of the first project (as discussed in chapter 5), it operates via control and interruption (as I detail in the analyses of the third project), expressing a simultaneous forwards-and-backwards alternation of (1) the two sections of a composition (*The Time Is out of Joint*), (2) the musical and the philosophical concerns of the analyses provided, and (3) a special case of different kinds of temporally-inflected silence that I call a "Rhythmicity of silences."

Time, considered with regard to the three-sided motion of a line-cycle alternation, and a Rhythmicity of silences, can be thought (and experienced) differently to the time conceptualised in Deleuze's Chronos-Aion system— and also in respect of time as understood via the widely referenced McTaggart A-theory model. The A-theory considers time to be in a constant process of transformation from future to present to past; Deleuze's Chronos-Aion uses an Aionic, eternally stretching past-future continuum as an incorporeal means of grounding the Chronic present in which we experience presents upon presents in an endless cycle. Both theories of time are dynamic, but Deleuze's is more nuanced than A-theory in so far as it syntheses his temporal perspectives (similar to how he constructs *Difference and Repetition*'s three syntheses) rather than placing them in series.

There is clearly a subjective aspect to Deleuze's Chronos, at least from the perspective of our (bodily) encounters of the living present as it enfolds countless presents within itself in the process of its operation. There is also a subjective aspect to A-theory, given that (as it postulates) we anticipate the future and remember the past as part of the becoming of time in its dynamic flow (from future to present to past). My own temporal model, as expressed via the Rhythmicity of the third project/*The Time Is out of Joint*, also offers a subjective perspective (three, in fact) into the temporal processes at work.

Where Rhythmicity expresses time a little differently to Deleuze's Chronos or McTaggart's A-theory, however, is in respect of its line-cycle movement in three dimensions of perspective (composer-me, performer-me, listener-me) and an understanding of silence(s) that interrelates with each perspective without being the exclusive privilege of any. The line-cycle is a rhythmic movement of the musical-philosophical, voiced in sounds and silences and multiperspective analyses. Moving by alternation, the musical-philosophical traces its rhythms via a process of control and interruption that brings together the temporalities of the composer-me, the performer-me, the listener-me, and the analyst-me that draws on each of its others, setting up a new movement of time that takes Deleuze's Chronos-Aion as one element in its construction, but without subsuming itself under Deleuze's temporal system—and likewise in respect of McTaggart's A-theory (and its relatives). As a result, the musical-philosophical Rhythmicity of the third project/*The Time Is out of Joint* is unique in its temporal expression—and part of that uniqueness is vested in the Rhythmicity of silences.

In the third project, I referred to the "ground and shroud" that silence provides in its different forms in relation to *The Time Is out of Joint*, its composition, performance, and the experience of listening to it (as performer, analyst, and for the reader-listener of this book). This is the Rhythmicity of silences. Its innovation in terms of our understandings of the nature of time comes from the inability to separate the personal/private from the performed. The duration of each section of silence can be measured (in seconds) after the event, as can the duration of each "Play" section, but the performer's private ten-count and its act of measuring out each section remains unknowable to anyone other than the performer at the time. This personal, subjective, experience of time as performed, in combination with listeners' personal, subjective experiences of time in the piece, problematises the notion that time is something we can understand in terms of second, minutes, and so on. It also problematises the conception of time as purely durational in the Bergsonian sense—that is, where time is thought as a "qualitative multiplicity, which bears no relation to number . . . a pure heterogeneity" (Guerlac 2006, 96). In *The Time Is out of Joint*, silence grounds the measurement of time in each of its two sections—silence as the silent ten-count, silence as one half of the alternating structure; silence also shrouds the measurement of time—the measurement being conducted in silence, inwardly to the performer. Neither a purely durational/internal or an externally measured approach to time suffice to encompass the temporal as practised (and theorised) in *The Time Is out of Joint*. The musical-philosophical, in this instance, provides insight into the nature of time in respect of Rhythmicity's threading together of silences that operate between the measured and the unmeasured, the objective and the subjective; the processual ever shrouded in its grounding of the various silences that move the music making.

Aside from its role in theorising and practising time, the Rhythmicity of silences brings the discussion of my book's original contributions to knowledge into an area of study that has fascinated experimental musicians since the mid-twentieth century (and has certainly gained pace in more recent decades). As noted in chapters 10 and 11, silence is a primary concern for many experimental musicians and experimental music theorists (including some who are both). Aside from the pioneering work undertaken by Cage (the piece *4'33*," and the writings collected in the *Silence* book, being only the better known of these outputs), we only need look to the Wandelweiser collective for ready inspiration as to the manifold possibilities offered by the study and practice of silence in music and music research into the twenty-first century. My own experiments with silence as part of the third project chime with certain of the ontological and epistemological foundations of the work of both Cage and certain musicians associated with Wandelweiser (for example, Pisaro and Frey)—for instance, in respect of the recognition of music as, at its most basic, the relation between sound and silence; of there being more than one kind of silence; and of silence's inherent overfullness (alongside its more commonly accepted emptiness). What my practice as research in Performance Philosophy brings to these ontological and epistemological perspectives, via the transformation of the Deleuzian conceptual pair of Chronos-Aion in the third project, is a theorisation of silence as a musical-philosophical rhythmic quality: my Rhythmicity of silences. Rhythmicity thus introduces into silence a movement between silences-as-experienced (in this case, as experienced by the performer-me and the listener-me). This movement between silences-as-experienced represents a making-dynamic of something that is typically considered as just that: silence as a thing, or a condition, rather than as a process (however silent). The process of experiencing the Rhythmicity of silences, then, in its movement between and across the alternations of the two sections of *The Time Is out of Joint*, from the perspective of performer and listener, enables a reconsideration of silence in both its more commonplace and its experimental music definition (as discussed above). Silence as rhythmic quality; the Rhythmicity of silences.

RHYTHMICITY, IN CLOSING, AND THE FUTURE IMPLICATIONS OF MY WORK

Taken together, the development of Rhythmicity across the three projects provides a musical-philosophical movement that explores the major research enquiry of my book, as well as offering fresh perspective and new knowledge in respect of a number of fields of study related to my research—studies in Deleuze and the philosophy of time, experimental music (including the work of certain musicians who use improvisation as part of their experiments in music), Performance Philosophy, and practice as research. In relation to the main drives of my enquiry, my project offers the following insights (summarised here from their explication, above, and numbered to reflect the primary objectives of my research):

1. The nature of the relationship I have engendered between my own solo-piano music-making and the Deleuzian concepts I have selected for investigation has been theorised and practised in a series of three projects, via an original concept I have called Rhythmicity. As a result, this book is both document and instance of Rhythmicity considered in musical-philosophical terms. Its composition bears testimony to my experiments in multimodality in respect of the musical-philosophical and expresses Rhythmicity at the same time as developing it. Given that any attempts toward a fixed ontology and epistemology of any thing or practice are bound to fail (given the ongoing nature of things and practices in that they change in time and are, therefore, resistant to fixture), my enquiry is a first step in the direction of a wider understanding of the process by which different practices/fields interrelate.

The interweaving of music practices and philosophical concepts undertaken in my enquiry is indicative of a determination to make the musical-philosophical my principal territory as a practitioner-researcher. But that territory is, of course, not mine alone to occupy, and neither is the musical-philosophical concept of Rhythmicity it has engendered mine alone to utilise. With regard to the philosophy of time, and the new insights my project has offered via practice as research in the musical-philosophical, there are, of course, a number of composers and performers who have been concerned with time and its nature as part of their work—certain of whom I have referenced in my book. For instance, Cage, Feldman, Boulez, Stockhausen, Young, Glass, Braxton, Coleman, Pisaro, and Lang have each explored time as a major part of their music-making methods. Of these, Feldman provides an important example of how a musician can undertake philosophical enquiry in and around their music practice, given that his own position was quite clear on the matter: he thought of his work as operating "between categories"—in other words, as neither musical nor any other kind of activity considered in isolation (2000, 88). Feldman's experiments with time, and those of others who have followed similar paths, are important forerunners and/or contemporaries to my own process of creating musical-philosophical expressions, in the three projects and chapters of this book. And it is in relation to the experiments of such practitioners (whether directly or more indirectly musical-philosophical in nature) that my concept of Rhythmicity can be positioned and utilised.

By creating Rhythmicity as a practice of the musical-philosophical, I have opened the way for further engagement on the issue of the nature of the relations between music and philosophy. I see no reason why future projects could not explore Rhythmicity in relation to other music practices, and also in duo, trio, and larger ensemble formats, as well as investigating other of the concepts of Deleuze (or another philosopher or philosophical field). That Rhythmicity is, first and foremost, a process of interrelation makes it more than suitable a concept for such enquiries.

Rhythmicity, then, is not something to be considered as being confined to my own music practice, and neither is it to be considered as being limited to the conceptual apparatus of Deleuze. Practitioner-researchers who approach any form of music-making as a means of providing insights into philosophical questions—Deleuzian or otherwise—may find Rhythmicity useful in that it offers a way of not only investigating, but of presenting such research. Where the focus of interdisciplinary work is on the operations of the two (or more) fields in relation, the rhythm occasioned by such movement between disciplines must not be relegated to solely a process (or by-product) of research, given that it can also function as a key presentational device. If the nature of the relationship between music and philosophy can be expressed via interdisciplinary rhythms (as I have argued in this book), then the composition of the manner in which that relationship is understood becomes an ontological and epistemological concern—that is, not purely a presentational decision. Which leads me to consideration of the next two research drives of my enquiry.

2. and 3. In respect of the Deleuzian concepts selected for investigation as part of my development of Rhythmicity, the insights garnered have come about as a result of practices of composition and interrelation—in the text of this book itself, and also in the three practice-as-research projects undertaken. Given the traditional format of presentation of Deleuze's original concepts—the printed page and the word (with a minimum of illustration in certain cases)—the format of presentation of my own encounters with difference and repetition, the fold and the incompossible, Chronos and Aion, in itself brings something fresh to our understandings of Deleuze's philosophical apparatus. The effect of the composition of the chapters, in combination with the insights generated by the practice as research projects and their analyses, brings to each conceptual pair an expression of the concerns of each. Expression, in this instance, is not taken as mere statement or supporting illustration of the concepts in question; rather, it is considered as a creative means of transforming that which is expressed by virtue of Rhythmicity. Accordingly, the concepts of difference and repetition investigated in the first project are differed and repeated in multiple ways via the composed inter-relation of the text and the audio (presenting the improvised music-making) created for the project/chapter. Similarly, in the second project, the concepts

of the fold and the incompossible are interrelated by means of the folding of incompossibles—that is, the audio of the performances given and the text of the analyses undertaken, neither of which can, or should, be considered independently of its other. Finally, in the last project, Deleuze's concepts of Chronos and Aion are taken as points of departure for an investigation analysed from the positions of the composer-me, the performer-me, and the listener-me—three angles on the enquiry that provide something new to the concepts in question: a Rhythmicity of temporal perspective not found in, and not possible through, Deleuze's original conception and presentation.

In each project, then, the concepts concerned are transformed beyond their original conceptions/presentations via the unique compositions and presentations adopted for the enquiry into each conceptual pair. Rhythmicity, in this respect, provides a rhythmic quality that works across disciplines and modes of engagement. While Deleuze's concepts provide the initial impetus for each project, they do not dominate or predetermine the scope of the investigation that follows. At every point in the musical-philosophical expression in my enquiry, the concepts utilised act as touchstones for the analyses undertaken; they are points of reference rather than explanatory apparatuses that are being applied to the musical and analytical practices undertaken. As a result, the musical-philosophical practices adopted for the music-making and the writing in the analyses made impact on Deleuze's concepts, transforming them in time with the Rhythmicity of each project, challenging them from their sedentary positions as fixed entities in conceptual space. On this matter: as much as Deleuze would have denied this description of conceptual fixity in his own work, it is certainly evident that much of the work undertaken in Deleuzian music research since his death has been concerned with expanding and illustrating his work further, rather than transforming his conceptual apparatus—even when certain authors have explicitly stated such a transformation as their primary intention (see, for instance, Campbell 2013; Buchanan and Swiboda 2004).

There are, of course, exceptions to this tendency in music research to expand and illustrate Deleuze's concepts rather than transform them—as I have noted in this book. For example, as referenced in chapter 2, Assis's (2018) micro-haecceity takes Deleuze and Guattari's (2004) concept of haecceity and reformulates it for the purpose of better understanding the forces at work in the time of music performance from the perspective of the performer—realising a goal that was not that of Deleuze and Guattari in their original conception. In addition, as noted in chapter 3, Hemment (2004) draws attention to how the stark minimalism inherent in popular electronic music of the 1980s problematises the distinction between Chronic and Aionic time conceptualised by Deleuze (2004b) and Deleuze and Guattari (2004), leading to deeper understanding of our perceptions of musical-temporal nuance. The conceptual transformations affected in my enquiry stand alongside, and build on, these kinds of appropriations and reformulations, and as such indicate a necessary move in practice as research in music that my project both practises and endorses. As demonstrated by the work I have undertaken and presented, such appropriation and reformulation perform a rhythm: a complex, interdisciplinary rhythm that cannot be limited to one or the other of the disciplines concerned.

The musical-philosophical, then, as investigated and practised in this book, is inherently rhythmic in its nature, expressing a rhythmic quality that I have chosen to conceptualise and practice as Rhythmicity. I would argue that future directions for both the musical-philosophical and Rhythmicity should include further interrelation of modes of investigation and presentation. By this, I mean that this book stands as one example (a founding project) among others possible—for instance, bringing together other music practices with other philosophical concepts. In short, musical-philosophical expression is to be encouraged, not solely as the coming-together of two disciplines for a single purpose, but instead as an example of a nascent field (or subfield) of practice: the musical-philosophical—with Rhythmicity as a major conceptual tool in its attendant apparatus. Aligned with the fields of Performance Philosophy and practice as research, and with implications for those studying the uses to which experimental music and improvisation can be put in the context of a research undertaking, *Rhythmicity and Deleuze* thus demonstrates how the expression of a set of research practices can provide insights by the means and modes, and rhythmic concept, of its (musical-philosophical) expression as much as through the words/analyses conveyed via that expression.

NOTES

1. Ongoing since, as I discuss later, any enquiry into the nature of a thing or a practice can never be entirely complete in its ontology or epistemology. Such enquiries, by their very nature, are open ended and (to use the Deleuzian term) ever in a condition of becoming.

2. In the first and third practice-as-research projects, this sense of Rhythmicity putting motion into the synthesis of past, present, and future time is discussed, respectively, in terms of Simondon's concept of *modulation* (and its related processes of individuation, disparation, and transduction) in Sauvagnargues (2016) and Assis (2018), and the concept of *kairos* in Coessens (2014), Coessens and Östersjö (2014b), Coessens et al. (2014), and Assis (2018).

Bibliography

Alperson, Philip. *What Is Music?: An Introduction to the Philosophy of Music*. New York: Haven, 1986.

Arom, Simha. *African Polyphony and Polyrhythm: Musical Structure and Methodology*. Cambridge: Cambridge University Press, 1991.

Assis, Paulo de. "Gilbert Simondon's 'Transduction' as Radical Immanence in Performance." In *On Stage: The Concept of Immanence in Contemporary Art and Philosophy*. Edited by Böhler, Arno, Eva-Maria Aigner, and Elisabeth Schäfer. *Performance Philosophy* 3, No. 3, 2017a: 695–717.

———. "Preface." In *The Dark Precursor: Deleuze and Artistic Research (Volume I: The Dark Precursor in Sound and Writing)*. Edited by Assis, Paulo de, and Paolo Giudici, Leuven: Leuven University Press, 2017b: 9–20.

———. "Rasch-24: The Somatheme." In: *Artistic Research in Music: Discipline and Resistance*. Edited by Impett, Jonathan. Leuven: Leuven University Press, 2017c: 15–42.

———. *Logic of Experimentation: Rethinking Music Performance through Artistic Research*. Leuven: Leuven University Press, 2018.

Assis, Paulo de, and Paolo Giudici. *The Dark Precursor: Deleuze and Artistic Research (Volume I: The Dark Precursor in Sound and Writing)*. Leuven: Leuven University Press, 2017.

———. *Aberrant Nuptials: Deleuze and Artistic Research 2*. Leuven: Leuven University Press, 2019.

Badiou, Alain. *Deleuze: The Clamour of Being*. Translated by Louise Burchill. Minneapolis: University of Minnesota Press, 2000.

Bailey, Derek. *Improvisation: Its Nature and Practice in Music (Revised Edition)*. New York: Da Capo Press, 1992.

Barnes, Robert. "Stoicism." In *Dictionary of Philosophy (2nd Edition)*. Edited by Mautner, Thomas. London: Penguin Books, 2005: 595–96

Barrett Estelle. "Introduction." In *Practice as Research: Approaches to Creative Arts Enquiry*. Edited by Barrett, Estelle, and Barbara Bolt. London: I. B. Tauris, 2010: 1–13.

Barrett, Estelle, and Barbara Bolt. *Practice as Research: Approaches to Creative Arts Enquiry*. London: I. B. Tauris, 2010.

Benson, Bruce Ellis. *The Improvisation of Musical Dialogue: A Phenomenology of Music*. Cambridge: Cambridge University Press, 2003.

———. "Phenomenology of Music." In *The Routledge Companion to Philosophy and Music*. Edited by Gracyk, Theodore, and Andrew Kania. London: Routledge, 2014: 581–91.

Bergson, Henri. *Matter and Memory*. Translated by Nancy Margaret Paul and W. Scott Palmer. Mineola, NY: Dover Publications, 2004.

———. *Time and Free Will: An Essay on the Immediate Data of Consciousness*. Translated by F. L. Pogson. Mineola, Mineola, NY: Dover Publications, 2001.

Berry, Wallace. *Structural Functions in Music*. New York: Dover, 1987.

Bidima, Jean-Godefroy. "Intensity, Music, and Heterogenesis in Deleuze." In *Sounding the Virtual: Gilles Deleuze and the Theory and Philosophy of Music*. Edited by Hulse, Brian, and Nick Nesbitt. Translated by Michael Wiedorn. London: Routledge, 2010: 145–58.

Biggs, Michael, and Henrik Karlsson. *The Routledge Companion to Research in the Arts*. London: Routledge, 2011.

Bogue, Ronald. *Deleuze on Music, Painting and the Arts*. London: Routledge, 2003.

Borgdorff, Henk. "The Production of Knowledge in Artistic Research." In *The Routledge Companion to Research in the Arts*. Edited by Biggs, Michael, and Henrik Karlsson. London: Routledge, 2011: 44–63.

———. *The Conflict of the Faculties: Perspective on Artistic Research*. Leiden: Leiden University Press, 2012.

Borgo, David. *Sync or Swarm: Improvising Music in a Complex Age*. New York: Continuum, 2007.

Boundas, Constantin V. "Subjectivity." In *The Deleuze Dictionary (Revised Edition)*. Edited by Parr, Adrian. Edinburgh: Edinburgh University Press, 2010: 274–76.

Bourdieu, Pierre. *Outline of a Theory of Practice*. Translated by Richard Nice. Cambridge: Cambridge University Press, 1977.

Bowie, Andrew. *Music, Philosophy, and Modernity*. Cambridge: Cambridge University Press, 2007.

———. "The Philosophy of Performance and the Performance of Philosophy." In *Performance Philosophy* 1. Edited by Cull Ó Maoilearca, Laura. 2015: 51–58.

Brown, Lee B. "Improvisation." In *The Routledge Companion to Philosophy and Music*. Edited by Gracyk, Theodore, and Andrew Kania. London: Routledge, 2014a: 59–69.

———. "Jazz." In *The Routledge Companion to Philosophy and Music*. Edited by Gracyk, Theodore, and Andrew Kania. London: Routledge, 2014b: 426–36.

Buchanan, Ian, and Marcel Swiboda *Deleuze and Music*. Edinburgh: Edinburgh University Press, 2004.

Burnham, Douglas. "Leibniz, Gottfried: Metaphysics." 2018. https://www.iep.utm .edu/leib-met.

Cage, John. *Silence: Lectures and Writings*. London: Marion Boyars, 1978.

Campbell, Edward. *Boulez, Music and Philosophy*. Cambridge: Cambridge University Press, 2010.

———. *Music after Deleuze*. London: Bloomsbury, 2013.

Caplin, William E. "Theories of Musical Rhythm in the Eighteenth and Nineteenth Centuries." In *The Cambridge History of Western Music Theory*. Edited by Christensen, Thomas. Cambridge: Cambridge University Press, 2002: 657–94.

Castro-Magas, Diego. "Deleze's Fold in the Performing Practice of Aaron Cassidy's *The Pleats of Matter*." In *The Dark Precursor: Deleuze and Artistic Research (Volume I: The Dark Precursor in Sound and Writing)*. Edited by Assis, Paulo de, and Paolo Giudici. Leuven: Leuven University Press, 2017: 56–66.

Chernoff, John Miller. *African Rhythm and African Sensibility: Aesthetics and Social Action in African Musical Idioms*. Chicago: Chicago University Press, 1979.

Cheyne, Peter, Andy Hamilton, and Max Paddison. "Introduction: Philosophy of Rhythm." In *The Philosophy of Rhythm: Aesthetics, Music, Poetics*. Edited by Cheyne, Peter, Andy Hamilton, and Max Paddison. Oxford: Oxford University Press, 2019: 1–12.

Chion, Michel. *The Voice in Cinema*. Translated by Claudia Gorbman. New York: Columbia University Press, 1999.

Chouvel, Jean-Marc. "Deleuze's Syntheses of Time and Their Aesthetical Prolongations: Form, Style, and Achievement." In *Aberrant Nuptials: Deleuze and Artistic Research 2*. Edited by Assis, Paulo de, and Paolo Giudici. Leuven: Leuven University Press, 2019: 25–46.

Clark, Suzannah, and Alexander Rehding. *Music in Time: Phenomenology, Perception, Performance*. Cambridge, MA: Harvard University Department of Music, 2016.

Clayton, Martin. *Time in Indian Music: Rhythm, Metre, and Form in North Indian Rag Performance*. Oxford: Oxford University Press, 2000.

Coessens, Kathleen. "Tiny Moment of Experimentation: Kairos in the Liminal Space of Performance." In *Artistic Experimentation in Music: An Anthology*. Edited by Crispin, Darla, and Bob Gilmore. Leuven: Leuven University Press, 2014: 61–67.

———*Experimental Encounters in Music and Beyond*. Leuven: Leuven University Press, 2017.

Coessens, Kathleen, Darla Crispin, and Anne Douglas. *The Artistic Turn: A Manifesto*. Leuven: Leuven University Press, 2009.

Coessens, Kathleen, Henrik Frisk, and Stefan Östersjö. "Repetition, Resonance, and Discernment." In *Artistic Experimentation in Music: An Anthology*. Edited by Crispin, Darla, and Bob Gilmore. Leuven: Leuven University Press, 2014: 349–63.

Coessens, Kathleen, and Stefan Östersjö. "Intuition, Hexis, and Resistance in Musical Experimentation." In *Artistic Experimentation in Music: An Anthology*. Edited by Crispin, Darla, and Bob Gilmore. Leuven: Leuven University Press, 2014a: 365–71.

———. "Kairos in the Flow of Musical Intuition." In *Artistic Experimentation in Music: An Anthology*. Edited by Crispin, Darla, and Bob Gilmore. Leuven: Leuven University Press, 2014b: 323–31.

Colebrook, Claire. *Gilles Deleuze*. London: Routledge. 2002.

———. "Expression." In *The Deleuze Dictionary (Revised Edition)*. Edited by Parr, Adrian. Edinburgh: Edinburgh University Press, 2010: 95–97.

Cook, Nicholas. "Between Process and Product: Music and/as Performance." In *Music Theory Online: The Online Journal of the Society for Music Theory* 7, No. 2, April 2001.

Cooper, Grosvenor, and Leonard B. Meyer. *The Rhythmic Structure of Music*. Chicago: University of Chicago Press, 1960.

Costa, Rogério. "Free Musical Improvisation and the Philosophy of Gilles Deleuze." In *Perspectives of New Music* 49, No. 1. 2011: 127–42.

Crispin, Darla, and Bob Gilmore. *Artistic Experimentation in Music: An Anthology*. Leuven: Leuven University Press, 2014.

Criton, Pascale, and Jean-Marc Chouvel. *Gilles Deleuze: La pensée-musique*. Paris: Centre de documentation de la musique contemporaine, 2015.

Cull Ó Maoilearca, Laura. "Performance Philosophy: Staging a New Field." In *Encounters in Performance Philosophy*. Edited by Cull Ó Maoilearca, Laura, and Alice Lagaay. London: Palgrave Macmillan, 2014: 15–38.

———. "Equalizing Theatre and Philosophy: Laruelle, Badiou, and Gestures of Authority in the Philosophy of Theatre." In *Philosophy on Stage: The Concept of Immanence in Contemporary Art and Philosophy*. Edited by Böhler, Arno, Eva-Maria Aigner, and Elisabeth Schäfer. *Performance Philosophy* 3, No. 3. 2017: 730–50.

———. "Performance Philosophy: An Introduction." In *Brazilian Journal of Presence Studies* 10, No. 1. 2020: 1–31.

———. Unpublished correspondence with the author. 6 June 2019.

Davies, David. *Philosophy of the Performing Arts*. Chichester: Wiley-Blackwell, 2011.

Davies, Stephen. *Themes in the Philosophy of Music*. Oxford: Oxford University Press, 2002.

Deleuze, Gilles. "La conception de la difference chez Bergson." In *Les Etudes Bergsoniennes* 4. Paris: Presses universitaires de France, 1956: 77–113.

———. *Nietzsche and Philosophy*. Translated by Hugh Tomlinson. New York: Columbia University Press, 1983.

———. *Cinema 1: The Movement Image*. Translated by Hugh Tomlinson and Barbara Habberjam. Minneapolis, MN: University of Minnesota Press, 1986.

———. *Bergsonism*. Translated by Hugh Tomlinson and Barbara Habberjam. New York: Zone Books, 1988a.

———. *Spinoza: Practical Philosophy*. Translated by Robert Hurley. San Francisco: City Lights. 1988b.

———. *Cinema 2: The Time Image*. Translated by Hugh Tomlinson and Robert Galeta. Minneapolis, MN: University of Minnesota Press, 1989.

———. *Expressionism in Philosophy: Spinoza*. Translated by Martin Joughlin. New York: Zone Books, 1990.

———. *Empiricism and Subjectivity: An Essay on Hume's Theory of Human Nature*. Translated by Constantin V. Boundas. New York: Columbia University Press, 1991.

———. *Negotiations: 1972–1990*. Translated by Martin Joughin. New York: Columbia University Press, 1995.

———. *Difference and Repetition*. Translated by Paul Patton. London: Continuum, 2004a.

————. *The Logic of Sense*. Translated by Mark Lester with Charles Stivale. London: Bloomsbury, 2004b.

————. *Francis Bacon: The Logic of Sensation*. Translated by Daniel W. Smith. London: Continuum, 2005.

————. *The Fold: Leibniz and the Baroque*. Translated by Tom Conley. London: Continuum, 2006a.

————. *Foucault*. Translated by Seán Hand. London: Continuum, 2006b.

————. *Two Regimes of Madness: Texts and Interviews 1975–1995*. Edited by David Lapoujade. Translated by Ames Hodges and Mike Taormina. New York: Semiotext(e), 2007.

————. *Kant's Critical Philosophy*. Translated by Hugh Tomlinson and Barbara Habberjam. London: Continuum, 2008.

Deleuze, Gilles, and Félix Guattari. *Kafka: Toward a Minor Literature*. Translated by Dana Polan. Minneapolis: University of Minnesota Press. 1986.

————. *What Is Philosophy?* Translated by Hugh Tomlinson and Graham Burchill. London: Verso, 1994.

————. *A Thousand Plateaus: Capitalism and Schizophrenia Volume 2*. Translated by Brian Massumi. London: Continuum, 2004.

Doğantan-Dack, Mine. *Artistic Practice as Research in Music: Theory, Criticism, Practice*. London: Routledge, 2015a.

————. "Introduction." In *Artistic Practice as Research in Music: Theory, Criticism, Practice*. Edited by Doğantan-Dack, Mine. London: Routledge, 2015b: 1–8.

Feitosa, Charles. "Borders between Performing Arts and Philosophy." In *Brazilian Journal of Presence Studies* 10, No. 1. 2020: 1–25.

Feldman, Morton. *Give my Regards to Eighth Street: Collected Writings of Morton Feldman*. Edited by B. H. Friedman. Cambridge, MA: Exact Change, 2000.

Feldman, Morton, and Chris Villars. *Morton Feldman Says*. London: Hyphen Press, 2006.

Fink, Robert. *Repeating Ourselves: American Minimal Music as Cultural Practice*. Berkeley: University of California Press, 2005.

Flaxman, Gregory. "Introduction: Deleuze: In Practice." In *Practising with Deleuze: Design, Dance, Art, Writing, Philosophy*. Edited by Attiwill, Suzie, Terri Bird, Andrea Eckersley, and Antonia Pont. Edinburgh: Edinburgh University Press, 2017: 1–15.

Foucault, Michel. "Theatrum Philosophicum." In *Critique*, No. 282, 1970: 885–908.

Frayling, Christopher. *Research in Art and Design*. London: Royal College of Art, 1993.

Freeman, John. *Blood, Sweat & Theory: Research Through Practice in Performance*. Farringdon: Libri Publishing, 2010.

Gallope, Michael. "The Sound of Repeating Life: Ethics and Metaphysics in Deleuze's Philosophy of Music." In *Sounding the Virtual: Gilles Deleuze and the Theory and Philosophy of Music*. Edited by Hulse, Brian, and Nick Nesbitt. London: Routledge, 2010: 77–102.

Gendron, Sarah. *Studies in Literary Criticism and Theory (Volume 19): Repetition, Difference, and Knowledge in the Work of Samuel Beckett, Jacques Derrida, and Gilles Deleuze*. New York: Peter Lang, 2008.

Goehr, Lydia. *The Imaginary Museum of Musical Works*. Oxford: Clarendon Press, 1992.

Gottschalk, Jennie. *Experimental Music Since 1970*. New York: Bloomsbury, 2016.

Gracyk, Theodore, and Andrew Kania. *The Routledge Companion to Philosophy and Music*. London: Routledge, 2014.

Grimshaw, Jeremy. *Draw a Straight line and Follow It: The Music and Mysticism of La Monte Young*. Oxford: Oxford University Press, 2011.

Gritten, Anthony. "Determination and Negotiation in Artistic Practice as Research in Music." In *Artistic Practice as Research in Music: Theory, Criticism, Practice*. Edited by Doğantan-Dack, Mine. London: Routledge, 2015: 73–90.

Guerlac, Suzanne. *Thinking in Time: An Introduction to Henri Bergson*. Ithaca, NY: Cornell University Press, 2006.

Hallward, Peter. *Out of This World: Deleuze and the Philosophy of Creation*. London: Verso, 2006.

Hamilton, Andy. "The Art of Improvisation and the Aesthetics of Imperfection." In *British Journal of Aesthetics* 40, No. 1. 2000: 168–85.

Hamilton, Andy, David Macarthur, Roger Squires, Matthew Tugby, and Rachael Wiseman. "Dialogue on Rhythm: Entrainment and the Dynamic Book." In *The Philosophy of Rhythm: Aesthetics, Music, Poetics*. Edited by Cheyne, Peter, Andy Hamilton, and Max Paddison. Oxford: Oxford University Press, 2019: 15–42.

Hannula, Mika, Juha Suoranta, and Tere Vadén. *Artistic Research: Theories, Methods and Practices*. Gothenburg: Academy of Fine Arts Helsinki, and Gothenburg University, 2005.

Harris, Tony. *The Legacy of Cornelius Cardew*. Burlington: Ashgate, 2013.

Haseman, Brad, and Daniel Mafe. "Acquiring Know-How: Research Training for Practice-Led Researchers." In *Practice-Led Research, Research-Led Practice in the Creative Arts*. Edited by Smith, Hazel, and Roger T. Dean. Edinburgh: Edinburgh University Press, 2009: 211–28.

Hasty, Christopher F. *Meter as Rhythm*. Oxford: Oxford University Press, 1997.

Hemment, Drew. "Affect and Individuation in Popular Electronic Music." In *Deleuze and Music*. Edited by Buchnan, Ian, and Marcel Swiboda. Edinburgh: Edinburgh University Press, 2004: 76–94.

Holland, Eugene. "Studies in Applied Nomadology: Jazz Improvisation and Post-Capitalist Markets." In *Deleuze and Music*. Edited by Buchanan, Ian, and Marcel Swiboda. Edinburgh: Edinburgh University Press, 2004: 20–35.

Hulse, Brian. "Thinking Musical Difference: Music Theory as Minor Science." In *Sounding the Virtual: Gilles Deleuze and the Theory and Philosophy of Music*. Edited by Hulse, Brian, and Nick Nesbitt. Farnham: Ashgate, 2010: 23–50.

Hulse, Brian, and Nick Nesbitt. "Introduction." In *Sounding the Virtual: Gilles Deleuze and the Theory and Philosophy of Music*. Edited by Hulse, Brian, and Nick Nesbitt. Farnham: Ashgate, 2010a: xv–xvii.

————*Sounding the Virtual: Gilles Deleuze and the Theory and Philosophy of Music.* Farnham: Ashgate, 2010b.

Jones, Timothy. "Variation Form." 2017. http://www.oxfordmusiconline.com.

Jude, Gretchen. "Vocal Performance through Electrical Flows." In *Performance Philosophy* 4, No. 2. Edited by Daddario, Will, and Eve Katsouraki. 2019: 393–409.

Jullander, Sverker. "Introduction: Creating Dialogues on Artistic Research." In *Special Issue on Artistic Research in Music.* Edited by Lund, Tobias. *Swedish Journal of Musicology* 95. 2013: 11–24.

Kant, Immanuel. *Critique of Judgment.* Translated by Werner S. Pluhar. Indiana: Hackett Publishing Company, 1987.

Kershaw, Baz. "Practice as Research through Performance." In *Practice-Led Research, Research-Led Practice in the Creative Arts.* Edited by Smith, Hazel, and Roger T. Dean. Edinburgh: Edinburgh University Press, 2009: 104–25.

Kivy, Peter. *Introduction to a Philosophy of Music.* Oxford: Oxford University Press, 2002.

Lachenmann, Helmut. "Philosophy of Composition: Is There Such a Thing?." In *Identity and Difference: Essays on Music, Language and Time.* Edited by Agsteribbe, Frank, Sylvester Beelaert, Peter Dejans, and Jeroen D'hoe. Leuven: Leuven University Press, 2004: 55–70.

Leibniz, Gottfried Wilhelm von. *Theodicy: Essays on the Goodness of God, the Freedom of Man, and the Origin of Evil.* Translated by E. M. Huggard. La Salle, IL: Open Court, 1985.

Lerdahl, Fred, and Ray Jackendoff. *A Generative Theory of Tonal Music.* Cambridge, MA: MIT Press, 1983.

Lester, Joel. *The Rhythms of Tonal Music.* Carbondale, IL: Southern Illinois University Press, 1986.

Levine, Mark. *The Jazz Theory Book.* Petaluma, CA: Sher Music Co., 1995.

Levinson, Jerrold. *Music, Art, and Metaphysics.* Ithaca, NY: Cornell University Press, 1990.

Lewis, George E., and Benjamin Piekut. *The Oxford Handbook of Critical Improvisation Studies (Volume 1).* Oxford: Oxford University Press, 2016.

Lock, Graham. *Forces in Motion: Anthony Braxton and the Meta-reality of Creative Music.* London: Quartet Book, 1988.

London, Justin. *Hearing in Time: Psychological Aspects of Musical Meter.* Oxford: Oxford University Press, 2004.

Look, Brandon C. "Leibniz's Modal Metaphysics." 2013. https://plato.stanford.edu/entries/leibniz-modal/.

MacArthur, Sally, and Judy Lochhead. "Introduction." In *Music's Immanent Future: The Deleuzian Turn in Music Studies.* Edited by MacArthur, Sally, Judy Lochhead, and Jennifer Shaw. London: Routledge, 2016: 1–16.

MacArthur, Sally, Judy Lochhead, and Jennifer Shaw. *Music's Immanent Future: The Deleuzian Turn in Music Studies.* London: Routledge, 2016.

Massumi, Brian. *Parables for the Virtual: Movement, Affect, Sensation.* Durham, NC: Duke University Press, 2002.

McAuley, Tomas. "Missing the Wrong Target: On Andrew Bowie's Rejection of the Philosophy of Music." In *Performance Philosophy* 1. Edited by Cull Ó Maoilearca, Laura. 2015: 59–64.

McGrath, John. *Samuel Beckett, Repetition and Modern Music*. London: Routledge, 2018.

Michon, Pascal. "A Short History of Rhythm Theory since the 1970s." 2011. http://www.rhuthmos.eu/spip.php?article462.

Moisala, Pirkko, Taru Leppänen, Milla Tiainen, and Hanna Väätäinen. *Musical Encounters with Deleuze and Guattari*. London: Bloomsbury, 2017.

Morris, Eilon. *Rhythm in Acting and Performance: Embodied Approaches and Understandings*. London: Bloomsbury, 2017.

Mullarkey, John. *Post-Continental Philosophy: An Outline*. London: Continuum, 2006.

Murphy, Timothy S. "What I Hear Is Thinking Too: The Deleuze Tribute Recordings." In *Deleuze and Music*. Edited by Buchanan, Ian, and Marcel Swiboda. Edinburgh: Edinburgh University Press, 2004: 159–75.

Murray, Michael J. "Leibniz on the Problem of Evil." 2013. https://plato.stanford.edu/entries/leibniz-evil/.

Nachmanovitch, Stephen. *Free Play: Improvisation in Life and Art*. New York: Tarcher/Penguin, 1990.

Nelson, Robin. *Practice as Research in the Arts: Principles, Protocols, Pedagogies, Resistances*. Basingstoke: Palgrave Macmillan, 2013.

Nicholls, Brett. "Leibniz, Gottfried Wilhelm von (1646–1716)." In *The Deleuze Dictionary (Revised Edition)*. Edited by Parr, Adrian. Edinburgh: Edinburgh University Press, 2010: 145=47.

Nicholls, David. *American Experimental Music: 1890–1940*. Cambridge: Cambridge University Press, 1990.

Nyman, Michael. *Experimental Music: Cage and Beyond*. London: Studio Vista, 1974.

———. *Experimental Music: Cage and Beyond (2nd Edition)*. Cambridge: Cambridge University Press, 1999.

Olewnick, Brian. *Keith Rowe: The Room Extended*. New York: powerHouse Books, 2018.

O'Sullivan, Simon. "Fold." In *The Deleuze Dictionary (Revised Edition)*. Edited by Parr, Adrian. Edinburgh: Edinburgh University Press, 2010: 107–108.

Parr, Adrian. "Preface." In *The Deleuze Dictionary (Revised Edition)*. Edited by Parr, Adrian. Edinburgh: Edinburgh University Press, 2010a: vii–viii.

———. "Repetition." In *The Deleuze Dictionary (Revised Edition)*. Edited by Parr, Adrian. Edinburgh: Edinburgh University Press, 2010b: 225–26.

Peters, Gary. *The Philosophy of Improvisation*, Chicago: Chicago University Press, 2009.

———. *Improvising Improvisation: From out of Philosophy, Music, Dance, and Literature*. Chicago: Chicago University Press, 2017.

Pluhar, Werner S. "Translator's Introduction." In *Critique of Judgment* by Kant, Immanuel. Translated by Werner S. Pluhar. Indiana: Hackett Publishing Company, 1987: xxiii–cix.

Pritchett, James. *The Music of John Cage*. Cambridge: Cambridge University Press, 1993.

Rawlins, Robert, and Nor Eddine Bahha. *Jazzology: The Encyclopedia of Jazz Theory for All Musicians*. Milwaukee, WI: Hal Leonard, 2005.

Ridley, Aaron, *The Philosophy of Music: Theme and Variations*. Edinburgh: Edinburgh University Press, 2004.

Roden, David. "Promethean and Posthuman Freedom: Brassier on Improvisation and Time." In *Performance Philosophy* 4, No. 2. Edited by Daddario, Will, and Eve Katsouraki. 2019: 510–27.

Roffe, John. "Gilles Deleuze (1925–1995)." 2005. http://www.iep.utm.edu/deleuze/.

Ross, Alison. "Plato." In *The Deleuze Dictionary (Revised Edition)*. Edited by Parr, Adrian. Edinburgh: Edinburgh University Press, 2010: 209–11.

Rothenberg, David. "The Concept of Humans and Nightingales: Why Interspecies Music Works." In *Performance Philosophy* 1. Edited by Cull Ó Maoilearca, Laura. 2015: 214–25.

Rush, Stephen. "Free Jazz, Harmolodics, and Ornette Coleman." 2017. http://www.jazzedmagazine.com/articles/focus-session/free-jazz-harmolodics-and-ornette-coleman/.

Ruthford-Johnson, Tim. *Music after the Fall: Modern Composition and Culture since 1989*. Oakland, CA: University of California Press, 2017.

Sarap, Madan. *An Introductory Guide to Post-Structuralism and Postmodernism (2nd Edition)*. New York: Harvester Wheatsheaf, 1993.

Saunders, James. *The Ashgate Research Companion to Experimental Music*. London: Routledge, 2017.

Sauvagnargues, Anne. *Artmachines: Deleuze, Guattari, Simondon*. Translated by Suzanne Verderber with Eugene W. Holland. Edinburgh: Edinburgh University Press, 2016.

Schwab, Michael. "Artistic Research and Experimental Systems: The Rheinberger Questionnaire and Study Day." In *Artistic Experimentation in Music: An Anthology*. Edited by Crispin, Darla, and Bob Gilmore. Leuven: Leuven University Press, 2014: 111–23.

Scruton, Roger. *The Aesthetics of Music*. Oxford: Oxford University Press, 1997.

———. "Rhythm, Melody, and Harmony." In *The Routledge Companion to Philosophy and Music*. Edited by Gracyk, Theodore, and Andrew Kania. London: Routledge, 2014: 24–37.

Sellars, John. "*Aion* and *Chronos*: Deleuze and the Stoic Theory of Time." In *Collapse* 3, 2007: 177–205.

Sim, Stuart, and Borin Van Loon. *Critical Theory: A Graphic Guide*. London: Icon Books, 2009.

Simons, Peter. "The Ontology of Rhythm." In *The Philosophy of Rhythm: Aesthetics, Music, Poetics*. Edited by Cheyne, Peter, Andy Hamilton, and Max Paddison. Oxford: Oxford University Press, 2019: 62–75.

Smith, Daniel W. "Gilles Deleuze." 2008. http://plato.stanford.edu/entries/deleuze/.

———. *Essays on Deleuze*. Edinburgh: Edinburgh University Press, 2012.

Smith, Hazel, and Roger T. Dean. "Introduction: Practice-Led Research, Research-Led Practice—Towards the Iterative Cyclic Web." In *Practice-Led Research, Research-Led Practice in the Creative Arts*. Edited by Smith, Hazel, and Roger T. Dean. Edinburgh: Edinburgh University Press, 2009a: 1–38.

———. *Practice-Led Research, Research-Led Practice in the Creative Arts*. Edinburgh: Edinburgh University Press, 2009b.

Spitzer, Michael. "Mozart's 'Dissonance' and the Dialetic of Language and Thought in Classical Theories of Rhythm." In *The Philosophy of Rhythm: Aesthetics, Music, Poetics*. Edited by Cheyne, Peter, Andy Hamilton, and Max Paddison. Oxford: Oxford University Press, 2019: 125–40.

Stagoll, Cliff. "Difference." In *The Deleuze Dictionary (Revised Edition)*. Edited by Parr, Adrian. Edinburgh: Edinburgh University Press, 2010a: 74–76.

———. "Duration." In *The Deleuze Dictionary (Revised Edition)*. Edited by Parr, Adrian. Edinburgh: Edinburgh University Press, 2010b: 81–83.

———. "Event." In *The Deleuze Dictionary (Revised Edition)*. Edited by Parr, Adrian. Edinburgh: Edinburgh University Press, 2010c: 89–91.

———. "Memory." In *The Deleuze Dictionary (Revised Edition)*. Edited by Parr, Adrian. Edinburgh: Edinburgh University Press, 2010d: 162–64.

Sterne, Jonathan. "Sonic Imaginations." In *The Sound Studies Reader*. Edited by Sterne, Jonathan. London: Routledge, 2012: 1–17.

Stevens, John. *Search & Reflect: A Music Workshop Handbook*. Milton Keynes: Rockschool, 2007.

Stockhausen, Karlheinz. *Stockhausen on Music: Lectures and Interviews*. Compiled by Robin Maconie. London: Marion Boyars, 1989.

Sudnow, David. *Ways of the Hand: The Organisation of Improvised Conduct*. Cambridge, MA: MIT Press, 1993.

Swiboda, Marcel. "Cosmic Strategies: The Electric Experiments of Miles Davis." In *Deleuze and Music*. Edited by Buchanan, Ian, and Marcel Swiboda. Edinburgh: Edinburgh University Press, 2004: 196–216.

Tartaglia, James. "Jazz-Philosophy Fusion." In *Performance Philosophy* 2, No. 1. Edited by Cull Ó Maoilearca, Laura, Theron Schmidt, and Daniel Watt. 2016: 99–114.

Teixeira, William, and Silvio Ferraz. "The Performance of Time (or the Time of Musical Performance)." In *Performance Philosophy* 4, No. 2. Edited by Daddario, Will, and Eve Katsouraki. 2019: 490–509.

Tromans, Steve, and Heidi Schmidt. "The Composite Incompossible: Forbidden Symmetries." In *Performance Philosophy* 7, No. 2. Edited by Daddario, Will, Laura Cull O Maoilearca, Eve Katsouraki, Diana Damian Martin, and Theron Schmidt. 2022: 145–48.

Turetsky, Phil. "Rhythm: Assemblage and Event." In *Deleuze and Music*. Edited by Buchanan, Ian, and Marcel Swiboda. Edinburgh: Edinburgh University Press, 2004: 140–58.

Watson, Ben. *Derek Bailey and the Story of Free Improvisation*. London: Verso, 2004.

Welsh, John. "*Projection 1 (1950)*." In *The Music of Morton Feldman*. Edited by DeLio, Thomas. New York: Excelsior Music Publishing Company, 1996: 21–38.

Williams, Alastair. *New Music and the Claims of Modernity*. London: Routledge, 2016.

Williams, James. "Event." In *Gilles Deleuze: Key Concepts (2nd Edition)*. Edited by Stivale, Charles J. London: Routledge, 2011a: 80–90.

———. *Gilles Deleuze's Philosophy of Time: A Critical Introduction and Guide*. Edinburgh: Edinburgh University Press, 2011b.

Winold, Allen. "Rhythm in Twentieth-Century Music." In *Aspects of Twentieth-Century Music*. Edited by Wittlich, Gary. Englewood Cliffs, NJ: Prentice-Hall, 1975: 208–69.

Yeston, Maury. *The Stratification of Musical Rhythm*. New Haven, CT: Yale University Press, 1976.

Žižek, Slavoj. *Organs without Bodies: On Deleuze and Consequences*. London: Routledge, 2004.

Index

About the Author

Dr Steve Tromans is a musician (pianist, composer) and an independent scholar working in the fields of practice as research and Performance Philosophy. As pianist, Tromans has given more than 6,000 performances in the UK and internationally. As composer, he has written 100+ works for various ensembles, including many solo projects. He has released over fifty albums to date, predominantly in improvised and experimental musics. As a researcher in the musical-philosophical, Tromans has been published in a number of edited collections and journals in music research, artistic research, and performance philosophy. He also gives frequent guest lectures at different institutions in the UK and internationally in music, philosophy, and the resonances between the two fields of practice. He received his doctorate from the University of Surrey (UK) in 2020.